I dedicate this series of books to all those who center their professional lives on fostering the development and practice of literacy.

LITERACY FOR THE NEW MILLENNIUM

Volume 2

Childhood Literacy

Edited by Barbara J. Guzzetti

Praeger Perspectives

Westport, Connecticut
London

Library of Congress Cataloging-in-Publication Data

Literacy for the new millennium / edited by Barbara J. Guzzetti.
   v. cm.
   Includes bibliographical references and indexes.
   Contents: v. 1. Early literacy — v. 2 Childhood literacy — v. 3 Adolescent
literacy — v. 4 Adult literacy.
   ISBN-13: 978–0–275–98969–9 (set : alk. paper)
   ISBN-10: 0–275–98969–0 (set : alk. paper)
   ISBN-13: 978–0–275–98992–7 (v.1 : alk. paper)
   ISBN-10: 0–275–98992–5 (v.1 : alk. paper)
   [etc.]
   1. Literacy.   2. Language arts.   I. Guzzetti, Barbara J.
   LC149.L4987   2007
   302.2'244—dc22   2007018116

British Library Cataloguing in Publication Data is available.

Library of Congress Catalog Card Number: 2007018116
ISBN-13: 978–0–275–98969–9 (set)   ISBN-10: 0–275–98969–0
ISBN-13: 978–0–275–98992–7 (vol. 1)   ISBN-10: 0–275–98992–5
ISBN-13: 978–0–275–98993–4 (vol. 2)   ISBN-10: 0–275–98993–3
ISBN-13: 978–0–275–98994–1 (vol. 3)   ISBN-10: 0–275–98994–1
ISBN-13: 978–0–275–98995–8 (vol. 4)   ISBN-10: 0–275–98995-X

First published in 2007

Praeger Publishers, 88 Post Road West, Westport, CT 06881
An imprint of Greenwood Publishing Group, Inc.
www.praeger.com

Printed in the United States of America

The paper used in this book complies with the
Permanent Paper Standard issued by the National
Information Standards Organization (Z39.48–1984).

10 9 8 7 6 5 4 3 2 1

CONTENTS

SET PREFACE

This set of four volumes—*Literacy for the New Millennium: Early Literacy; Literacy for the New Millennium: Childhood Literacy; Literacy for the New Millennium: Adolescent Literacy;* and *Literacy for the New Millennium: Adult Literacy*—presents a current and comprehensive overview of literacy assessment, instruction, practice, and issues across the life span. Each volume presents contemporary issues and trends, as well as classic topics associated with the ages and stages of literacy development and practice represented in that text. The chapters in each volume provide the reader with insights into policies and issues that influence literacy development and practice. Together, these volumes represent an informative and timely discussion of the broad field of literacy.

The definition of literacy on which each of these volumes is grounded is a current and expanded one. Literacy is defined in this set in a broad way by encompassing both traditional notions of literacy, such as reading, writing, listening, and speaking, and the consumption and production of nonprint texts, such as media and computer texts. Chapters on technology and popular culture in particular reflect this expanded definition of literacy to literacies that represents current trends in the field. This emphasis sets this set apart from other more traditional texts on literacy.

The authors who contributed to this set represent a combination of well-known researchers and educators in literacy, as well as those relatively new to the profession of literacy education and scholarship. Contributors to the set represent university professors, senior scientists at research institutions, practitioners or consultants in the field, teacher educators, and researchers in literacy. Although the authors are experts in the field of literacy, they have written their chapters to be reader friendly, by defining and explaining any professional jargon and by writing in an unpretentious and comprehensible style.

Each of the four volumes shaped by these authors has common features. Each of the texts is divided into three parts, with the first part devoted to recent trends and issues affecting the field of literacy for that age range. The second part addresses issues in assessment and instruction. The final part presents issues beyond the classroom that affect literacy development and practice at that level. Each of the texts concludes with a chapter on literacy resources appropriate for the age group that the volume addresses. These include resources and materials from professional organizations, and a brief bibliography for further reading.

Each of the volumes has common topics, as well as a common structure. All the volumes address issues of federal legislation, funding, and policies that affect literacy assessment instruction and practice. Each volume addresses assessment issues in literacy for each age range represented in that text. As a result of the growing importance of technology for instruction, recreation, information acquisition, communication, and participation in a global economy, each book addresses some aspect of literacy in the digital age. Because of the importance of motivating students in literacy and bridging the gap between students' in-school literacy instruction and their out-of-school literacy practices, each text that address literacy for school-age children discusses the influence and incorporation of youth and popular culture in literacy instruction.

In short, these volumes are crafted to address the salient issues, polices, practices, and procedures in literacy that affect literacy development and practice. These texts provide a succinct yet inclusive overview of the field of literacy in a way that is easily accessible to readers with little or no prior knowledge of the field. Preservice teachers, educators, teacher trainers, librarians, policy makers, researchers, and the public will find a useful resource and reference guide in this set.

In conclusion, I would like to acknowledge the many people who have contributed to the creation of this set. First, I recognize the outstanding contributions of the authors. Their writings not only reflect the most informative current trends and classic topics in the field but also present their subjects in ways that take bold stances. In doing so, they provide exciting future directions for the field.

Second, I acknowledge the contributions to the production of this set by staff at Arizona State University in the College of Education. My appreciation goes to Don Hutchins, director of computer support, for his organizational skills and assistance in the electronic production of this set. In addition, I extend my appreciation to my research assistant, Thomas Leyba, for his help in organizing the clerical aspects of the project.

Finally, I would like to thank the staff and editors at Praeger Publishers, who have provided guidance and support throughout the process of producing this set. In particular, I would like to thank Marie Ellen Larcada who has since left the project but shared the conception of the set with me and supported me through the initial stages of production. My appreciation also goes to Elizabeth Potenza, who has guided this set into its final production, and without whose support this set would not have been possible. My kudos extend to you all.

Barbara J. Guzzetti

PREFACE

LITERACY FOR THE NEW MILLENNIUM: CHILDHOOD LITERACY

This book, the second in a series of four, addresses the literacy needs, interests, development, and practices of and for children in the intermediate grades of elementary school. Most often this includes students in grades 4 and 5, with some overlap to grade 6. A chapter in the text on adolescent literacy addresses specific areas of interest for middle school and junior high school students in the upper grades.

Children in the intermediate grades not only differ physically from their peers in the primary grades, but they also have different literacy interests and practices as well. They also have their own childhood culture and changing interests in popular culture. Their needs and interests set them apart from early readers as they grow more sophisticated in their understandings and acquisitions of reading and writing processes. Yet they are not ready for the experiences and interests of adolescents. Hence, this is a unique age group that requires appropriate support and recognition.

This text is crafted to address the unique topics and issues related to childhood literacy. To that end, this book is divided into three main parts. These parts range from two to seven chapters and provide an overview of topics related to childhood literacy. The topics were chosen to reflect and address the concerns of a variety of stakeholders, including those considering a career in education, graduate students in literacy, teachers, researchers, librarians, policy makers, and members of the interested public.

The first part, "Recent Issues in Childhood Literacy," presents current trends and issues that affect instruction and assessment in childhood literacy. It begins with a chapter by James Hoffman and Misty Sailors who emphasize that teachers are crucial to the support of students as they learn to read, and that all children deserve effective teachers. The authors provide readers with a summarization of effective teaching and effective teacher preparation in literacy and offer a set of "lessons learned" that can be used to describe effective teachers and teacher preparation. They conclude by identifying propositions to guide reading instruction for teacher education.

The second chapter in this part by Terry Salinger and Barbara Kapinus provides background on the National Assessment of Educational Progress (NAEP) in reading, an achievement survey done every four years to measure students' progress in reading. These authors trace the changes that have occurred in the design of the NAEP reading measure and provide information on the results of special studies carried out as part of the NAEP administrations. They conclude their chapter by describing the content of the NAEP assessments that will be used beginning in 2009.

The last chapter in this part by Randy Bomer discusses high-stakes tests of reading and writing. Bomer describes the nature and effects of standardized tests used to make important educational decisions. He discusses the probable motives of the politicians who decide to use such tests and accountability systems as a concern for those students whom the school does not serve well—the poor, African Americans, and those whose first language is not English. Bomer points out that, ironically, there is evidence that many of the very students that the accountability systems are supposed to help are the ones most harmed by constant testing. Bomer also describes the perspective of many teachers on such policies—that the tests force them into unprofessional practices that they know to be against the interests of their students' learning. This chapter also describes the ways that educators are coping with the difficulties imposed by these political policies.

The second part of this text, "Assessment and Instruction in Childhood Literacy," addresses a range of topics related to elementary literacy instruction and assessment. These topics begin with a chapter by James Baumann and T. Lee Williams on popular approaches and methods in reading instruction used by teachers in grades 3 to 6. The authors discuss eight different methods for reading instruction that are considered to be either skills-based methods (i.e., basal reading programs and direct instruction reading programs), holistic methods (i.e., the language experience approach, reading-writing workshop, and literature-based reading programs), or balanced methods (i.e., guided reading instruction and the four blocks approach).

The next chapter in this part describes and explains the various kinds of formal and informal assessments used to measure reading ability. Jerry Johns and Janet Pariza begin with a discussion of standardized reading tests and issues of reliability and validity of these tests and introduce the reader to the technical language associated with standardized measures. After they describe achievement, diagnostic, and criterion-referenced tests, they explain the limitations of formal measures. They then describe various informal methods, including commercially produced informal reading inventories and other methods, concluding with advice on the best use of reading assessments.

In the third chapter in this part, Robert Calfee and Kim Norman review research, textbooks, writing assessments, and state and national standards to describe writing development for the intermediate grades. The authors describe the nature of writing tasks in regard to content, genre, organization, and complexity. They make the point that writing is the means by which students demonstrate their acquisition of content. They conclude the chapter with a discussion on instruction and assessment and by suggesting practices that support the development of writing across disciplines.

The fourth chapter in this part, written by Kathy Short, explains the potential of children's books to transform children's lives through connecting their hearts and minds. Because readers construct their own understanding and interpretations as they engage with books, children's literature must be examined not only for itself, but also for the ways in which children engage with these books as readers. Short provides an overview of literary and aesthetic considerations, multicultural and international issues, the selection of fiction and nonfiction; she concludes with a brief list of recommended literature.

In the next chapter in this part, Shane Templeton and Bob Ives characterize spelling or orthographic knowledge as more than a skill for writing, but as an underpinning for word recognition, as well. These authors posit that the spelling system of American English is more regular than often believed and that this regularity is evident by considering the three principles that govern the spelling system—alphabet, conceptual pattern, and meaning. Spelling instruction supports vocabulary and vice versa. Templeton and Ives offer general tenets for instruction that develops students' spelling abilities.

The sixth chapter in this part by Rachel Washington, John Bishop, Emma Bailey, and JoBeth Allen present a fictionalized narrative of a 3rd-grade teacher's attempts to meet the needs of her culturally and linguistically diverse students. This vignette focuses on two aspects of teaching for social justice—educational equity or ensuring that all students have equal opportunity to learn and succeed, and involving students in issues that affect their lives. The chapter includes issues such as learning the academic and cultural expectations of parents and children, building on students' strengths and interests, and language diversity. Resources for multicultural children's literature, as well as teaching for social justice and educational equity, are included.

The last chapter in this part by David Reinking and Amy Carter describes shifts in reading print to digital texts, the digital revolution, and digital literacies. These authors summarize how literacy educators and researchers have responded to increasing digital literacies and identify the factors that have limited those responses. They provide references to other perspectives, particularly to studies on digital writing.

The third and final part is "Childhood Literacy Beyond the Classroom." This section addresses topics that relate to literacy outside the school and represent recent trends and resources in consideration of childhood literacy. The first chapter by Thomas Newkirk describes the intersections of childhood culture and popular culture. This chapter draws on research documenting the media exposure of children and young adults, and presents the concerns of groups who claim that engagement in popular culture contributes to youth violence and other social pathologies. These views are balanced by opposing positions of scholars who take a less alarmist stance by arguing that involvement in popular culture has cognitive and social benefits. Newkirk concludes the chapter by exploring the permeable curriculum, a concept posited by scholar Anne Dyson who claims that these affiliations to visually mediated popular culture can provide scaffolding for literacy learning.

The second and final chapter in this part by Denise Morgan and Wendy Kasten provides an overview of the literacy resources available for the reading development of students of elementary school age. Morgan and Kasten pose questions to serve as a guide to assist adults in selecting appropriate print materials and online resources and Web sites. The authors describe such resources and journals provided by professional organizations. They offer books, periodicals, and online resources in reading, writing, and language arts.

Part One

RECENT ISSUES IN CHILDHOOD LITERACY

Chapter One

EFFECTIVE TEACHING AND TEACHER PREPARATION IN READING: LESSONS THAT MATTER

James V. Hoffman and Misty Sailors

We believe that teachers are crucial in supporting children as they learn to read. We believe in the power of quality teacher education programs to prepare professionals who can serve effectively in this role. These are assertions that reflect our passion as teacher educators and our experiences as classroom teachers. These are also assertions grounded in a growing body of research on teachers, teaching, and teacher education. To be clear, these are not claims toward the status quo. We firmly believe that teacher educators can and must do better. Our claims are set in a vision of the high quality that exists in some particular cases today, and what should become the reality for all children in the near future. All children deserve effective teachers, and all of those who aspire to become teachers deserve to be prepared well.

Who would take issue with these statements? Surprisingly, there are many. As literacy educators, we surround ourselves in the discourse of "teachers matter" in the lives of the students whom they serve. National polls tell us that teachers are among the most trusted professionals. The fact is, however, that we live within institutions that treat teachers as if they cannot be trusted with instructional decisions. Teachers are valued insofar as they preserve and protect what exists. They are devalued when they question or teach their students to question the status quo. We do not believe, on most days, that this protectionism is a conscious conspiracy of the "haves" against the "have-nots." Rather, we believe there are institutional realities that constrain decision making in ways that too often determine the answers (and outcomes) of education. This underbelly of control and manipulation has been revealed more clearly as the metaphors of "accountability" and "outcomes" have become dominant in schools. Productivity and not democracy is the stuff of schools today. For the underserved, reading has become a set of skills to be mastered. The "democratic" creation and interpretation of texts in schools are rare in this community (Hoffman, 2000).

The recent attacks on teacher preparation programs suggest that teacher educators are even less trusted than teachers—portrayed as the "culprits" in a system that is failing (National Council on Teacher Quality, 2006). Some would argue that teacher education is being systematically dismantled. Alternative programs of preparation and "instant" certification programs are replacing university-based programs of preparation. The case for these programs is made on the basis of "need" for fully certified teachers in classrooms. The "No Child Left Behind Act" requires that all teachers be instructed with fully certified teachers. What easier path to reach this objective than providing a quick path to certification for anyone and everyone? Where do these fast-track teachers enter the profession? They enter through the classrooms that serve economically disadvantaged communities. Policy makers find it convenient to ignore research showing that these teachers are far less effective than the teachers who have been certified through university-based programs. Rather, they focus on the development of programs that are scripted and teacher proof.

We believe that the case for what counts as effective teaching and effective teacher preparation has not been made in nearly as public a manner as is needed. These issues have become mired in debates that don't really matter. There are camps created around fires that offer no light or warmth. We write this chapter to summarize what we have learned about effective teaching and effective teacher preparation through personal experience and research. We offer a set of "lessons learned" that can be used to describe a consensus around effective teachers and teacher preparation.

We offer these "lessons learned" as a source of support for beginning teachers as they develop a personal "vision" of learning and teaching. A vision, according to Duffy (2002), is a teacher's "moral compass." That is, a vision helps a teacher make instructional decisions for the children with whom she or he works. What a teacher believes to be real and true about teaching and learning is a personal perspective and is guided by what that teacher wants children to become long after they have left the classroom. A teacher's vision is influenced by who he or she is personally and politically and is shaped by personal history. Visions of teachers can and do change over time and are influenced by ever-growing professional and personal development.

In this chapter, we write directly to those who are considering or planning, or who have already started preparation to enter teaching. We off a set of propositions that are specific to teaching and teacher preparation in reading instruction, although we suspect that the model could easily be generalized to most teaching contexts. We have organized this presentation around 10 "lessons learned" and one grand lesson.

EFFECTIVE TEACHERS: LESSONS THAT MATTER

1. Effective Teachers Understand Reading

Effective teachers understand the reading process and reading development (situated within a broader understanding of language processes) and that reading is a means to a larger end—that of learning. The literature on reading instruction is filled with the great debates in reading, forever replaying the differences in various approaches to teaching reading. Some argue that the best way to begin reading instruction is to teach children to learn to read by first learning to sound words out (commonly referred to as "phonics"); others argue that the best way to begin reading instruction is through the teaching of reading as part of a system of language (commonly referred to as "whole language"). These debates are not helpful to teachers who must meet the needs of their students. There must be careful representations of the consensus on the reading process and development that draw on multiple methods of research.

We do not envision this representation taking the form of a "checklist" of facts to be learned or skills to be mastered. Rather, we envision a complex representation of the development of strategic reading that is explained clearly to children, especially those who struggle with reading. We believe that reading is not a set of skills that are to be taught in isolation from learning, and so instruction must be purposeful and meaningful to students. Assertions that are *not* widely supported by research (e.g, context is not important in word recognition) should be addressed and challenged, as well as incomplete representations of the process as those included in the National Reading Panel Report (Allington, 2002). At the same time, however, a consensus must be reached that can guide instruction. There will always be enough uncertainty within our models to drive further inquiry.

2. Effective Teachers Use Informal Assignments

Effective teachers are in touch with the ever-changing interests, strategies, skills, and instructional needs of their students through the application of a variety of informal assessment tools. Early on in Donald Graves's (1994) *A Fresh Look at Writing*, Graves asks readers to write down everything they know about their students. Our undergraduates almost always comment on how much the classroom teachers they work with know about their students—deep knowledge that reaches across domains of skills, interests, family history, aspirations, frustrations, and on and on. This is true of most outstanding teachers. In an early study of portfolio assessment (Hoffman et al., 1998), we asked teachers to rank order the students in their classrooms in terms of how well they would score on a standardized reading test at the end of first grade before the students took the test. We then correlated the teachers' rankings with the rankings of the students in the class after they had taken the test. The correlation was extremely high. This is, of course, a crude demonstration of teachers' knowledge of students. It is much more important to look specifically at what they know, value, and act on in their teaching. Effective teachers do not need a test, in particular a standardized test, to guide them. They know their students.

They know their students through the application of systematic assessment strategies that include careful observations, interviews (conversations), focus assessments (such as those used during reading instruction that document the strengths of readers), and the analysis of classroom work/artifacts (portfolios). They document carefully. They are able to use multiple sources to capture and see the strategies used by their readers across reading opportunities. They are in a constant state of dynamic assessment during instruction. In fact, the lines between what is "instruction" and what is "assessment" are often blurred so much that the observer—even the teacher—may not know when one ends and the other begins. Assessment (not testing) drives their teaching.

3. Effective teachers teach to strengths.

Before the "accountability" movement of the1980s took control of education, there were decades of "clinical"/deficit models of teaching reading (that persist as undercurrents to this day). The diagnostic-prescriptive model set teachers on the path of "find the needs" (usually through some kind of testing) and teach what the student doesn't know to mastery. Those who cannot recall the skills-based management systems of the 1980s are fortunate—unless this means they are doomed to relive it.

Today, we have come to believe in the power of assessment to guide instruction as it reveals what the student "needs" (i.e., in the sense of motivation to learn, to reach out for, to experiment with). Good assessment leads to identification of what the learner knows and is exploring and then helps the teacher make instructional decisions to move the learner toward greater control over what is being learned. We have seen this as expert teachers of writing "notice" learners experimenting with a particular "form" of written language (such as quotation marks). These teachers recognize that this is the moment for the mini-lesson that extends and refines the writer's control over that convention. The assessment is based on careful kid watching (Goodman, 1985), not on the application of some scope and sequence that is tested then taught. This is more than just a matter of perspective (the glass half full; the glass half empty). This is a case of looking for something entirely different to guide instruction.

4. Effective teachers have high expectations for themselves and for the students they teach.

The notion of "high expectations" as part of effective teaching is rooted in both the mythology of teaching (How many movies can you name in which the teacher believed in students where no one else did and made a difference?) and in empirical data. Good (1987), for example, describes a "can do attitude" as a hallmark of effective teaching (i.e., teachers associated with high gains for students on achievement test. Here is the understanding that is almost always lost in the "posters" and "testimonies." Anyone can espouse a "high expectation" philosophy, but can it be enacted? Research that has explored the relationship between teachers' high expectations for students' success and their students' growth typically shows a low relationship when the measures of teachers' expectation are in the abstract. It is only when the "expectations" of teachers are assessed in relation to the children that they work with and are responsible for—in particular students who struggle within the academic curriculum—that the relationship between teachers' expectation and students' achievement grows.

It is not simply the expectations for students that make a difference. It is the expectation that the teacher can and will that makes a difference in students' learning .Failure on the part of students is viewed as a failure on the part of their teachers—and these teachers will not stick to the same plan. These are classrooms without "labels" and without excuses. These teachers will change and they will make a difference.

5. Effective teachers plan, organize, and instruct within a variety of classroom routines and activity structures.

The principal walks into a classroom to conduct an unannounced observation. The teacher is reading aloud to the children. The school principal shuffles back out the door whispering, "It's ok. I'll come back later when you're teaching." We have not made this up. We have observed it. One of the tremendous shortcomings of the "process-product" effective teaching literature is the extreme focus on direct instruction (Hoffman, 1986). Direct instruction is important, but it is only one of several models of teaching that effective teachers use. Joyce and Showers (1994) describe "models" of teaching ranging from "Information Processing" to "Social" to "Personal" and the many representations of these models within a classroom. Information processing models (e.g., a "Madelyn Hunter" seven-step lesson) emphasizes the transfer of specific information (knowledge) and skills with the teacher in control. Social models (e.g., cooperative learning, book clubs) emphasize the importance of social interaction and language in building inferences and insights. Personal models (e.g., workshops, inquiry) emphasize the role of the learner in making significant choices in the curriculum.

It is unfortunate, from many perspectives, that the literature positions these models of teaching as antithetical to one another and incompatible within a teaching philosophy. Effective teachers do not see instruction in such black-and-white terms. At one point, Joyce's model was seen as a kind of "choice" list arrayed along a continuum that the effective teacher selected from based on learning goals. More recently, the model has been viewed not along the lines of a continuum of a circle. Apparent contradictions become complementary. In pragmatic terms it is the "mini-lesson" (an information processing/direct instruction model) that takes on its power within a "writers workshop" (a personal/indirect model). Effective teachers create spaces where instruction supports learners seeking to fulfill needs.

6. Effective teachers use individual and collective reflection as processes that support the creation of professional knowledge.

Effective teachers learn from their students. John Dewey (1938) described it long ago: experience plus reflection are the key ingredients in learning for children and adults. David Shon (1987) and others have taken this notion to an empirical level. Professionals, educators included, use reflection on experience to shape their learning and their actions. The reflection is not just personal but social as well. The discourse community within a profession creates language and theories that lift us above the daily experience (Schon's "swamp") to discover principles and patterns that guide us to greater effectiveness.

We do not underestimate the role that language plays in this learning. The crucial interplay of language and thought and social discourse is enormous (Wertsch, 1991). We have found Peter Johnston's (2004) book, "*Choice Words*," is inspiring in this regard. Teachers who examine carefully the words that they use as they interact with children have a tremendous resource for change. Where does professional language come from? What does it represent at a deep level? How can teachers become better in saying what they mean? Effective teachers recognize the wealth of learning that can come through reflection.

7. Effective teachers enjoy learning with their students.

We have read a few too many essays on "Why I want to become a teacher" where the dominant theme is "I love to be around children." We find this motivation of "love to be around children" as weak in sustaining effective teaching. We recently attended a ceremony honoring a group of outstanding teachers. Teacher after teacher talked about their love for children. The last teacher honored began by saying that she felt guilty around the other teachers who were so expressive of their love for children. She "confessed" that her love of teaching was largely selfish. She described herself as "addicted" to learning, and that teaching was the only way to satisfy her habit. That expression of addiction rang true to us as an explanation for the rewards of teaching.

Moving out of the process-product movement, research on teaching shifted to focus on "teacher knowledge" (Shulman, 1986) but not nearly enough on "teacher learning." Measuring knowledge is a priority among those who strive to develop "tests" to certify teachers. The flaw here is similar to the flaw in tests designed to measure "intelligence" with a focus on knowledge accrued. Vygotsky (1978) argued that "intelligence" is revealed through the inspection of "learning" much better than through the examination of fossilized learning. The same is true of excellence and effective teachers. It's not what is known as much as it is the willingness and inclination to learn and to find joy in doing that with students.

8. Effective teachers struggle.

There is a "flow" to good teaching (Csikszentmihalyi, 1996). It looks so easy. This apparent ease leads to all sorts of misconceptions (e.g., anyone can do it, good teachers are born to teach, teaching is an easy job). These are far from the truth of teaching. Teachers are learners. They are learning about their students, about their craft, and about the content they teach. They are learning to "cope" with institutional barriers and hurdles (e.g., high-stakes tests, summer "vacations," labeling of children, grouping and scheduling practices). The life of a teacher is filled with struggles that frustrate and may even drive teachers out of their chosen profession.

Effective teachers survive by adapting and negotiating. They become, as Ayers (2001) describes, "creatively compliant." Ayers offered an example from his own teaching to illustrate this point. He was bothered constantly by the interruption of announcements from the office into his classroom. Complaining about this would do no good, he reasoned. So he climbed up and pulled the wire from the back of the speaker. He submitted a request to have the speaker repaired knowing this would take forever. Problem solved. Duffy uses the metaphor of a cross-country skier attacking a difficult hill to get over. The fool attacks directly and typically fails. The expert learns to traverse and be patient. In the end, the one who traverses is the one who prevails. We have seen this play out in teaching again and again—in particular in these times of severe policy pressure.

9. Effective teachers tend to see the whole child and the whole curriculum.

We all make mistakes. In the first author's (Jim's) teaching experience, he devised and implemented a "Joplin plan" system for an elementary school that divided students, based on their instructional level, into classrooms for two hours of reading instruction each day. He trained teachers in how to administer and interpret an informal reading inventory. He sorted children across grade levels. He saw excellent teachers frustrated by a system that limited their opportunities to integrate instruction, to stay flexible in their teaching, and to be responsive to their students. Jim saw the teachers who were less excellent compliment him on how great this system was and how their teaching was so much easier now. He saw the effects of labeling on children's self-concept and motivations. Jim lost focus on the child and on the teacher. He placed the curriculum in the foreground. It's one of those experiences that he is constantly apologizing for as he reflects on his career. Confession is good for the soul, but he looks forward to the time that he can improve without compromising the learning of others.

Whole language swept the country in the 1990s, in part, as a reaction to the severe fractioning of the curriculum, the overlabeling of children, and the overemphasis on standardized testing (Goodman, 1986). Whole language offered an alternative that was child-centered, a curriculum focused on processes, with huge attention to responsive teaching. Whole language has lost its momentum in recent years, but the message is no less valid today than it was a decade ago. The movement will in time reappear, perhaps under a new label or perhaps even an old one. It will reappear because it frames teachers and teacher education in a way that reflects research in teaching.

10. Effective teachers serve.

Teaching is a service profession. Teachers serve the students in our classrooms and their families. Teachers do not work for principals. They do not even work for school districts. Teachers are professionals contracted to teach. Teachers are focused on their students, which can become difficult with the pressures of testing the "closing the gap" rhetoric. Too many educators have become more focused on the scores and the "percent" of kids passing than on the children. Too many schools have come to accept the "triage" model for schooling. Students who will pass the tests are left on their own. Students who will not pass the test, regardless of instruction, are also left on their own. Students who might pass the test if offered intense instruction are given the bulk of the attention. This ethic may be defended in the case of medical emergencies, but not in education. The scores, the schools, the districts, and the system become the focus. We have failed.

One other benefit of the service ethic is the influence it has on the individual to learn about and learn to appreciate students from backgrounds different from the teacher's. The intense, personal commitment of service leads to significant contact that helps the teacher step outside his or her own life and move into another (Eyler & Giles, 1999). These connections provide the teachers with a base to begin to build from the known to the new.

EFFECTIVE TEACHER EDUCATION

For every person who believes the best teachers are those who move on to become teacher educators there is another who subscribes to the view that: "Those who can't teach, teach teachers." Neither of these claims is true. Teacher educators are no more or no less smarter, harder working, higher paid, or valued than other teachers. The qualities that mark effective teacher educators are no different from those I have used to describe effective teachers. Their students are sometimes taller and older. Their institutions are no less challenging to effective practice than public schools (e.g., course structures). It is all the same and always a challenge. We have recently completed a study of teacher preparation in reading education that followed teachers through their first years of teaching. We recently reported on the qualities of effective programs and the impact of effective preparation on the transition into teaching. Teacher educators inside quality programs make a difference (International Reading Association, 2005).

We teach in teacher preparation programs that are nontraditional. We take students into our programs in cohorts. We teach most of their courses and we organize the experiences that our students have in classrooms working with teachers and children while they take our courses. We have a classroom in the elementary school where we tutor and work with teachers. We follow the schedule of the public schools and not the university. We try to blur the lines between courses, much to the concern of students at times. We make contact with the parents of our students (or their children in some cases). We work to create a real learning community that is like the ones they will create in their own professional lives as teachers. The qualities and impact of our program have been demonstrated and informed by numerous studies. A quality teacher preparation is more than a set of courses that the student completes in order to graduate.

The only differences we can detect between effective teaching and effective teacher education are the institutional barriers we have to accommodate. At the university, we struggle with course descriptions, course schedules, programs of work, academic calendars, certification standards/tests, accreditation agencies, and admission criteria to programs. Classroom teachers have their own set of institutional struggles that are both similar and different. In the end, however, we both serve learners, and all of the other principles we have described apply as much to teacher educators as to teachers.

THE GRAND LESSON

The need to value teachers and teacher educators

If quality teachers and teacher educators are not valued and supported, they may leave the profession. Teachers and teacher educators have never received the financial support they deserve. Teachers' salaries are considerably lower than other professions that require similar levels of preparation and effort. Teacher educator salaries are typically the lowest within colleges and universities. Sadly, this realty is not likely to change in the short term. The good news is that salaries have never been one of the factors that support teachers and teacher educators in their choice of a professional career or in sustaining their engagement over time. The bad news is that conditions of teaching are changing rapidly, and many of these changes are driving the best teachers out of the profession. Mandated curricula, standard course syllabi, high-stakes testing, and other forms of "accountability" are part of an effort to de-professionalize teaching.

Significant responsibilities for professional decision making are being replaced by scripted and standardized programs for teachers in reading instruction. These changes remove the professional obligation to be strategic and responsive to individual differences. This is particularly the case in working in schools of poverty and programs that prepare teachers to work in these schools. The best teachers are leaving because they can no longer teach in the ways that they know best.

Who will replace them? If the trends toward standardization continue, we envision the next generation of teachers as technocrats who will easily step in and out of slots. The "fast food" nation will become the "fast schooling" nation, with commercial programs that are targeted to create a standardized product that everyone recognizes. Unfortunately, this standardized product approach will underestimate the potential of learners to achieve and will only perpetuate inequities that exist within our society.

This is not just a projection about the future. It is a reality in many schools today. Teachers are dropping out of the profession at alarming rates (Quality Counts, 2003). The track into teaching has become faster and easier. Preparation has become less professional and more technical. Inner-city teaching has become the testing ground to see whether these fast-track teachers can survive. If not, they drop out. If they continue, they move on into the suburbs. Teacher shortages in inner-city schools are not due to a lack of teachers; they are the result of teachers not being supported to teach in these settings (Darling-Hammond, 2003).

No single group can reverse this trend. It will take a conscious effort of teachers, parents, researchers, and policy makers working together to redirect teaching and teacher education back on the track of professionalism that has been the focus over a century in this country. Not that long ago, most elementary school teachers were high schools graduates (or less), elementary schools were the terminal degree for the majority of learners, and the expectation for schools was to prepare individuals to function effectively in the same setting and the same roles as their parents (Hoffman & Pearson, 2000). The American dream for public education as the great liberator and equalizer is "at risk." The dream has been hijacked by a public agenda for accountability and standardization. The "Nation at Risk" that warned us of the threat of peril from within has become strangely and sadly prophetic. It is time to take what we have learned through research that matters on effective teaching and teacher preparation to reenvision a future for public education in America and for literacy for all.

REFERENCES

Allington, R. (2002). *Big brother and the national reading curriculum: How ideology trumped evidence.* Portsmouth, NH: Heinemann.

Ayers, W. (2001). T*o Teach: The Journey of a Teacher* (2nd ed.). New York: Teachers College Press.

Csikszentmihalyi, M. (1996). *Creativity: Flow and the psychology of discovery and invention.* New York: HarperCollins Publishers.

Darling-Hammond, L. (2003). Keeping good teachers: Why it matters, what leaders can do. *Educational Leadership, 60* (8), 6–13.

Dewey, J. (1938). *Experience in education.* New York: Macmillan.

Duffy, G. (2002). Visioning and the development of outstanding teachers. *Reading Research and Instruction, 41,* 331–344.

Eyler, J., & Giles, D. E. (1999). *Where's the learning in service-learning?* San Francisco: Jossey-Bass.

Good, T. L. (1987). Two decades of research on teacher expectations: Findings and future directions. *Journal of Teacher Education, 38,* 32–47.

Goodman, K. (1986). *What's whole in whole language?* Portsmouth, NH: Heinemann.

Goodman, Y. (1985). "Kid Watching: Observing Children in the Classroom" In A. Jaggar and M. T. Smith-Burke (Eds.), *Observing the language learner* (pp. 9–18). Newark, DE: International Reading Association.

Graves, D. H. (1994). *A fresh look at writing.* Portsmouth, NH: Heinemann.

Hoffman, J. V. (1986). *Effective teaching of reading: research and practice.* Newark, NJ: International Reading Association.

Hoffman, J. V. (2000). The de-democratization of schools and literacy in America. *Reading Teacher, 53* (8), 616–623.

Hoffman, J. V., & Pearson, P. D. (2000). Reading teacher education in the next millennium: What your grandmother's teacher didn't know that your granddaughter's teacher should. *Reading Research Quarterly, 35* (1), 28–45.

Hoffman, J. V., Worthy, J., Roser, N., McKool, S., Rutherford, W., & Strecker, S. (1998). Challenging the assessment context for literacy instruction in first grade classrooms: A collaborative study." In C. Harrison, M. Bailey & A. Dewar (Eds.), *New approaches to reading assessment.* London: Longman.

International Reading Association (2005). *Prepared to make a difference: A report of the national commission of excellence in the preparation of elementary teachers in reading.* Newark: International Reading Association.

Johnston, P. (2004). *Choice words: how our language affects children's learning*. Portland, ME: Stenhouse Publishers.

Joyce, B., & Showers, B. (1994). *Student achievement through staff development*. White Plains, NY: Longman, Inc.

National Council on Teacher Quality (2006). *Increasing the odds: How good policies can yield better teachers*. Washington, DC: NCTQ.

Quality Counts. (2003): If I Can't Learn From You. . . . : Insuring a highly qualified teacher-for every classroom. *Education Week*. Bethesda, MD. Retrieved March 26, 2003, from www.edweek.org/qc03

Shon, D. (1987). *Educating the reflective practitioner*. San Francisco: Jossey-Bass.

Shulman L. (1986). Paradigms and research programs in the study of teaching. In M. C. Wittrock (Ed.), *Handbook of research on teaching* (3rd ed.). New York: McMillan.

Vygotsky, L. V. (1978). *Mind in society*. Cambridge, MA: Harvard University Press.

Wertsch, J. V. (1991). *Voices of the mind: A sociocultural approach to mediated action*. Cambridge, MA: Harvard University Press.

Chapter Two

THE NATIONAL ASSESSMENT OF EDUCATIONAL PROGRESS IN READING

Terry Salinger and Barbara Kapinus

The National Assessment of Educational Progress (NAEP) is a federally funded, nationally representative assessment of what American students know and can do in numerous content areas, including reading. NAEP is administered at three points along the kindergarten to grade 12 span (grades 4, 8, and 12) to provide information about students in elementary, middle, and high schools. NAEP assessments have been part of the education landscape since 1969, as data have been used to report on students' achievement in numerous subjects, including reading, and to contrast achievement according to various demographic groups. Perhaps its most important role has been to report the upward and downward trends in achievement, which are often used as a measure of the success of educational reform efforts.

This chapter begins with a general overview of the NAEP, with particular attention to the reading assessment. It continues by discussing how NAEP is developed, what it measures, and how data are reported. The chapter ends with a contrast of the 1992 form of the assessment and the changes that will be made as a new framework is implemented for the 2009 assessment.

OVERVIEW OF THE NATIONAL ASSESSMENT OF EDUCATIONAL PROGRESS

The original impetus for NAEP was the 1963 congressional mandate that established the U.S. Office of Education. Representatives of the Office of Education, the Carnegie Foundation, and the Center for Advanced Studies in the Behavioral Sciences were tasked with devising a mechanism to provide data on the condition and progress of education across the country. Their challenge was to devise an assessment system that would differ from the norm-referenced cognitive testing approach that was prevalent at the time and has continued on into the present. Assessments would be developed to measure achievement in reading, writing, mathematics, science, literature, social studies, art, music, citizenship, and career/occupational development, using mostly open-ended, constructed-response items (Jones, 1996). The assessments stay independent of particular curricular approaches, and resulting data were intended to provide information for policy makers, educators, and parents. As discussed later, until fairly recently, the original plan for open-ended items was abandoned in favor of the less expensive multiple-choice items, and item format continues to be a point of tension as NAEP specifications are periodically revised. Over time, reading and mathematics have been the most frequently tested subjects of all the NAEP subjects.

Although independent of curricular approaches, NAEP in many ways is the closest representation there is to national standards or a national curriculum in the United States. Frameworks that guide assessment development for each NAEP subject area and the achievement levels that shape reporting have been agreed on by nationally representative committees and seek to affect national policy. NAEP reports, often referred to as "The Nation's Report Cards," are widely cited, primarily because the data they provide document both trends in student achievement and differentials in achievement of students from different demographic groups.

Since 1990, the nonpartisan, presidentially appointed National Assessment Governing Board (NAGB) has had oversight for NAEP's design, administration, and reporting. NAGB's 25 members include governors, state legislators, educators at the state and local level, curriculum and measurement experts, and representatives of the business community and of the general public. The National Center for Educational Statistics administers the assessment program, which is developed and carried out by several testing companies.

NAEP seeks to be a rigorous assessment. Its reporting mechanism, referred to as achievement levels and described later, sets high standards for proficiency. Some critics have said that the standards set by the achievement levels are too high (Shepard, 1993). Many states have adopted the proficiency level labels—basic, proficient, and advanced—for use in their own test score reporting, probably because these terms seem to be more easily understood than grade level equivalents. Studies of ways in which states set standards to determine what the levels mean on their state tests, however, suggest that NAEP's rigorous standards are not always adopted along with the labels (National Research Council, 1999b).

Since 1990, NAEP has provided state-level data for comparative purposes. NAEP also administers assessments to samples of students in large urban districts so that cities like Washington, DC or Los Angeles have their own data for analysis and comparative purposes. With passage of the No Child Left Behind Act (NCLB) of 2000, NAEP has taken on even more importance. NCLB stipulates that NAEP assess reading in grades 4 and 8 every two years and reading in grade 12 every four years. NCLB further states that state participation in NAEP is prerequisite for Title I funding, and districts selected for inclusion in the NAEP sample must also participate or forfeit Title I funds. Because by law, NAEP scores cannot be reported for individual students, schools, or districts (other than the participants in the Trial Urban Assessment), data for individual schools in the NAEP sample do not contribute to determining their progress toward Adequate Yearly Progress goals. Nonetheless, state results on NAEP are considered important indicators of upward or downward achievement "trends" and often provide a sobering contrast to inflated state reading test scores.

DIFFERENT FORMS OF NAEP

Many of the people who use NAEP data do not realize that there are actually two independent forms of the assessment, both serving different goals. One goal for NAEP is to report students' achievement in a subject such as reading at a specific point in time and trends in achievement over relatively brief periods. This is often referred to as "main" NAEP. Thus, since 1992, students have taken the NAEP reading assessments developed to align to the 1992 framework. Beginning in 2009, students will take a newly designed NAEP that is aligned to a new framework.

Data from each administration of "main" NAEP assessment can be compared to provide information on students' achievement over the period for which a framework is in use. For example, scores for 4th graders have shown no dramatic upward or downward trends on NAEP reading assessments administered from 1992 to 2005 (Perie, Grigg, & Donahue, 2005). Graphic representations of the scores on administrations during this period would show a relatively flat line. To make an even shorter term comparison, the average national score for 4th graders taking the 2005 NAEP reading assessment was only one point higher than the national average in 2003; this change was statistically insignificant and could not really be heralded as improvement. Eighth- and 12th-grade trends show similar patterns with minimal movement. In fact, short-term results found a modest decline in reading achievement from 2003 to 2005.

The second goal for NAEP is to report trends over longer periods, in fact, to document changes in achievement back to the first NAEP administrations. Accomplishing this goal requires administering a different form of NAEP to a smaller sample of students. This is referred to as "long-term trend" NAEP. These NAEP forms consist of items that have been carried forward unchanged from the original administration of the assessment. Thus students in 2006 who took the NAEP reading assessment designed to measure the long-term trend responded to the same items that were administered to the first cohort of comparable-age students and to every other cohort of students who participated in the long-term assessment. Administration of this original NAEP form allows for statements about whether students' reading scores have improved, declined, or remained "flat" from administration to administration over long periods. Such data can be especially interesting when compared against current curricular trends or policies, such as the current focus on scientifically based early reading instruction and extended periods of instruction as required by the Reading First guidance.

HOW NAEP IS PLANNED AND DEVELOPED

Two documents are developed for each subject that will be assessed: an assessment framework and test specifications. The frameworks and specifications are reviewed periodically, and major revisions occur every 10 to 12 years. For example, even though the 1992 NAEP reading framework was "revisited" and somewhat revised to respond to criticisms about the labels of the "aspects of reading," committees were assembled in 2002 to begin the process of deciding whether the existing framework should go forward or a new framework should be developed for the assessment to be administered in 2009 (see Salinger, Kamil, Kapinus, & Afflerbach, 2005, for a discussion of this process). There are several purposes for the NAEP frameworks and specifications, not the least of which is to explain in plain language the aspects of each subject area that will be assessed along with the format of the assessments, the anticipated difficulty level of assessments, and the procedures for scoring and reporting test results.

As was the case for the 1992 and the proposed 2009 reading frameworks, nationally representative advisory committees were convened to review the existing framework and make recommendations for the two documents. The committees include experts in the specific content areas, measurement experts, teachers and school administrators, and policy makers who will eventually use NAEP data to make recommendations for the assessments.

The frameworks present an organization of the domain agreed on by the committee members and make public the nature of the tasks that will appear on a test. For example, NAEP reading frameworks present the aspects of reading that will undergird the assessment. A continuing tension has existed about whether NAEP should include aspects of basic reading such as word attack skills on the assessment, but framework developers have consistently chosen to measure only comprehension. The specifications describe the characteristics of the tests more fully by giving detailed information to test developers. In reading, such information includes the length, characteristics, and sources of passages students will read.

The frameworks for NAEP assessments are subjected to wide public review to ensure that they are comprehensible and acceptable to educators and policy makers. They are also presented to the National Assessment Governing Board, which must approve them before they can be used for test development. The NAEP frameworks are readily available, along with NAEP reports, on the NAEP Web site, www.naep.org

The actual process of moving from framework and specification documents to actual test items, test booklets, and data is long and complicated. Once a framework and specifications have been reviewed and approved by the NAGB, commercial testing firms develop items, which again are thoroughly reviewed. Items are pilot tested before they are included on test forms. Commercial testing firms conduct the NAEP administrations nationwide and score the tests to create the databases from which reports are developed and made available electronically for secondary and specialized analyses. The National Center for Education Statistics and NAGB provide oversight of the entire process.

WHAT NAEP MEASURES

The NAEP assessments for all subjects attempt to sample the entire content area or domain that is being measured as thoroughly as possible. For reading, the domain includes the various strategies for comprehending literary and informational continuous text, poetry, and some documents. At the same time, NAEP seeks to exert a minimum of burden on students who take the assessment and on their teachers. The challenge of being able to sample the huge domain of reading in a short amount of time—less than one hour for the entire assessment process—is met through a process called matrix sampling. Thus a large assessment is developed that consists of approximately 10 "blocks" of items each of which takes about 25 minutes to complete on the current NAEP reading assessment. Through matrix sampling, each student actually receives about one-tenth of the entire assessment; that is, the blocks are intermingled so that there are many different "forms" of the assessment to administer. Aggregate data from all students who take the assessment at each grade contribute to total NAEP results.

In addition to the so-called cognitive items that assess a particular subject area, students respond to background surveys that gather information about their perceptions of topics such as instructional approaches used in their classes, the amount of homework they are assigned, the support they receive at home, their television viewing or computer use, or other topics of interest to researchers and policy makers. By linking responses to the cognitive items and the background surveys, researchers can make interesting generalizations about the student population as a whole and about different demographic sub-groups. For example, comparison of responses to background questions about quantity of reading and students' reading scores on NAEP showed a positive relationship between the amount of reading completed inside and outside of school and achievement in reading at the 4th-, 8th-, and 12th-grade levels (Donahue, Voelke, Campbell, & Mazzeo, 1999).

HOW NAEP DATA ARE REPORTED

NAEP results are reported in many different forms and for many different audiences. The aggregate results—for the nation as a whole—constitute the primary "message" reported after each NAEP administration, but data are also disaggregated by several groupings, such as region of the country; urban, rural, or suburban locations; or students' race/ethnicity, socioeconomic status, or gender.

The actual results—how students perform on the assessments—are reported as average scores and percentiles on 500-point, subject-specific scales. Specific points along the scale differentiate the achievement levels at each grade level. Students' scores are divided according to three main bands, the NAEP achievement levels. These are labeled basic, proficient, and advanced. NAGB has adopted generic descriptors for achievement levels across all NAEP assessments, and these are elaborated for the individual subject areas (Perie et al., 2005). The generic descriptor for advanced is "superior performance;" for basic it is "partial mastery of prerequisite knowledge and skills that are fundamental for proficient work." The middle band, proficient achievement, is the most comprehensive of the generic achievement level descriptors. It is shown in Table 2.1 along with the current descriptors of proficient reading at grades 4, 8, and 12.

The statistical procedures for setting the achievement levels have been strongly criticized (National Research Council, 1999a). Recommendations from a National Academy of Education study of the achievement levels suggested that any reporting of student achievement in terms of the NAEP achievement levels be accompanied by "clear and strong warnings that the results should be interpreted as suggestive rather than definitive because they are based on a methodology that has been repeatedly questioned in terms of its accuracy and validity" (National Research Council, 1999a, p. 167). Yet use of the achievement levels is common on state and commercially developed

Table 2.1
Generic and Reading-Specific Descriptors of the NAEP Proficient
Achievement Level

Generic Descriptor of Proficient Reading	Grade 4 Descriptor of Proficient Reading
This level represents solid academic performance for each grade assessed. Students reaching this level have demonstrated competency over challenging subject matter, including subject-matter knowledge, application of such knowledge to real-world situations, and analytical skills appropriate to each subject matter.	Fourth-grade students performing at the *proficient* level should be able to demonstrate an overall understanding of the text, providing inferential, as well as literal information. When reading text appropriate to 4th grade, they should be able to extend the ideas in the text by making inferences, drawing conclusions, and making connections to their own experiences. The connection between the text and what the reader infers should be clear. For example, when reading **literary** text, *proficient* level students should be able to summarize the story, draw conclusions about the characters or plot, and recognize relationships such as cause and effect. When reading **informational** text, *proficient* level students should be able to summarize the information and identify the author's intent or purpose. They should be able to draw reasonable conclusions from the text, recognize relationships such as cause and effect or similarities and differences, and identify the meaning of the selection's key concepts.

tests, perhaps because the terms seem to imply more certainty about students' actual achievement than they actually do.

Another frequent criticism of the NAEP achievement levels, especially as applied to reading, is that there is no comprehensive description of what students who score "below basic" actually can do. The media and the general public have often misinterpreted reports about the percentage of students whose NAEP scores are below the scale score cut off for basic, assuming incorrectly that students who read at the "below basic" level cannot read at all. Although some students in any cohort of "below basic" readers may have severe reading deficits, most students scoring in this band do have some fundamental, although low level, skills.

Some indication of what these low level, "below basic" skills can do is actually shown on another NAEP reporting device, the item maps that are developed for each assessment. Item maps lay out a full range of score points for each grade that is assessed; they show where the cut points are for the achievement levels; and they give short summary statements about the multiple choice and constructed response items at various points along the "map" (Perie et al., 2005). For example, the cut point for "basic" for the grade 4 NAEP is 208, and students scoring below this point are considered to be "below basic" readers. Table 2.2 shows the brief summary statements for items below the 208 cut point, that is, items that students scoring below basic could answer about informational and literary text. That some of the items are constructed response is important because it shows that they were able to construct some meaning from text and not merely make lucky guesses from among the options following a multiple choice item.

SPECIAL STUDIES

NAEP administrations provide an excellent opportunity to conduct special studies of smaller samples of students, and these are reported as in-depth analyses of relevant issues. Although researchers are encouraged to conduct postadministration secondary analyses of NAEP data, the special studies are planned before the assessment is given. They may or may not involve collecting additional data from students who take the actual assessment, but data can never be tracked back to specific individuals or schools.

One of the most ambitious studies, the Integrated Reading Performance Record, was conducted after the 1992 NAEP reading was administered. Interviews were conducted with more than 1,300 grade 4 students who had recently taken the NAEP reading assessment. They were asked about their reading habits, preferences, in- and out-of-school reading experiences, and their perceptions of their reading instruction. Also, "portfolios" of students' products from their reading work were collected, and students were recorded as they read orally one of the passages from the NAEP reading.

Two published reports detailed the results of this investigation: *Listening to Children Read Aloud* (Pinnell et al., 1995) and *Interviewing Children about Their Literacy Experiences* (Campbell et al., 1995). A rubric was developed to measure students' reading fluency (Pinnell et al., 1995), and analysis of the

Table 2.2
"Below Basic" Entries in a Grade 4 NAEP Reading Item Map

Score Point	Item Type	Task
207	Multiple choice	Identify a trait describing a main character
202	Constructed response	Provide story detail to support an opinion
201	Multiple choice	Recognize the main idea of an article
200	Constructed response	Provide text-based explanation of characters' importance to story
193	Constructed response	Retrieve and provide a text-related fact
172	Constructed response	Recognize the central problem faced by story character

recordings of oral reading for 4th graders' overall oral reading fluency, but not necessarily accuracy, was related to comprehension: students who comprehend well read with expression and good intonation, but their word-for-word accuracy was not perfect. The interview data showed that students who had been exposed to more diverse types of reading materials had higher reading achievement than students whose reading experiences were more limited (Campbell, Kapinus, & Beatty, 1995), and information about participating students suggested that "reading outside of school for enjoyment and reading self-selected books in school may be related to reading fluency" (Pinnell et al., 1995, p. 59). The oral reading fluency study was repeated in 2002, with the same reading passage and rubric but with more sensitive recording instruments. Results have not yet been released.

HOW NAEP HAS CHANGED OVER TIME

Some things about NAEP assessments have remained the same since their first administration, but other aspects have evolved to reflect changes in thinking about instruction and assessment (Jones, 1996; Salinger & Campbell, 1998). This is true for all the major subjects that NAEP assesses, and the changes in the reading assessment are especially illustrative of the process. The changes in many ways mirror the pedagogical and policy milieus in which four NAEP reading assessment frameworks were created. What has not changed over time is that scores still cannot be tracked back to individual schools, teachers, or students.

Another notable consistency across all administrations has been that NAEP is a low-stakes test; that is, there are no consequences for students, their teachers, or the schools that participate in the assessment. The stakes attached to NAEP changed somewhat when state NAEP was introduced and state-by-state comparisons became possible. Since then, the Trial Urban Assessment that tests students in large city schools has made another set of comparisons inevitable. Even though some states and districts will always come out "at the bottom" on NAEP, comparisons of this sort can be positive if they leverage local discussion about the need for educational reform.

In spite of the numerous changes that have shaped NAEP reading, reading comprehension has remained the primary outcome that is measured; however, the ways in which comprehension is conceptualized and measured and the ways in which results are reported have varied over the years. The introduction of large numbers of constructed response items into NAEP reading represented one significant change. Although the original architects of the NAEP system had envisioned the inclusion of many constructed response items (Jones, 1996), it was not until 1992 that NAEP reading really acknowledged the power of this item type. The most frequently cited drawback to constructed response items is the time required to develop and refine scoring rubrics and to train scorers, and then for scorers to read and evaluate written answers. The advantage of these items is that they can be designed to measure aspects of students' comprehension that most multiple-choice items cannot.

Beginning in 1992, students had to spend up to 50 percent of their time (for grade twelve) responding to items that asked them to write anywhere from a short sentence or two to extended paragraphs about what they had read. In adopting the proposed framework for the 2009 NAEP reading, the NAGB unanimously affirmed continuation of the use of constructed response items on NAEP. It is interesting to note that the other subject areas have adopted use of constructed response items as well.

Even more important than the shift in item formats have been the changes in how the NAEP frameworks have conceptualized reading comprehension and operationalized it through test development. The best way to illustrate the changes over time is to compare how the domain of reading has been delineated in a succession of NAEP reading frameworks. Table 2.3 contrasts the primary headings used to describe the aspects of reading that students have been asked to demonstrate on assessments developed from the three frameworks that have shaped NAEP so far (Council of Chief State School Officers [CCSSO], 1992; National Assessment of Educational Progress, 1970, 1981) and on the framework proposed for introduction in 2009 (American Institutes for Research, 2004).

The table is arranged to show reading behaviors that seem to be of a similar nature, but it is misleading in that there are no equivalent cells for "uses what is read" or "applies study skills in reading." The 1992 framework recommended that some of the materials included on the assessment be documents such as schedules or tables or other "practical" material that would lend themselves to questions measuring how well students could "read to perform a task." The proposed 2009 framework discusses how students "understand" text and how they "use" text, and it, too, includes procedural texts and documents, including the kinds of graphic material that students encounter in text books.

The contrast across these four sets of NAEP reading objectives reflects 40 years of changes in reading research and practice. The relatively straightforward sets of objectives published for the 1970–1971 and 1979–1980 assessments align with the management-by-objective or criterion-referenced reading programs that were prevalent in the period. The Wisconsin Design is a good example of such a program. The 1979–1980 assessment measured reading and literature, hence the background items assessing the value students place on reading and literature.

As Table 2.3 indicates, development of the 1992 framework represented a major shift in thinking about reading to reflect the ways in which thinking about reading instruction and assessment was changing (Langer,

Table 2.3
Primary Headings of Categories of Reading on Four NAEP Reading Frameworks

1970–71 Framework	1979–80 Framework	1992/2003 Framework Aspects of Reading	2009 Framework Cognitive Targets
Comprehend what is read	Comprehends written words	Forming an initial understanding/ Forming a general understanding	• Locate/recall • Integrate/infer
• Analyze what is read • Reason logically from what is read • Make judgments concerning what is read	Responds to written works in interpretative and evaluative ways	• Developing an interpretation • Demonstrating a critical stance (to text)/Examining content and structure	• Analyze/apply • Critique/evaluate
Use what is read	Applies study skills in reading		
		Personal reflection and response (toward text)/Making reader/ text connections	
Have attitudes about and an interest in reading	Values reading and literature		
		Stances: • Reading for a Literary Experience • Reading for Information • Reading to Perform a Task	

Campbell, Neuman, Mullis, Persley, & Donahue, 1995). Reading researchers, teacher educators, and many classroom teachers thought that the criterion-reference reading programs and standardized multiple choice reading tests had reduced the construct of reading comprehension to a set of discrete skills. Many were concerned that the teaching and measurement of reading seemed to deal more with the mechanics of getting meaning from text rather than with the individual meaning, relevance, or growth. A constructivist interpretation of reading—termed *reader response*—was coming to be accepted (Langer, 1995), and developers of state reading assessments were exploring new ways to measure reading (Wixson, Peters, Weber, & Roeber, 1987).

The developers of the 1992 NAEP reading framework sought to operationalize reader response and to take advantage of some of the ideas being used in innovative state assessments. They defined reading as "a dynamic, complex interaction among three elements: the reader, the text, and the context [of the reading act]" (CCSSO, 1992, p. 10). Concern about the context of the reading act was addressed through the division of types of reading into classifications that combined purpose and genre; thus readers were assumed to read certain kinds of texts for different purposes, and the choice of stimulus material was guided by these considerations.

The developers of the 1992 framework discussed "reading literacy" to expand the sense of reading beyond functional behaviors to "a broader sense of reading, including knowing when to read, how to read, and how to reflect on what has been read" (CCSSO, 1992, p. 6). They recommended that the best way to assess this broader sense of reading would be through the use of lengthy, authentic texts that are similar to what students at the three grade levels would actually encounter in their in- and out-of-school reading. They also recommended that the assessment include constructed response items, as the original NAEP design had intended. Students in 12th grade were estimated to spend approximately half their assessment time writing in response to open-ended prompts. Using a large number of constructed response items on an assessment with the magnitude of NAEP was a major challenge and required creating a new set of technical guidelines.

The 1992 NAEP Reading Framework had a powerful effect on state and commercial reading assessments and was praised because it so clearly aligned with the constructivist and literacy-based approaches to literacy instruction that were widely used. It had declared at a national level what the gold standards of reading tests should be during the 1990s: extensive use of constructed response items; long and diverse passages from literature, informational texts, and even documents, especially for the "reading to perform a task" stance; and items that reflected a reader-response perspective on reading.

Nevertheless, there were many criticisms. The underlying perspective on reading was difficult to translate into measurement items. According to the framework, items were to be classified according to "aspects of reading" to reflect a theoretical perspective that reading involves a process of moving in and out of text to gain meaning and then standing back to evaluate and analyze not just the meaning per se but also the way in which authors have crafted text (Langer, 1995). Although from a theoretical and perhaps even pedagogical perspective, this interpretation of how one reads is indeed elegant, reviewers trained on the meaning of the framework found it almost impossible to classify items reliably according to the stance to which item writers had assigned them (Pearson & DeStefano, 1994). As shown in Table 2.3, the labels were changed in the "revisited" framework, but the underlying constructs represented by the stances remained the same.

CHANGES PROPOSED FOR THE 2009 NAEP READING ASSESSMENT

When committees were convened in 2002 to develop the new framework and specifications for the 2009 NAEP Reading Assessment, they faced one important question: Should the taxonomy for item development and definition of reading embodied in 1992 NAEP be continued? Dramatic movement away from the existing framework would mean that the "trend line" of data from 1992 would be "broken" because even if many of the characteristics of the existing assessment were maintained, the item types included on assessments administered in 2009 and beyond would be different enough that student scores could not be compared. So-called "bridging studies" could be conducted to determine how the assessment results compared, and the regular "long-term trend" NAEP would be administered as usual, but in many ways a new conceptualization of the framework always means a new assessment.

As was the case with the 1992 NAEP reading assessment, developers of the 2009 framework were aware that the political climate in which they would do their work was fraught with strong opinions about why students seemed to be graduating from high school with reading skills that did not serve them well in postsecondary education or the workplace. Debates about what constituted "scientific evidence" for the effectiveness of approaches to reading instructional were also rampant. The passage of the *No Child Left Behind* legislation, introduction of the Reading First program, and general acceptance of the National Reading Panel's (National Institute for Child Health and Human Development, 2000) definition of reading as phonemic awareness, phonics, fluency, vocabulary, and comprehension all contributed to the political landscape in which the framework was developed. Further, policy makers at all levels were clamoring for more data more quickly than ever before, and NAEP's inclusion of constructed response items requiring human scoring was viewed as one obstacle to speedy test scoring and reporting.

Developers of the 2009 framework rejected the 1992 taxonomy in favor of one that is grounded in cognitive science rather than literary theory. For the new framework, reading would be defined as "an active and complex process that involves: understanding written text, developing and interpreting meaning, and using meaning as appropriate to type of text, purpose, and situation" (American Institutes for Research [AIR], 2004, p. 2). This definition views reading as involving the reader, texts, and purposes for reading, much as the 1992 framework had done, but it recommends changes in the way this interaction is assessed.

The broad reading categories are referred to as "cognitive targets" to ground them firmly in the cognitive science research on what readers do when they read. The terms used as labels of the cognitive targets—*locate/recall, integrate/ infer, analyze/apply, and critique/evaluate*—are deceptively simple. Developers of the framework worked hard to delineate the specific kinds of reading that could be classified under the broad headings and have further recommended that the reading behaviors be distinguished in three ways: those common across all text types, those specific to literary texts, and those elicited specifically by informational texts. Table 2.4 shows the extensiveness of the behaviors subsumed under the general category of "integrate and interpret" for both literary and informational texts at the 4th-grade level.

The 2009 framework has recommended the continued use of both multiple choice and constructed response items, with students in grade 4 spending approximately half the assessment time responding to multiple-choice items and half the time responding to constructed-response items; students in grades 8 and 12 spending even more time responding to constructed-respond items. Texts will continue to be long, authentic representations of the literary and informational texts student frequently encounter. Literary texts may be fiction, literary nonfiction (such as essays), or poetry; informational texts include exposition, argumentation and persuasive texts, and procedural texts and documents.

Changes in the taxonomy of reading behaviors would alone have been enough to necessitate that a new trend line be established when the new NAEP is administered in 2009, but they were not the only major change

Table 2.4
2009 NAEP Reading Grade 4 Cognitive Targets for Integrate and Infer by Text Type

Cognitive Targets for Integrate and Interpret at Grade 4	
Literary texts	**Informational texts**
Form a general idea	Form a general idea
Identify theme	Identify purpose
Describe a character	Identify problem and solution
Identify a character's motivation	Predict events
Predict events	Identify causation
Connect ideas within or across text	Identify various levels of text
Relate setting to development of theme or characters	
Describe relationships between and among characters	
Interpret character's motivation	
Provide paraphrases	
Identify symbols or symbolic language in literary text	

to the assessment. Past assessments have allowed for, but not required, some items that asked about vocabulary. The committees designing the 2009 framework recommended that items be developed to assess vocabulary on every NAEP passage. As the framework makes clear, the focus of vocabulary items on NAEP will be to measure students' "meaning vocabulary," that is, the ways in which students apply their understanding of word meanings in comprehending what they read (AIR, 2004; Beck, McKeown, & Omanson 1987). The words within NAEP passages that will be assessed must be central to passage meaning; not knowing or being able to approximate the meaning of these words will disrupt students' full comprehension of what they mean. The proposed framework and specifications give clear guidelines for selecting words to assess and for developing items.

The introduction of vocabulary assessment to NAEP reading is an important innovation because it emphasizes the essential role vocabulary knowledge plays in comprehension. Merely learning definitions or use of context clues is not enough to produce strong readers. Students must also learn strategies for figuring out word meaning as part of their entire set of comprehension skills.

CONCLUSION

The National Assessment of Educational Progress in reading has changed dramatically over the years, just as reading research and instruction have changed. NAEP short- and long-term trend data were always available for use, but it was probably not until the introduction of state NAEP testing in reading that policy makers and educators really wanted to know more details about the actual assessment instruments. The introduction of the 1992 framework provided this information, and many state and commercial tests followed its model. It remains to be seen whether introduction of the 2009 framework, with its definition of reading as a cognitive process and its assessment of vocabulary, will be equally as powerful. NAEP reading data, however, will continue to play an important role in educational decision making.

REFERENCES

American Institutes for Research (AIR). (September 2004). *Reading Framework for the 2009 National Assessment of Educational Progress.* Prepared for the National Assessment Governing Board in Support of Contract # ED-02-R-0007. Washington, DC: Author.

Beck, I. J., McKeown, M.G., & Omanson, R.C. (1987). The effects and use of diverse vocabulary instructional techniques. In M. G. McKeown & M. Curtis (Eds.), *The nature of vocabulary acquisition* (pp. 147–163). Hillsdale, NJ: Erlbaum.

Campbell, J. R., Kapinus, B., & Beatty, A.S. (1995). *Interviewing children about their literacy experiences.* Washington, DC: National Center for Education Statistics.

Council of Chief State School Officers. (1992). *1992 NAEP reading objectives.* Washington, DC: Author.

Daane, M. C., Campbell, J. R., Grigg, W. S., Goodman, M. J., & Oranje, A. (2005). *Fourth-grade students reading aloud:NAEP 2002 Special Study of Oral Reading* (NCES 2006-469). U.S. Department of Education. Institute of Education Sciences, National Center for Education Statistics. Wachington, DC: Government Printing Office.

Donahue, P. L., Voelke, K. E., Campbell, J. R., & Mazzeo, J. (1999). *NAEP 1998 report card for the nation and the states.* Washington, DC: National Center for Education Statistics.

Jones, L. J. (1996). A history of the National Assessment of Educational Progress and some questions about the future. *Educational Researcher, 27*(7), 15–22.

Langer, J. A. (1995). Envisioning literature: Literacy understanding and literacy instruction. New York: Teachers College Press.

Langer, J. A., Campbell, J. R., Neuman, S. B., Mullis, I.V.S., Persley, H. R., & Donahue, P. L. (1995). *Reading assessment redesigned.* Princeton, NJ: Educational Testing Service.

National Institute of Child Health and Human Development (2000). *Report of the National Reading Panel.* Washington, DC: Author.

National Research Council. (1999a). Grading the Nation's Report Card: Evaluating NAEP and transforming the assessment of educational progress. Washington, DC: National Academy Press.

National Research Council. (1999b). *Uncommon measures: Equivalence and linkages of educational tests.* Washington DC: National Academy Press.

Pearson, P. D., & DeStefano, L. (1994). Content validation of the 1992 NAEP in reading: Classifying items according to the reading framework. (pp. 285–314). In R. Glaser, R. Linn, & G. Bohrnstedt (Eds.), *The trial state assessment: Prospects and realities: Background Studies.* Stanford, CA: National Academy of Education.

Perie, M., Grigg, W., & Donahue, P. (2005). *The nation's report card: Reading 2005.* Washington, DC: National Center for Education Statistics.

Pinnell, G. S., Pikulski, J. J., Wixson, K. K., Campbell, J. R., Gough, P. B., & Beatty, A. S. (January 1995). *Listening to children read aloud: Data from NAEP's Integrated Reading Performance Record (IRPR) at Grade 4.* Washington, DC: National Center for Education Statistics.

Salinger, T., & Campbell, J. (1998). The national assessment of reading in the USA. In C. Harrison & T. Salinger (Eds.), *Assessing reading: Theory and practice.* (pp. 96–109). London: Routledge.

Salinger, T., Kamil, M., Kapinus, B., & Afflerbach, P. (2005). Development of a new framework for the NAEP reading assessment. In B. Maloch, J.V. Hoffman, D.L. Schallert, C.M. Fairbanks, & J. Worthy (Eds.), *The 54th yearbook of the National Reading Conference.* (pp. 334–348). Oak Creek, WI: National Reading Conference.

Shepard, L. (1993). *Setting performance standards for student achievement. A report of the National Academy of Education Panel on the Evaluation of the NAEP Trial State Assessment: An evaluation of the 1992 achievement levels.* Stanford, CA: National Academy of Education.

Wixson, K. K., & Peters, C. P., Weber, E. M, & Roeber, E. D. (1987). New directions in statewide reading assessment. *The Reading Teacher, 40,* 749–754.

Chapter Three

HIGH-STAKES TESTING OF READING AND WRITING AT THE ELEMENTARY LEVEL

Randy Bomer

The other chapters in this book discuss elements of literacy instruction that the education profession has developed thoughtfully and carefully across years of research, theory, and expertly crafted teaching. This chapter is different. It is about a practice that has been developed by people who are not educators, with no research about how it will affect young people. The subject of this chapter, however, has exerted a stronger impact on literacy instruction than any one of the others, especially in recent years. Nothing at present conditions the nature of literacy in school as much as so-called *high-stakes testing.*

The term is easy enough to define: it refers to the use of standardized tests to make significant decisions in an education system. A high-stakes test, then, is not a particular kind of test; the term is about the *use* to which a test is put. If a child's promotion from 3rd to 4th grade is determined by a test, then that is a high-stakes test—whether that test is a multiple choice test, a writing test, or a spelling test. Such consequences are not determined by the makers of the test or by educators. They are determined by elected officials or appointees—often through law and sometimes through administrative regulations and policies. Attaching stakes to a test, therefore, is a political decision.

The consequences of a particular test can be directed at the student or at the teacher, principal, school, district, or state. Stakes for educators and systems have included advancement in or loss of either pay or employment, the labeling of schools as good or bad, the requirement that schools provide additional services or options to transfer, or simply the publication of scores in newspapers. Whether a particular consequence should be considered *high stakes* is in the eye of the beholder.

In this chapter, I explain what high-stakes testing is, where it comes from, and the impact it has on teachers, students, and what goes on in schools. I begin with a consideration of what makes a test a high-stakes test and describe the range of things that can be called one. I then discuss the tangle of issues around high-stakes testing including social promotion, accountability, motivation of teachers and students, and political calculations. Next I review some research about the attitudes of teachers toward high-stakes testing and the reasons for those attitudes, and I describe some of what we know so far about the effects that these testing programs are having on teachers, students, and the sort of things that go on in schools. Finally, I describe some of the things teachers and other educators seem to be doing to respond to the policy realities.

In literacy and its learning, there is nothing more important than assessment: it is part of everything we do. But assessment does not always mean testing; it does not always mean someone outside the classroom does it; and it does not even mean the teacher instead of the student always does it. When students are learning to write, they must learn to assess the quality of what they have written so far in a piece of writing, so that they can know what and how to revise. For a writer, assessment is the activity that provides a map of the process. When reading, a person must monitor her or his own thinking to ensure that she or he is understanding the text and thinking in ways appropriate to the context for reading. When a reader assesses that he or she is on the wrong track or has made a mistake about the meaning, it is essential that the reader be able to self-correct. There is no way to learn to be a better reader or writer without assessing all along the way.

Teachers of literacy, too, must continually assess. Because literacy is thinking, its nature differs from one student to another, and the particular elements are learned in intricately individual ways. Consequently, a teacher must monitor each student's habits and progress, noting gains and planning what to do next. A classroom depends on a continual exchange of information—flowing from students to teacher as much as from teacher to students—as education unfolds in dialogue. Although assessment is essential to the teaching of reading and writing across all ages, it is never more crucial than in elementary education, where children are first establishing the meaning of literacy, developing habits and identities, and covering greater distances as learners than they ever will again in their literate lives.

Because assessment is so important to literacy and its teaching, it is especially significant that forces outside the classroom demand particular forms of assessment of teachers and children. If people who support increased testing are right, then such intensification might promote more learning, as students become more concerned about the quality of their reading and writing, and as teachers become more informed and supported by formal assessment systems that are backed up by the power of the state. On the other hand, if those opposing intensified testing are correct, then the imposition of high-stakes tests as a way of assessing diverse students and classrooms could actually impede the flow of accurate information and judgments within classrooms. This would occur because tests, written and determined by people far away from the classroom, move decision making to a place distant from the interactions that matter most.

FEDERAL LAW AND THE NEW PERVASIVENESS OF HIGH-STAKES TESTING

High-stakes tests are not particularly new. Even in the nineteenth century, teachers in some cities and towns in the United States lost their jobs over their students' scores on standardized tests (U.S. Congress, 1992). Certain states, such as New York, have had tests with serious consequences in high school for much of the twentieth century, including a competency test that students had to pass to graduate. When the National Council of Teachers of English asked me to chair a task force in 1999 to think about high-stakes testing and recommend responses to it, there were high-stakes tests in about 28 states. Now there are high-stakes tests in 50 states, because the federal government requires them of all states receiving federal education funds. Whereas in the past, high-stakes tests were mainly confined to high school students, they are now universally applied to elementary schools.

Since the passage of the No Child Left Behind Act in 2002, America's children are subject to high-stakes tests of literacy as soon as they move out of the primary grades in school. All 3rd graders are tested in reading, according to the provisions of No Child Left Behind, as are all 4th, 5th, 6th, 7th, and 8th graders. The main event of grades 3 to 5 in education policy is that at this age, the induction into the testing culture and its high stakes begins. Current federal law requires that schools make steady progress every year until 2014 when all students must have achieved a score designated as "proficient" in reading and math, as measured on the state's chosen tests. In addition, schools must show this "adequate yearly progress" with subgroups that include these social categories of children, among others: low-income, English language learners, Latinos/as, African Americans, American Indian, and special education. (By the time many readers encounter these words, this law will have changed substantially.) For now, let us just say that these requirements are difficult for schools, and they create a good deal of stress about the testing performance of students. The adults in the building respond to the *consequences* of the tests, and that is what makes them high stakes. These adults' responses are what create the environment for the children in their care. It is an environment characterized mostly by anxiety and fear. People often teach what and how they do because they are afraid of consequences, not because they believe their curriculum tells the truth, or because they have thought through what is important, or because it creates the most meaningful, thoughtful, democratic, or beautiful forms of life possible for their students.

High-stakes testing also creates authoritarian social relations. Because funding or status is at stake, people in positions of power manage in a more authoritarian way, so they introduce more and more prescriptive procedures for curriculum, teaching, and assessment; and they introduce more surveillance to ensure their control mechanisms are working. When stakes of one test are high, districts impose more test benchmarks to manage the risk that something unexpected will occur on the test that carries drastic consequences. My home district requires monthly benchmark testing of students in grades that have high-stakes tests, and some individual schools schedule even more frequent tests so that they will not be surprised by the outcomes of the benchmark tests that must be reported to the district. This level of information flow, of surveillance and control, dominates teachers' thinking; it takes over what they can imagine, consider, plan, or even notice. The position of managing information about students' levels of strength or weakness also positions students as providers of information about themselves. Their quality is always in question, and their competence is always under scrutiny.

Of course, the clearest examples of high stakes are those in which students' promotion to the next grade or graduation from high school is determined. For a 3rd, 4th, or 5th grader, 8 to 11 years old, not being promoted with one's friends to the next school grade is more than just a matter of educational policy: it can mean loss of friends, loss of status with siblings, or being prevented from progressing through life—arrested in the process of growing up. There may be consequences for identity—one's sense of self as competent and strong—and for social and emotional health. These are high stakes indeed. These uses of tests, of course, create stress for educators, too, especially teachers who know the children and want the best for their students.

Technically, the term *high-stakes testing* refers to the attachment of significant consequences to test scores. It seems a relatively straightforward concept, but it isn't. In fact, the term *high-stakes testing* in conversations about education in the United States carries with it an amalgam of conceptual assumptions, attitudes, histories, policies, technologies, and practices. An insistence on educational equity and impatience with the gap in achievement and opportunity among different social groups, especially races, are compressed inside the term, as is a faith in the technology of testing. These ideas share space, too, with beliefs about the motivations of teachers and students, and with others about promotion and retention of students. The term stands in for ideas about the accountability of public employees to the public and to powerful political entities and about the public's need, in a democracy, for information and involvement about the future being composed in the minds of its children. Technical dimensions of assessment are also contested in this term, including questions of whether every student must be tested in order to assess the system's progress, and whether a one-shot direct assessment of reading or writing can possibly produce a valid picture of what a learner can do. In other words, much of American history, politics, and culture is jammed into this single element of education policy or assessment practice.

EQUITY: THE PUTATIVE REASON FOR HIGH-STAKES TESTS

A public education system is answerable to the public, and elected representatives have a responsibility to make sure the schools are serving public purposes. This was evident in the nineteenth-century origins of the common schools; it was the expressed project of the progressive movement in the United States; and it was the reason that the schools were (and still are) a site of struggle for civil rights. The story of progress in education has often been about access for all—women, African Americans, those who speak first languages other than English, and people with disabilities.

Evidence persists, however, that the system does not serve all social groups equally well, or even close to it. African Americans, Latino(a)s, and students from economically disadvantaged families, on a statistical average, score lower on tests, drop out more, and are less likely to attend college. Scholars and researchers do not agree about why this is so, but politicians have bypassed explanation, seizing on the achievement gap itself as not a product of many other social inequities, but an enemy that can be defeated with sufficient political will. The programmatic shape given to that political will has most often been accountability, along with experimental research as proof of program effectiveness and phonics as the only trusted approach to reading. In his 2000 presidential debates with Al Gore, George W. Bush said:

> [R]eading is the new civil right.... [T]o make sure our society is as hopeful as it possibly can be, every single child in America must be educated. I mean every child. It starts with making sure every child learns to read. K-2 diagnostic testing so we know whether or not there's a deficiency. Curriculum that works and phonics needs to be an integral part of our reading curriculum. Intensive reading laboratories, teacher retraining. I mean, there needs to be a wholesale effort against racial profiling, which is illiterate children. We can do better in our public schools. We can close an achievement gap, and it starts with making sure we have strong accountability, Jim. One of the cornerstones of reform, and good reform, is to measure. Because when you measure you can ask the question, do they know? Is anybody being profiled? Is anybody being discriminated against? It becomes a tool, a corrective tool. And I believe the federal government must say that if you receive any money, any money from the federal government for disadvantaged children, for example, you must show us whether or not the children are learning. And if they are, fine. And if they're not, there has to be a consequence. And so to make sure we end up getting rid of basic structural prejudice is education. There is nothing more prejudiced than not educating a child. (Commission on Presidential Debates, 2000)

Although this was a debate in a famously contentious election, there was no difference between the candidates in their attitude toward educational testing and accountability. Al Gore said:

I agree with Governor Bush that we should have new accountability, testing of students. I think that we should require states to test all students, test schools and school districts, and I think that we should go further and require teacher testing for new teachers also. (Commission on Presidential Debates, 2000)

There was no debate over whether accountability was necessary or desirable, or whether testing would be the most appropriate mechanism for accountability. When "testing" and "accountability" appear together in language, we have to assume that we are talking about "high-stakes testing," because "accountability" would not be very meaningful without at least publication of scores, and probably more serious consequences, being attached to tests. It would not seem to be an accountability system if the main use of tests was simply to inform instruction. In other words, a particular way of thinking about education and accountability has developed among policy makers.

The Democratic legislators who later helped turn Bush's program into the No Child Left Behind law saw it the same way. Democrat Edward Kennedy was the chair of the Senate committee that worked on the law. His Web site states: "The bipartisan No Child Left Behind Act created a national commitment to public education—a commitment to improve America's schools through accountability for results." He goes on to criticize the lack of funding that the programs have received, but he presents the accountability theme in much the way Bush would. George Miller, the ranking Democrat on the House Committee on Education and the Workforce is passionate in his defense of the law:

No Child Left Behind's philosophical roots go back to the Supreme Court's 1954 Brown vs. Board of Education decision. The reason we needed No Child Left Behind in the first place was that, five decades after Brown, our country still fails to offer poor and minority children the same educational opportunities as their peers.

Poor and minority children are still much more often assigned to less-challenging classes and less-qualified teachers than are higher-income and white students.

This opportunity gap or lack of access to an equal education affects academic achievement: seventy-four percent of white fourth graders read well—nearly twice the rate of black fourth graders. Latino and Native American fourth graders fare only slightly better.

More than half a century after this nation committed itself to educational equality, fewer than half of all minority children can read proficiently. It was this two-class education system that No Child Left Behind was intended to put an end to, once and for all. (Miller, 2006)

In discussions of the reauthorization of the law, congressional members from both parties have insisted that any revisions cannot compromise on reducing the achievement gap by holding schools accountable for students' test scores. In other words, absent some political sea change that is hard to imagine at this moment, high-stakes testing will remain a requirement for all states receiving money from the U.S. Department of Education. For now, those states number 50. And even if the federal government reduced its emphasis on high-stakes testing, the policy originated in states to begin with and would be likely to continue there as long as it remained politically advantageous for politicians to appear tough on education.

There are a number of assumptions in this approach to the problem of equity. It assumes that students have not been scoring as high as they might because either they or their schools were not trying hard enough. It also assumes that fear of humiliation will motivate the educators in schools, and the students they teach, to score better on tests. It assumes that existing tests accurately measure students' reading in ways that matter.

DO HIGH-STAKES TESTS PROMOTE EQUITY?

If the motive for introducing high-stakes tests is that they will improve the quality of learning for poor, minority, and vulnerable students, then we should attend to whether that is the case. Are high-stakes tests advancing civil rights? What are the consequences of high-stakes tests for African American, Latino(a), and children from low-income homes? These are empirical questions, and we may look to research for answers, although, as with most research questions, we will not find a single, uniform answer.

Several researchers have examined the question of whether high-stakes tests work to raise the level of student achievement overall. Comparing the results of high-stakes tests to other assessments, Amrein and Berliner (2002) found that although scores on high-stakes tests have risen in many states, those gains have not been reflected in other kinds of assessments taken by the same cohorts of students. Findings like these suggest that various patterns of behavior might be influencing the reported scores on the high-stakes tests: from variations in the level of difficulty in the test itself, to teaching directly to the kinds of questions on the high-stakes test, to outright cheating and deception on the part of school officials afraid of losing their jobs. Green, Winters, and Forster (2004) critiqued these findings and argued that high-stakes tests are reliable indicators of students' growth, but even they found only a moderate level of confidence in the Florida tests' reliability. That high-stakes tests may not be reliably measuring student growth is an important point, as the promise of the policy is that disadvantaged students will get a higher quality education, not simply that their scores can be made to climb on a particular test.

Some researchers have found that high-stakes testing is doing some good for schools with large minority populations. Skrla and Scheurich (2004) found that some school and district administrators believed the Texas accountability system had helped raise teachers' expectations for students. According to these principals and district personnel, schools' test scores rose as a result of changes in the attitudes and intentions of school faculties. They also said that the requirement that schools report the scores of various ethnic groups and poor students, as well as the knowledge that there would be consequences for those scores, brought issues of race, equity, and access to education into the foreground of the schools' work. The authors concluded that testing and accountability (which is another word for consequences being attached to tests) were a useful part of a system designed to bring more equity to education.

Their respondents and critics, admirably included in the same volume (Skrla & Scheurich, 2004), posit that the effects of high-stakes testing cannot be determined only by looking at scores and talking to principals. They believe that other measures must be examined, such as dropout rates and other assessments of learning. If the dropout rate is increasing, as Valencia (2002), Valenzuela (2004), Haney (2000), and others say it is, then it may be that the tests have added pressures and obstructions to students' lives in ways that actually result in their receiving less education. Moreover, if other means of assessing students' learning, including other tests, do not show the kinds of improvement that the high-stakes test seems to show, then it may be the case that the students are being taught to pass a test without really being taught to read and write in a variety of situations. These effects are most pronounced in the very schools that the policy was supposed to help—those with poor and minority students—because those are the schools most frequently under threat of the consequences of the test.

Another glimpse into how testing affects poor and minority students is provided by several studies of the impact of high-stakes testing in Chicago. Roderick and Nagaoka (2005) found that African American students were retained much more frequently than other ethnic groups. Furthermore, they found that retaining students, giving them a "second dose" of what they had struggled with before, did not make them learn more; sometimes resulted in lowered achievement; and made it more likely that they would drop out later or that the school would place them in special education. Furthermore, the testing policy lowered the achievement rates in reading of moderate and high-achieving African American children, although it did raise the lowest scores (Roderick, Jacob, & Bryk, 2002). The lower scores of the stronger readers could be a result of a curriculum narrowed toward test demands.

Diamond and Spillane (2004) found that high-stakes accountability in Chicago had a much greater impact on the lives and work of administrators, teachers, and students in low-performing elementary schools than those in high-performing schools. The latter, with a few exceptions, went about their business in the usual way. Low-performing schools, however, focused their efforts on whatever superficial adjustments they needed to make to get "off probation" or to avoid mid-level bureaucratic sanctions. They did worry, as they were expected to do, but they did not necessarily worry more about the learning of their students. Consequently, the accountability system, perhaps designed with the intention to improve the educations of minority and low-income students, actually ended up distracting their teachers toward the system itself.

In her research, Booher-Jennings (2005) reported that schools in Texas perform "educational triage" by analyzing data to figure out exactly which students will get them the most return for their efforts at raising scores. Generally, those closest to, but below, the cut score—"the bubble kids"—get more attention, and the most struggling students are written off. Once again, poor and minority students are disproportionately represented among the lowest-achieving students, and the radical redistributive intentions of accountability are thwarted. Because policy makers are not putting more money into education as they increase accountability, resources in the form of teacher time and effort are rationed to do more with less. This is just one of the ways of "gaming" the accountability system that Booher-Jennings points out. Others include reclassifying students as special education so that they will not have to take the test and retaining low-performing students so they cannot advance to the grade where a high-stakes test is given.

Zip codes predict test scores. Neighborhoods with expensive houses will have high test scores, and neighborhoods with housing projects will have low ones. If we believe the rhetoric of the politicians who design testing policy, this inequity is what high-stakes testing is intended to address, but it may turn out that the consequences of high-stakes testing only add to the vulnerability of the poor and further disadvantage them.

TEACHERS' PERSPECTIVES

Seven women, three men, and I gather close to listen to Perla, an eight-year-old girl, talk about what she has written in her writer's notebook. We see her as the little girl she is. We are trying to drop the roles assigned to us by the institution of school and be people together—so *that* we can arrive with her at a place of confidence and expertise, where meaning for her is thick and dense and so writing is easier, especially quick, ample, fluent writing. She has crystalline blue eyes and black hair, very fair skin, and, visible only close up, a constellation of pale freckles scattered across the bridge of her nose. There is a little gap between her front teeth through which her tongue flickers in and out as she speaks. Everyone in the room adores her.

She has been writing in her notebook in both English and Spanish. Most of her entries are memories of when she was very little, many, in fact, not so much her own direct memories as accounts given to her by her mother, aunt, and grandmother. Most of the entries are about her life in Mexico, told to her in Spanish, and so it seems natural and intelligent that she writes them in the most fitting language for her. We ask about some of the themes we think we see in her notebook, and whether they might remind Perla of still other memories. She moves easily between the concrete particulars of her memories—how her *abuela's* (grandmother's) face looked that day she was so surprised—and more abstract ideas—feeling close to people in her family, feeling like she was growing up.

It is in connection with this latter theme—growing up, getting bigger and stronger—that she relates the memory about the remedial reading class. In second grade, because she hadn't made a high enough score on the district's test and so was deemed at risk of failing the high-stakes third-grade state reading test, Perla was placed in a special class where she practiced answering questions about stories they read together and received a system of points with candy rewards when she got enough questions right. She looked a little embarrassed to be admitting to her difficulties in front of these teachers who thought she was so smart, but she reported that she had gotten lots of candy because she got the questions right. She had been scared of failing the test and failing the grade, but she had gotten through it.

She finished this story, and the women and men in the room continued to gaze softly, thanked her for talking with us, and whispered our wishes that she have a nice day. Then, as the door closed, the room erupted. Through clenched teeth, people exclaimed how angry they were at a system that could be so stupid as to miss Perla's brilliance and put that child in a remedial environment just for the sake of the test. Outraged that the system would aggress in that way on this specific child, threatening her sense of herself as strong and competent and embarrassing her in front of her friends, family, and teacher by identifying her as in need of treatment, the teachers felt protective of Perla. They believed that her multilingualism, which most of the world would view as a deep strength, caused her to be placed in a diminished intellectual environment, subjected to behaviorist tricks to earn candy. It was insulting, to her, to her teachers, and to the work we believed we as educators should be engaged in.

As teachers, we know children as particular people; we recognize their bodies, the colors of their eyes, the texture of their hair. We hug them in the mornings and predict the moments of their days. If we are any good at all, we recognize what they love, what they are good at, what excites them—we recognize them as exactly the people they are. Teachers tend to be skeptical of distant, formal, mechanized forms of coming to know what children can do. The ways we view our students places many teachers on a collision course with education policies that favor high-stakes tests.

These perceptions have been supported in some of the recent research on teachers' attitudes toward testing. Jones and Egley (2004) found that most teachers in a survey of more than 700 educators in Florida believed that high-stakes testing was taking schools in the wrong direction, and that the scores were not an accurate assessment of what their students knew and could do. They reported that the test was having negative effects on the curriculum, on teaching and learning, and on their own motivation, as well as on that of their students. The teachers made clear that they did think accountability was necessary, and that teachers should be held accountable. The principle of accountability, from the respondents in this study, was not under attack; the teachers simply had professional and technical objections to the tests and their uses. Similarly, Mathison and Freeman (2003), in a set of interviews conducted in New York schools, found that teachers favored accountability in principle but thought that the high-stakes tests frequently forced them to act in ways they considered unprofessional and not in the best interests of their students. They reported teaching in ways that they did not think resulted in high-quality learning but did result in higher test scores, which represented a lowering of their educational standards. They often felt themselves to be in a dilemma, choosing between providing a quality education and doing what the state education system required of them. In previous research, surveys of teachers working under the Texas accountability system revealed teachers' morale to be very low, for many reasons similar to those cited in the previous studies (Gordon & Reese, 1997; Hoffman, Assaf, & Paris, 2001). Observational and interview studies of literacy teachers have shown them to experience serious conflicts between their professionally valued practices in the teaching of writing and reading against the demands of a testing system (Ketter & Pool, 2001; Larson & Gatto, 2004; Rex & Nelson, 2004). Teachers' attitudes toward accountability systems are complex, but there can be no doubt that the quality of the system, particularly when it contains high-stakes tests, can create conflict, stress, and difficulty for many teachers.

VALIDITY PROBLEMS

If literacy tests are simply finding out how well students can read or write, why would teachers experience conflict if they do the best job they can at teaching reading and writing? What could be wrong with saying that 6th graders should prove on a test that they can read at a 6th-grade level? Why would that level of literacy be too hard for anyone to achieve after so many years in the school system? These kinds of questions force us to ask what it is, really, that tests can do, Because if a test is not really revealing a simple and pure essence of *reading* or *writing*, then it is important to understand what it is doing.

As most people grow up and go through school, they get used to the idea that some of their friends are smart and knowledgeable, but just not good at tests, whereas others are great at scoring high on tests, but not especially thoughtful or well informed. People are good at different things, and it's possible just to be a good test-taker. If that is so, then a test is not a transparent instrument that can find out about another ability called, say, "reading."

A person could be just fine with reading but not be so fine with test situations for a number of reasons. Some people, for instance, don't respond well to being asked direct questions; it makes their minds shut down. Similarly, some people get unusually nervous in testlike situations. Other people do not respond positively to the experience of being compared to other people, exactly what tests are designed to do. (This problem with being compared against others, so that others' stereotypes become threats to how one can anticipate being perceived socially, has been suggested as one factor in the test performance of different genders and races [see the work of Claude Steele, 1997].) For these and lots of other reasons, some people underperform on tests; that is, they seem to be worse readers or writers than they really are because of problems with the way their abilities are being measured.

Literacy research over the past few decades has shown that "reading" and "writing" are not simple abilities that an individual learns once and for all like riding a bike. The nature of each of these language practices depends on the context in which it is being done. Reading is different when a person is reading a medicine bottle to decide if it's safe for a child than it is when that person is reading a novel on an airplane to pass the time (Gee, 1996). Reading is different when people feel oppressed than when they feel free and powerful. Writing, likewise, is a completely different activity when a person leaves a note to a partner about what's for dinner and when that person writes to prove to an authority that required reading has been done. Because literacy is different for its users at different times, it makes sense that literacy on a test would be a special form of literacy—not a dipstick that can reveal a generalized "level."

In social science research and in testing, there is a concept known as *validity* that concerns the degree to which the phenomenon under investigation can really be understood using those particular methods. There are many issues in regard to validity in high-stakes testing, but I focus here on one crucial issue. Many people in literacy education, even many people who work in the field of educational measurement, have grave doubts about the validity of standardized tests when it comes to finding out the most important things about children's reading and writing. That makes a huge difference in results. If the tests aren't really determining whether students can read or write well, if high-stakes decisions are being made on that basis, and if teachers are teaching how to take tests rather than reading and writing, then the current policies are doing immeasurable harm to the education of children and to the habits and values of teachers. In that case, we have a big problem.

CURRICULAR CONSEQUENCES

If tests do not align well with other forms of reading and writing, but the tests are what count in the system, then most forms of reading and writing stand to suffer at the hands of high-stakes tests. People in life outside of school read and write for a host of reasons: social, emotional, artistic, spiritual, informational, practical, civic, career-oriented, and many others. If education is preparation for life, then children ought to have opportunities to read and write for all of these purposes in school. If intense consequences are being attached to a few, limited kinds of reading and writing, what are the chances that these more expansive and ultimately more important forms of literacy will find a place in the curriculum?

The curriculum is *the course to be run* in education, and it is made up of all the things that teachers and children do together. We often use the term to refer to plans for instruction and their reasons, but in the end, the curriculum is what happened—what the teacher and the students did with their minutes. Quite a bit of research, consisting of careful observation of what goes on in classrooms, has shown us that high-stakes testing constricts the range of activities teachers take up with their students (e.g., McNeil, 2000; Smith, Edelsky, Draper, Rottenberg, & Cherland, 1991). Just as art, music, and, in places where it isn't tested, even science are dropped out of the school day, so are varied forms of literacy that are not on the test. Traditional pursuits, like the reading of poetry and novels, begin to seem like frills. Perhaps even more costly, this narrowing squeezes out cutting-edge practices, such as writing and reading for social and political action, forms of reading and writing that are only beginning to be developed through new technologies and the Internet, and an expanded understanding of literacy as combining words with pictures, sounds, and moving images. Teachers, already harried by the demands of reporting test scores and preparing for the next round of testing, hardly have the attention, time, or energy to learn about whole new ways of doing reading and writing. High stakes, in effect, freeze innovation and progress in place, causing the academic literacy in the memories of politicians educated in the 1950s to limit the ambitions teachers can entertain for twenty-first-century children.

HOW TEACHERS COPE AND HOPE

Despite the contradictions in high-stakes testing policies, teachers can and do make a difference in the ways that they approach the dilemmas of their teaching. Some teachers and schools see the test as requiring that they do nothing but drill students on a narrow range of reading and writing tasks. These are the responses that amplify the harmful effects of a high-stakes testing policy, not only depriving students of a quality education, but also weakening them as readers and writers and consequently producing lower test scores (Roderick & Engel, 2001). There is a temptation to panic, to run as fast as possible in exactly the wrong direction, to hurl energies senselessly against the test format, rather than to concentrate on making students strong and effective users of literacy.

Effective school leaders have been able to turn the challenge of improving students' achievement into opportunities for professional development and for bringing teachers together around the shared project of making students into powerful readers and writers. In most cases, that kind of project, one of real curriculum development, allows students to become more engaged and thoughtful, and even allows them the space to develop the skills, knowledge, and confidence that will make them perform better on the tests (Langer, 2004). Some research indicates that students who have been given a quality curriculum are able to develop real strength in the use of literacy, despite the mismatch between the forms of literacy they study and the tests (e.g., Reyes, Scribner, & Scribner, 1999).

Furthermore, some approaches to work on the tests themselves offer more promise than does a curriculum reduced to practice for the test. Some teachers have found success getting students to study tests as a form of writing, to try writing test questions to come to a better understanding of what they are being asked when they encounter something confusing on a test, and to practice tests with a degree of sophistication that comes from trying to understand what the makers of the test are *doing* and how they, the test-takers, are supposed to respond (Calkins, Montgomery, Santman, & Falk, 1998). Teachers have also helped children draw on the content of writing that they have done previously in class to write a more developed composition on a test. By learning to use their own memories, about which they have already written several times in journals and literary works, as the kernel for a writing test response, students with deeper writing experience from a rich curriculum can use the resources their past work has given them (Bomer, 2005). These approaches are embedded in a curriculum rich with varied opportunities to write and read in a wide range of forms and for diverse, authentic purposes—a course of study designed to make students strong in real life, rather than merely for a test.

Even as teachers make these promising compromises with an unfortunate reality, many of them work actively to inform policy makers in order to create better policy. By working through professional organizations like the National Council of Teachers of English (www.ncte.org), the International Reading Associations (www.reading.org), and their state and local affiliates, teachers come together to attempt to inform politicians and their appointees about the consequences of high-stakes testing and the impact that it sometimes has on children and schooling. They ask for accountability to be based on multiple measures rather than a single test. They ask that consequences for individual students be mitigated, such as retention for scoring beneath a particular number on the test. They ask that specific conditions of their school context, like massive international transmigration or special risks of dropping out, be taken into account when a school is being judged. In conversations with policy makers, they keep their ambitions modest and try to practice what the German statesman Bismarck called "the art of the possible."

In other conversations among themselves, and in the visions of a better world they hold secretly in mind, teachers imagine an education policy that is committed to making sure no child under five goes hungry on a consistent basis, as no other single thing we could do would raise educational achievement more than that. They hope, too, for a different kind of accountability, one in which adults in a country hold themselves accountable for the quality of life of each child growing up there. They imagine that someday, the word *accountability* will invoke in their fellow citizens' minds not punishing an eight-year-old for the score on a reading test, but responding with resources when it is clear that a school building is falling apart, with information and education to curious and bewildered teachers, and with caring support for children who want nothing more than to learn, do well, and be happy. What would it look like if a society realized that the stakes are very high indeed for helping children find joy?

REFERENCES

Amrein, A. L. & Berliner, D. C. (2002). High stakes testing, uncertainty, and student learning. *Educational Policy Analysis Archives, 10* (18).

Bomer, K. (2005). *Writing a life: Teaching memoir to sharpen insight, shape meaning—and triumph over tests.* Portsmouth, NH: Heinemann.

Booher-Jennings, J. (2005). Below the bubble: "Educational triage" and the Texas accountability system. *American Educational Research Journal, 42*(2), 231–268.

Booher-Jennings, J. (2006). Rationing education in an era of accountability. *Phi Delta Kappan, 87*(May 16, 2006).

Calkins, L. M., Montgomery, K., Santman, D., & Falk, B. (1998). *A teacher's guide to standardized reading tests: Knowledge is power.* Portsmouth, NH: Heinemann.

Commission on Presidential Debates. (2000). Debate Transcript. October 11, 2000. Available: http://www.debates.org/pages/trans2000b.html, accessed: December 9, 2006.

Diamond, J. B., & Spillane, J. (2004). High-stakes accountability in urban elementary schools: Challenging or reproducing inequality? *Teachers College Record, 106*(6), 1145–1176.

Gee, J. P. (1996). *Social linguistics and literacies: Ideology in discourses* (2nd ed.). London: Falmer Press.

Gordon, S. P., & Reese, M. (1997). High stakes testing: Worth the price? *Journal of School Leadership, 7*(4), 345–368.

Green, J., Winters, M., & Forster, G. (2004). Testing high-stakes tests: Can we believe the results of accountability tests? *Teachers College Record, 106*(6), 1124–1144.

Haney, W. (2000). *The Myth of the Texas Miracle in Education.* Chestnut Hill, MA: Center for the Study of Testing, Evaluation, and Educational Policy.

Hoffman, J. V., Assaf, L. C., & Paris, S. G. (2001). High-stakes testing in reading: Today in Texas, tomorrow? *The Reading Teacher, 54*(5), 482–492.

Jones, B. D., & Egley, R. J. (2004). Voices from the frontlines: Teachers' perceptions of high-stakes testing. *Education Policy Analysis Archive, 12*(39).

Ketter, J., & Pool, J. (2001). Exploring the impact of a high-stakes direct writing assessment in two high school classrooms. *Research in the Teaching of English, 35*(3), 344–393.

Langer, J. A. (2004). *Getting to excellent: How to create better schools.* New York: Teachers College Press.

Larson, J., & Gatto, L. A. (2004). Tactical underlife: Understanding students' perceptions. *Journal of Early Childhood Literacy, 4*(1), 11–41.

Mathison, S., & Freeman, M. (2003). Constraining elementary teachers' work: Dilemmas and paradoxes created by state mandated testing. *Education Policy Analysis Archive, 11*(34).

McNeil, L. M. (2000). *Contradictions of school reform: Educational costs of standardized testing.* New York: Routledge.

Miller, G. (2006). Rep. Miller Statement on Committee Hearing on No Child Left Behind. June 13, 2006, available: http://www.house.gov/apps/list/press/ed31_democrats/RelJune13NCLB.html, accessed: December 9, 2006.

Rex, L., & Nelson, M. (2004). How teachers' professional identities position high-stakes test preparation in their classrooms. *Teachers College Record, 106*(6), 1288–1331.

Reyes, P., Scribner, J. D., & Scribner, A. P. (1999). *Lessons from high-performing Hispanic schools: Creating learning communities.* New York: Teachers College Press.

Roderick, M., & Engel, M. (2001). The grasshopper and the ant: Motivational responses of low achieving students to high stakes testing. *Educational Evaluation and Policy Analysis, 23*(3), 197–227.

Roderick, M., Jacob, B. A., & Bryk, A. S. (2002). The impact of high-stakes testing in Chicago on student achievement in promotional gate grades. *Educational Evaluation and Policy Analysis, 24*(4), 333–357.

Roderick, M., & Nagaoka, J. (2005). Retention under Chicago's high-stakes testing program: Helpful, harmful, or harmless? *Educational Evaluation and Policy Analysis, 27*(4), 309–340.

Skrla, L., & Scheurich, J. J. (Eds.). (2004). *Educational equity and accountability: Policies, paradigms, and politics.* New York: RoutledgeFalmer.

Smith, M. L., Edelsky, C., Draper, K., Rottenberg, C., & Cherland, M. (1991). *The role of testing in elementary schools* (No. 321). Los Angeles: UCLA Center for Research on Evaluation, Standards, and Student Testing.

Steele, C. M. (1997). A threat in the air: How stereotypes shape the intellectual identities and performances of women and African-Americans. *American Psychologist, 52,* 613–629.

U.S. Congress, Office of Technology Assessment (1992). *Testing in American schools: Asking the right questions.* Washington, DC: US Government Printing Office.

Valencia, R. (Ed.). (2002). *Chicano school failure and success.* London: Falmer.

Valenzuela, A. (Ed.). (2004). *Leaving children behind: How "Texas-style" accountability fails Latino youth.* Albany, NY: State University of New York Press.

Part Two

ASSESSMENT AND INSTRUCTION IN CHILDHOOD LITERACY

Chapter Four

METHODS FOR READING INSTRUCTION IN GRADES 3–6

James F. Baumann and T. Lee Williams

> No single method or single combination of methods can successfully teach children to read. Instead, each child must be helped to develop the skills and understandings he or she needs to become a reader. ... Because children learn differently, teachers must be familiar with a wide range of proven methods ... They also must have thorough knowledge of the children they teach, so they can provide the appropriate balance of methods needed for each child.

The purpose of this chapter is to provide an overview of methods available for teaching reading to children in the elementary school years. As noted in the preceding statement, it is generally accepted that there is no single method that ensures success in reading for all children. Instead, methods must be carefully selected to match children's needs. We believe that the most critical factor in successful reading instruction is the informed, artful teacher behind the methods and materials. That said, we do not suggest that reading methods are irrelevant. Rather, decisions must be made thoughtfully, considering both the students and methods simultaneously, by a knowledgeable reading professional.

We begin by presenting an overview of reading methods. Next, we describe various methods for teaching reading to children in grades 3–6. We conclude by briefly discussing the importance of teacher decision making when selecting reading methods.

METHODS OF READING INSTRUCTION

Sadoski (2004) organizes reading instruction according to three perspectives: skills-based, balanced, and holistic. We use this structure to describe methods of reading instruction in the following sections. Skills-based methods assume that reading is composed of a set of skills that can be taught in a sequenced, explicit manner. Skills-based methods emphasize phonics instruction, fluent oral reading, and comprehension skills. Skills are taught directly by the teacher, often in a highly structured and sometimes scripted manner. Skills-based methods are usually found in elaborate published programs that suggest that they provide all the materials and instructional guidance teachers need to effectively teach children to read.

Like skills-based methods, balanced methods provide instruction in reading skills, but they also provide students with many opportunities to read quality children's literature and many opportunities to write in response to what they read (Pressley, 2006). Reading and writing skills are taught explicitly, but through authentic literacy tasks that focus on meaning. Balanced methods use different types of instructional materials, including children's books, collections of children's literature, graded readers ("little books") designed especially for reading instruction, and various electronic texts.

Holistic methods provide children many opportunities to read, write, and talk about texts. The primary emphasis in holistic methods is on seeking meaning and responding to literature, with students assuming a great deal of responsibility over what they read and write . Reading and writing strategies are taught through mini-lessons or teachable moments when the teacher determines that students will benefit from lessons connected to what they are reading or writing. Reading materials include children's books and stories the students have written themselves.

Eight reading methods are described in this review, organized by Sadoski's (2004) skills-based↔balanced↔holistic framework. There are many reading methods available to teachers in grades three through six. Because of space limitations, we discuss selected classic and contemporary methods that are representative of the various positions on the framework. Thus this is not a comprehensive presentation of all methods of reading instruction. Finally, particular methods may not fit precisely under a given category, and they may be placed in adjacent categories depending on the manner in which reading professionals implement them.

SKILLS-BASED METHODS

Basal Reading Programs

A basal reading program is a commercially produced "collection of student texts and workbooks, teachers' manuals, and supplemental materials for developmental reading." Basal readers are published in levels of increasing difficulty according to readability formulas. Basals are usually published for students in kindergarten through grade 8.

Most basal textbooks are collections of complete or excerpted selections (sometimes adapted) from published children's books. Selections in the beginning readers may be written especially for inclusion in the basal program. Beginning-level selections are often predictable in nature, feature repetitions of high-frequency words, and include words that are "decodable" when students apply corresponding phonics instruction.

Basal reading programs usually include supplemental children's books that connect to thematic units in the anthologies. Little books that have controlled vocabulary or decodable text are usually included at the early basal levels to provide additional reading practice. Basal programs also include workbooks or reproducible worksheets to provide opportunities for students to practice reading skills. Interactive CD/DVD and other technology, elaborate teacher manuals to guide instruction, and assessment materials for students' placement in a program and their evaluation are also components of most basal reading programs.

Basal instruction includes teaching reading skills, strategies, and content that, depending on the basal level, may include phonemic awareness; high-frequency words; phonics; structural and contextual analysis; meaning vocabulary; literal, inferential, and critical reading comprehension; and content reading strategies. Most basal reading programs use some variation of the directed reading activity (DRA), which usually consists of five steps: (1) preparation for reading, (2) guided silent reading, (3) skill development, (4) oral rereading of the selection, and (5) follow-up extension activities.

As a basal DRA example, consider one lesson from a 3rd-grade level of a basal reading program called Trophies . This lesson is built around the children's book *Nate the Great, San Francisco Detective*, which is included in the 3rd-grade basal textbook. Activities that prepare students for reading include developing knowledge about detectives and mysteries and teaching key vocabulary included in the story. The teacher guides students' reading by asking comprehension questions, followed by lessons on several phonics skills and comprehension strategies. For oral rereading, the teacher's manual suggests having pairs of students reread the story as a radio play. Finally, the teacher's manual provides follow-up writing, grammar, and spelling lessons, and it suggests that students read accompanying children's books that connect to the Nate the Great story.

Direct Instruction Reading Programs

Direct instruction (DI) involves sequenced, teacher-directed lessons that emphasize decoding skills and comprehension strategies. DI comes in two forms. In the first form, the teacher provides explanation, modeling, guided application, and independent practice in reading skills. DI lessons of this type are structured but not scripted. For example, Duke and Pearson described a lesson on predicting in which the teacher defines predicting and then demonstrates it with a reading selection. Next, the teacher and students make predictions together as they read on in the selection, after which the students try the strategy on their own with teacher support. Finally, students practice the prediction strategy independently.

In the second form of DI, teachers provide sequenced, scripted lessons in reading skills to small groups of children (Kame'enui et al., 1997). The teacher reads from a lesson that provides exact wording. Students often respond in unison, and the teacher provides corrective feedback. DI of this type is often provided to children with reading disabilities.

Strengths and Limitations

There are strengths and limitations to skills-based methods. Generally, skills-based methods provide a great deal of guidance and resources for teachers, but such highly structured approaches may leave little room for the teacher to exercise flexibility and professional judgment . As with any method of reading instruction, common sense suggests that skills-based approaches should be used only when they are consistent with educational goals, the nature of the learners, and teachers' preferences and expertise.

BALANCED METHODS
Guided Reading Instruction

Guided reading is an instructional approach that engages students of similar reading abilities in small groups. The purpose of guided reading is to teach specific decoding and comprehension strategies. Although originally designed for the primary grades, this method was modified for use in the upper elementary grades as well.

In guided reading, groups of four to six students are formed based on students' reading levels. These groups change frequently throughout the school year. In guided reading instruction, the teacher works with one group at a time, usually around a kidney-shaped or circular table. There is a general structure for each guided reading lesson. Before the lesson begins, the teacher selects a leveled book that challenges students slightly, but does not frustrate them. Next, the teacher previews the book to engage the readers. Each student then reads the book silently. After all of the students have finished reading, the group discusses the book. Next, the teacher presents one skill or strategy that is needed by group members and is relevant to the particular book just read (e.g., teaching plot, characters, and setting for a narrative selection). The lesson may conclude with an extension activity such as personal reflections or artistic responses.

As an example, consider a guided reading lesson for a group of five students reading the book *Flossie and the Fox*. The teacher previews the story, explains the author's use of African American dialect of the rural South, and discusses the portrayal of the fox as a trickster. Students then read the book silently under the teacher's supervision, after which there is a group discussion. Next, students and teacher create a map or diagram of the story documenting how Flossie outsmarted the fox. Although this would conclude the day's lesson, students might reread this text on subsequent days, focusing on fluency or other aspects of the story, such as the author's use of descriptive language.

Four Blocks Literacy Model

The four blocks literacy model is a structure for reading instruction designed to meet the complex needs of all children in a classroom. There are two related premises of this approach: literacy instruction must occur in heterogeneous ability groups, and instruction must include activities on multiple levels to accommodate students of differing reading abilities. The four blocks model was designed for reading instruction in the primary grades, but its success has prompted adaptation for use in the upper elementary grades. Reading and language arts instruction is divided into four daily segments, or blocks, each lasting between 30 and 40 minutes.

1. Self-selected reading. First students engage in independent reading of self-selected books and other materials that pique their individual interests. As a result, the classroom is filled with a variety of materials and genres on multiple reading levels. Students share and respond to the materials they read in a variety of ways, such as discussing their reading with the teacher or constructing a written or artistic response to a book.
2. Guided reading. In this block, the teacher provides direct instruction in comprehension strategies by using an assortment of reading materials (e.g., basal readers, magazine articles, children's books, science textbooks). Typically, students work in small groups with a particular text for several days, analyzing the text to make meaning and rereading the text to promote fluency. Guided reading was previously discussed as a stand-alone method, but in the four blocks approach, guided reading is just one component.
3. Working with words. In the third block, the teacher focuses on word identification, usually through the use of Word Walls and Making Words activities . The Word Wall is a large, alphabetized collection of high-frequency words displayed on a classroom wall. Each week, new words are introduced and become the primary focus for phonics, spelling, and sight-word instruction. Making Words is an activity in which students create increasingly more complex words by arranging letter tiles. For example, given the letters c, e, p, i, l, n, s, students could create the words is, in, pen, nip, sip, snip, pale, pine, clip clips, spine, eventually solving for the "mystery word" pencils.
4. Writing. In the final component, students produce original pieces of writing on topics of their choice, publish their compositions, and share them with classmates. The teacher writes with the students, modeling composition by thinking aloud as she writes on an overhead projector or white board. Based on observations and individual conferences, the teacher leads a mini-lesson on a composition strategy needed by the class, such as character development, use of interesting adjectives, or punctuation.

Basal-Trade Book Reading Approaches

Another type of balanced reading instruction involves combining skills instruction with more meaning-centered activities by relying on both basal readers and children's books. Consider, for example, a 4th-grade teacher who has initiated a unit on ecology by working from a basal reader textbook titled *Nature Guides*. Before reading the first basal selection, an excerpt from Jean Craighead George's *The Moon of the Alligators*, students make predictions based on what they already know about alligators. After reading, the students engage in a teacher-guided discussion, and they refer to the selection to check their predictions.

Next, the teacher conducts two skill lessons. First, the teacher models how to chunk words into meaningful phrases, after which pairs of students reread aloud *The Moon of the Alligators*, practicing this fluency strategy. Second, the teacher teaches prefixes by drawing example words from the story (e.g., semi in semitropical; sub in submerged).

The teacher has secured multiple copies of several books on ecology suggested in the basal. Students select one of the books for independent reading, and they keep a reading-response journal in which they record what they are learning about nature and ecology. As a culminating activity, students use the Internet site The WebQuest Page to complete a project in which groups of students explore and report on different ecosystems.

Strengths and Limitations

Strengths of balanced methods include the amount of choice of reading materials that students have and the use of small groups that promote individualized instruction. Limitations include the substantial cost of the large number of books required. Balanced methods also have been criticized for failing to capture the complexity of effective literacy instruction.

HOLISTIC METHODS

Language Experience Approach

The language experience approach (LEA) is an instructional method in which children's oral language is transcribed to print and used as texts for reading instruction. LEA integrates students' writing, speaking, and listening with reading instruction; and it builds on students' knowledge of language and the world around them to generate familiar, readable texts. Allen states the rationale for LEA as follows:

> What I can think about, I can talk about.
> What I can say, I can write (or someone can write for me).
> What I can write, I can read.
> I can read what others write for me to read. (p. 1)

The LEA often includes the following six activities:

1. Initiating experience: A teacher engages students in some experience to initiate an LEA lesson. For example, a class might visit a children's zoo on a morning field trip.
2. Discussion and dictation: The teacher and children discuss their experience and compose a group story about it. Individual children offer sentences, which the teacher writes on a chart or white board. For instance, the children might compose a story titled "Our Trip to the Zoo."
3. Rereading for meaning: The group rereads the story aloud, with the teacher using a pointer to track print and promote fluency.
4. Working with words: Words from the story are used for instruction. For example, specific phonic elements may be taught (e.g., the consonant digraph *sh* in sheep). Words from the story could be added to a classroom Word Wall, for example, high-frequency words (e.g., look, fun) or interesting content words (e.g., monkey, zebra).
5. Individual stories: Students write individual stories (e.g., "The Monkeys Were Funny"), often with assistance from the teacher or a classroom helper.
6. Extension activities: Extension activities involve more reading, writing, speaking, and listening. For example, the teacher might read aloud children's books related to zoo animals, or the children could research specific zoo animals.

LEA is usually considered as a beginning-reading instructional method, but it can be used effectively for teaching older, struggling readers. LEA is often recommended for students of all ages whose first language is not English. LEA has been adapted to accommodate new technologies. For example, Labbo, Eakle, and Montero (2002) described "digital language experience," in which teachers and children use tools such as digital cameras, computers, the Internet, and electronic whiteboards to capture images and to record print and audio texts.

Reading and Writing Workshop

Artwell (1989) was one of the first to promote a workshop approach, which provides students' considerable voice and choice in literacy instruction. Using a large block of time (1 1/2 to 2 hours), students select, read, and write about books of interest to them. Students also confer with one another and the teacher about their reading and writing. A workshop approach usually integrates reading and writing; however, because some teachers choose to use just one or the other, we discuss them separately.

Reading workshop. There are three general components to a reading workshop. First, students read by themselves in books at their independent reading levels. To expose students to a wide variety of texts and authors, the teacher previews books or reads aloud excerpts from them. Second, students respond to books, often through a dialogue journal, in which teachers and students correspond with one another about books. Responses might also be artistic or dramatic, or simply involve group discussion. Third, the teacher conducts mini-lessons in reading skills and strategies based on observations of students' needs.

Writing workshop. There are three components to the writing workshop. First, based on students' needs, the teacher conducts a mini-lesson on a writing skill, such as proper punctuation, paragraph formation, or use of figurative language. Second, students write independently on self-selected topics, progressing through the writing process, which involves prewriting, drafting, revising, editing, and publishing. Students receive feedback in conferences with the teacher or with peers. Finally, students share their writing with classmates informally or through published works.

Literature Circles and Book Clubs

A new perspective on reading instruction became popular in the early 1990s in which students read quality children's literature and engaged in student-centered literature discussions. This perspective was implemented in two different formats: literature circles and book clubs.

Literature circles. In literature circles (Daniels, 2002), students are presented with three or four books by the same author (e.g., books by Katherine Paterson) or around a similar theme (e.g., titles related to the American Revolution), and students join a group or circle based on what they would like to read. Because the groups are formed according to students' choices, they include students of differing reading abilities. Group members, rather than the teacher, determine how much each member will read before the next regularly scheduled meeting of the circle. Group members also assume responsibility for the discussion by taking on specific roles—such as a discussion director, a word master, or an illustrator (Daniels, 2002)—that rotate among the members. The roles encourage personal responsibility and help to provide a structure for discussion, although the roles may be dropped after students get accustomed to the circle routine. After the circle completes a book, new groups are formed around different books, and the process is repeated.

Book clubs. Like literature circles, students in book clubs choose from three to four titles selected by the teacher to support a theme or author study. Unlike in literature circles, however, the teacher, not the students, assigns the amount of daily reading to be completed in book clubs. Students use a reading log to write about their books, and they are encouraged to make personal connections to the text, use graphic organizers to promote comprehension, and list words of interest. The teacher takes on a more active instructional role, teaching comprehension, fluency, and vocabulary in connection with the book. The teacher models how to engage in discussions to promote thoughtful dialogue.

Strengths and Limitations

Holistic methods have the advantage of promoting students' motivation, engagement, and interest, which can enhance reading development and independence in literacy learning. A great deal of individualized planning is needed to implement holistic approaches, however, and familiarity with a varied collection of books is essential. In addition, parents and administrators may need to be convinced of the benefits of student-centered, holistic methods. Nevertheless, holistic methods provide teachers a useful, viable alternative to skills-based or balanced methods.

CONCLUSION

As we have shown, methods for reading instruction in grades 3–6 vary in multiple ways. As a result, the methodological choices for educators are many, including the eight we that have discussed, various combinations of those methods, and even others not discussed because of space constraints. Given the methodological options available, how do school district superintendents, principals, or classroom teachers decide which method (or methods) to use for reading instruction?

We argued at the beginning of this chapter that although reading methods do matter, the more important factor for successful reading instruction is the knowledge, competence, and experience of the teacher (International Reading Association, 2000). In an article titled "In Pursuit of an Illusion: The Flawed Search for a Perfect Method," Duffy and Hoffman concur, stating that "there is no perfect method" (p. 10). Instead, they argue, "the answer is not the method; it is in the teacher. It has been repeatedly established that the best instruction results when combinations of methods are orchestrated by a teacher who decides what to do in light of children's needs" (p. 11).

In other words, quality teaching and learning occur when teachers identify, select, and combine instructional methods based on their knowledge of effective reading instruction and their assessment of the unique needs of the students they are teaching. Thus we hope that educational administrators and policy makers encourage and support teachers to exercise their professional responsibility to construct and assemble reading methods suited for the particular students they teach.

REFERENCES

Allen, R. V. (1968). How a language-experience program works. In E. C. Vilscek (Ed.), *Approaches to beginning reading* (pp. 1–8). Newark, DE: International Reading Association.

Allington, R. L., & Johnston, P. H. (2002). *Reading to learn: Lessons from exemplary fourth-grade classrooms.* New York: Guilford.

Atwell, N. (1989). *In the middle: Writing, reading, and learning with adolescents.* Portsmouth, NH: Boynton/Cook Publishers.

Beck, I. L., Farr, R. C., & Strickland, D. S. (2003). *Trophies.* Orlando, FL: Harcourt.

Cunningham, P.M. (1999). *The teacher's guide to the four blocks: a multimethod, multilevel framework for grades 1–3.* Greensboro, NC: Carson-Dellosa Publishing.

Daniels, H. (2002). *Literature circles: Voice and choice in book clubs and reading groups.* Portland, ME: Stenhouse Publishers.

Duffy, G. G., & Hoffman, J. V. (1999). In pursuit of an illusion: The flawed search for a perfect method. *The Reading Teacher, 53,* 10–16.

Duke, N., & Pearson, P. D. (2002). Effective practices for developing reading comprehension. In A. Farstrup & S. J. Samuels (Eds.), *What research has to say about reading instruction* (Vol. 3, pp. 205–242). Newark, DE: International Reading Association.

Fountas, I. C., & Pinnell, G. S. (1996). *Guided reading: good first teaching for all children.* Portsmouth, NH: Heinemann.

Gambrell, L. B., Hamilton, V., Hartman, D. H., Kirby-Linton, K., & Mitchell, A. H. (1996). *Nature guides (Literacy Place Reading Program).* New York: Scholastic.

George, J. C. (1991). *The moon of the alligators.* New York: Harper Collins.

Goodman, K. S. (2002). Whole language and whole language assessment. In B. A. Guzzetti (Ed.), *Literacy in America: An encyclopedia of history, theory, and practice* (pp. 673–677). Santa Barbara, CA: ABC-CLIO Publishers.

Graves, M. F., Juel, C., & Graves, B. B. (2004). *Teaching reading in the 21st century* (3rd ed.). Boston: Allyn & Bacon.

Hammond, D. (1994). Directed reading activities. In A. C. Purves (Ed.), *Encyclopedia of English studies and language arts* (pp. 378–380). New York/Urbana, IL: Scholastic/National Council of Teachers of English.

Harris, T. L., & Hodges, R. E. (Eds.). (1995). *The literacy dictionary: The vocabulary of reading and writing.* Newark, DE: International Reading Association.

International Reading Association. (2000). Making a difference means making it different: Honoring children's rights to excellent reading instruction. Retrieved April 17, 2006, from http://www.reading.org/downloads/positions/ps1042_MADMMID.pdf

Kame'enui, E. J., Simmons, D.C., Chard, D., & Dickson, S. (1997). Direct reading instruction. In S. A. Stahl & D. A. Hayes (Eds.), *Instructional models in reading* (pp. 59–84). Mahwah, NJ: Lawrence Erlbaum.

Labbo, L. D., Eakle, A. J., & Montero, M. K. (2002, May). Digital language experience approach: Using digital photographs and software as a language experience innovation. *Reading Online, 5*(8).

McIntyre, E., & Pressley, M. (Eds.). (1996). *Balanced instruction: Strategies and skills in whole language.* Norwood, MA: Christopher-Gordon.

McKissack, P. (1986). *Flossie and the fox.* New York: Dial.

McMahon, S. I., & Raphael, T. E. (1997). *The book club connection.* New York: Teachers College Press.

Pearson, P. D., & Gallagher, M. C. (1983). The instruction of reading comprehension. *Contemporary Educational Psychology, 8,* 317–344.

Pearson, P. D., & Raphael, T. E. (2003). Toward a more complex view of balance in the literacy curriculum. In L. M. Morrow, L. B. Gambrell & M. Pressley (Eds.), *Best practices in literacy instruction* (Vol. 2, pp. 23–39). New York: Guilford.

Pressley, M. (2006). *Reading instruction that works: The case for balanced teaching* (3rd ed.). New York: Guilford.

Sadoski, M. (2004). *Conceptual foundations of reading.* New York: Guilford.

Shannon, P. (1989). *Broken promises: Reading instruction in twentieth century America.* Granby, MA: Bergin & Garvey.

Sharmat, M. W., & Sharmat, M. (2000). *Nate the great, San Francisco detective.* New York: Delacorte.

Chapter Five

INFORMAL AND FORMAL ASSESSMENT IN LITERACY

Jerry L. Johns and Janet L. Pariza

With the advent of Reading First, a federal program established as part of the No Child Left Behind (NCLB) Act of 2000, reading assessment has gained more widespread attention than ever before. The primary goal of NCLB is to ensure that students learn to read well by the end of 3rd grade. Systematic monitoring of progress is an important part of NCLB, and students' performance on reading tests has never had such serious consequences for the school or the individual student as it does today. Sound academic assessment depends on multiple measures because no single test can wholly measure the complex text-based cognitive activity called reading. Valid reading assessment involves the dynamic interaction among tests, classroom literacy experiences, teachers, and students.

In this chapter, we explain various kinds of assessments used to measure reading ability. We first turn our attention to standardized or formal measures of reading assessment because this is the area of reading assessment that garners much media attention. Then we look at criterion-referenced tests. Finally, we address informal reading assessment. We explain the basic concepts associated with, as well as the uses and misuses of, both formal and informal reading assessment.

STANDARDIZED READING TESTS

Standardized reading tests are part of the broad range of commercially produced tests that represent formal assessment. Most students encounter standardized tests regularly from kindergarten through 12th grade. Today, in our culture of academic accountability, some students are tested multiple times each year with standardized, norm-referenced tests. We want this chapter to help develop or increase the wise and appropriate use of these types of tests.

The primary purpose of standardized or norm-referenced reading tests is to compare the reading ability of a group of students to that of the large sample population that was used to standardize the test. Test manufacturers create large comparison groups that include students from various parts of the country, from both urban and rural schools, from different races and ethnic groups, and of different socioeconomic status. Students in the comparison group are carefully chosen so that they share similar characteristics with the students who will eventually be given the test. From this large sample, norms are established that represent average performance of the students in different grades. Scores are interpreted in comparison to the norming group. For example, the reading performance of the 3rd-grade students may be said to be above the norm if their average scores on the test are higher than those of the 3rd-grade students in the norming sample.

To ensure that comparisons are valid, test manufacturers attempt to control for as many variables as possible. Therefore the test instructions require that each administration of the test is consistent, with the same oral instructions given to the students and the same time constraints honored. "Testing that maintains a high degree of control attempts to approach the measure of student achievement in a scientific manner" (Criswell, 2006, p. 118). Just as with scientific investigation, there are concerns of reliability and validity in standardized testing. Of the two terms, reliability is the easier to understand, but validity is of greater importance. *Reliability* tells us how consistently a test measures whatever it measures. For example, if students in a class were retested on the same reading test, we would expect that their performance would be similar to that of the first testing. Of course, we would expect that students had remembered some of the questions and had perhaps "learned" from the testing situation, but we would expect that those students who performed well the first time would have done well the second time, and that those students who performed poorly the first time would have done so on the second testing. We would not expect that students who performed well the first time would perform poorly the second time. That their scores remained relatively consistent is a measure of reliability.

Validity, generally considered the single most important characteristic or attribute of a good test, refers to whether a test measures what it claims to measure. Four kinds of validity can be considered:

1. Deciding whether the test is appropriate for the age or grade for which it is intended calls for making a judgment about *face validity*. For example, if several passages on a reading test deal with pastoral and agricultural issues, you may question the face validity of this test when it is administered to students in an inner-city school.

2. Questioning whether the items on the test are consistent with specific curriculum, objectives, textbooks, or course of study involves making a judgment about *content validity*. Does the content of the test match the content of the instruction?

3. Questioning whether the test scores might be used to predict a student's later scholastic achievement involves making a judgment about *criterion-related validity*. For example, college entrance exams are used to predict academic success in college programs.

4. Questioning the underlying concepts of reading that are evident in the test construction involves making a judgment about *construct validity*. For example, some tests treat reading as a compilation of discrete subskills. Some experts question the validity of such tests because reading is a holistic process that is greater than the sum of individual subskills.

Students' performance on standardized tests is often reported in multiple ways. The number of items to which a student responded correctly is his or her *raw score*. A student's raw score can be compared with those of students in the norming or standardization group. These scores, referred to as *norms*, represent an average. By using the norms section of the test manual, raw scores can be converted to various derived scores that make it possible to understand and interpret test results. Derived scores are based on a standard score scale and are representative of continuous ranking along a normal distribution curve. Common derived scores include stanines and percentiles.

Stanines are derived scores that report student performance using a nine-point scale. The word *stanine* comes from the term *standard nines*. Stanines 1, 2, and 3 are considered below average; stanines 4, 5, and 6 are considered average; and stanines 7, 8, and 9 are considered above average. Stanines for an individual can be compared within the same level of a test, but not within different levels of a test or with different tests. For example, Jeff, a 4th-grade student, achieved a stanine of 6 in vocabulary, showing that his vocabulary knowledge as measured by the test is in the high-average range when compared to the norming group; however, he achieved a stanine of only 4 on the comprehension subtest. Because both scores were achieved on the same level of the test, they can be compared. A difference of two or more stanines is considered statistically significant. Because comprehension is the goal of reading, Jeff's teacher may want to further investigate his needs in that area.

Percentiles are also derived scores. A percentile rank tells the percentage of students in the comparison group that scored at or below a certain raw score. A percentile rank is not the same as the percentage of correct items; rather, percentiles allow for rank comparisons between a student and those in the norming group. For example, a student in the 4th grade with a percentile rank of 75 scored as high or higher than 75 percent of all 4th-grade students in the norming group. It is also true that this student's raw score was lower than 25 percent of all 4th-grade students in the norming group.

Percentiles can be used to identify the relative standing of the students in a class. Students who score in the lower percentile ranks may need further assessment to determine their specific areas of instructional need. Students who score in the upper percentiles may be considered for enrichment programs or instructional adjustments to further challenge them.

Some tests also report students' performance in terms of *grade equivalents*. Of all derived scores, grade equivalents are perhaps the most widely misinterpreted, misunderstood, and abused. Grade-equivalent scores describe reading performance in terms of a particular grade and month. Grade-equivalent scores are mathematical extrapolations of a student's raw score and do not represent the level at which the student is reading.

Grade equivalent scores can be quite misleading. Let's look at two different students to gain a better understanding of these scores. Lisa, a student in 3rd grade, achieved a grade-equivalent score of 7.3 on a 3rd-grade reading test. Because she was administered a level of the test designed for 3rd graders, there were most likely no passages on the test at the 7th-grade level. Lisa probably could not handle 7th-grade reading material and should not be instructed with material written for 7th grade. The score, however, does indicate that Lisa is reading well above her peers and should be given materials at a level that will promote her continued reading development. On the other hand, Marcus, an 8th-grade student, achieved the same grade equivalent score of 7.3 on a reading test. For Marcus, the score is more meaningful because it is within one year of his grade placement and some of the passages on the 8th-grade level of the test were appropriate for 7th graders. His score indicates that he is reading below his peers, but his percentile rank or stanine would be more useful for determining his reading progress in relation to others of his grade level. Unlike percentiles and stanines, grade equivalent scores do not represent equal units. They are not scaled scores. Grade equivalents are easily misunderstood and should be used with caution.

In addition to the methods of standardizing tests and the ways scores are reported, norm-referenced tests share other common characteristics. The tests are usually presented in different forms for different grade levels or for a range of levels. Occasionally, two or more forms for testing and retesting are provided. Standardized tests have manuals that contain explicit instructions for administration, tables for translating raw scores into derived scores, information on the norming process, and explanations of the reliability and validity of the test. Many test companies offer provisions for scoring the tests and for the production of various reports, including those on individuals, classes, and larger groups. Two kinds of standardized tests are commonly used to measure reading ability: achievement tests and diagnostic tests.

Achievement Tests

Achievement tests are norm-referenced batteries that assess the depth of students' knowledge in a variety of subject areas. They are sometimes referred to as survey tests and are most commonly administered to groups of students. Sometimes, all students in a school district are tested during the same week. These kinds of tests typically measure mathematics, science, social studies, and language usage in addition to reading ability and vocabulary. The *Iowa Tests of Basic Skills,* the *California Achievement Test,* and the *Stanford Achievement Test* are examples of comprehensive academic achievement tests.

Other achievement tests focus specifically on reading and include only reading-related subtests. The *Gates-MacGinitie Reading Tests,* with test forms for 1st through 12th grades, have subtests in vocabulary and reading comprehension; there are also assessments for use in kindergarten. The *Nelson-Denny Reading Test,* with test forms for high school and college, has subtests in vocabulary knowledge and reading comprehension with an added provision to measure reading rate. Raw scores on these achievement tests can be converted to grade equivalents, stanines, and/or percentiles.

Achievement tests are almost always group tests that are used to evaluate groups of students rather than individuals; for this reason, they have limited potential as diagnostic instruments. These tests should be carefully evaluated for content validity. The test will yield little useful information if the content of the test does not match school curricula or instructional materials. Achievement tests are designed to measure reading development by assessing what the student has already mastered, and, for this reason, they are most useful when administered near the end of the school year.

Diagnostic Reading Tests

Diagnostic reading tests are designed to assess areas in need of further instruction and are most useful when administered near the beginning of the school year. Subsequent instruction can then focus on assessed needs. Like achievement tests, diagnostic reading tests are norm referenced and standardized. Unlike reading achievement tests, diagnostic tests have numerous subtests, each designed to measure a specific aspect of reading development. Also, unlike achievement tests, diagnostic reading tests are commonly individually administered, generally only to those students who are struggling with delayed progress in reading. There are, however, some diagnostic tests that can be given to groups. The underlying goal of diagnostic testing is similar to that of medical diagnosis: to determine the problem and remediate it. These tests are designed to identify the reading strengths and needs of the student being tested.

An example of a diagnostic test designed for individual administration is the *Diagnostic Assessment of Reading* (DAR). This test has subtests that assess word recognition, word analysis, oral reading, silent reading comprehension, spelling, and word meanings. The multilevel format allows for testing beginning readers through high school students. Another individually administered diagnostic test is the *Gates-McKillop-Horowitz Reading Diagnostic Test*. With forms for grades 1 through 6, this test assesses skill areas including auditory discrimination, letter knowledge, blending, decoding, word recognition, spelling, oral reading, and comprehension.

The *Stanford Diagnostic Reading Test* (SDRT) is an example of a group diagnostic test. The SDRT has four levels appropriate for students in 1st grade through the first year of college. Subtests include auditory discrimination, word recognition, phonetic and structural analysis, auditory vocabulary, and literal and inferential comprehension. Test levels for older students also include comprehension of textual, functional, and recreational reading materials; word parts; reading rate; and skimming and scanning. The tests can be hand scored or machine scored, and raw scores can be converted to stanines, percentiles, and grade equivalents.

Student performance on a diagnostic test can be compared to that of the norm population, but comparison is not the primary purpose of diagnostic tests. They are designed to assess key areas of reading development in greater depth than can survey or achievement tests to identify specific areas of strength or need. When reading is divided into discrete subskills for purposes of diagnostic assessment, however, questions of construct validity arise. It is important with diagnostic assessments to further validate the results of the test with other assessment measures. When areas of instructional need are determined, the teacher can develop a plan for reading instruction that meets the assessed needs of the student.

Limitations of Standardized Tests

Standardized reading tests are constructed with care, and the norming process may include thousands of students; yet formal reading assessments have a number of limitations. They can measure only those aspects of reading performance that can be quantified. Standardized tests "can't measure initiative, creativity, imagination, conceptual thinking, curiosity, effort, irony, judgment, commitment, nuance, good will, [or] ethical reflection" (Ayers, 1993, p. 116). Standardized reading tests measure the product of reading rather than the processes students use to construct meaning from written text. The multiple-choice items require the student to "select rather than create responses" (Gunning, 2006, p. 69).

Another concern often voiced by educators is that standardized reading tests do not reflect current teaching methodology, and the test scores do not reflect what students do in authentic literacy experiences. Because they measure product rather than process, there is no way to determine what strategies students are using to make meaning of the text and no way to adequately quantify the higher-order thinking skills often required in the process of reading. A final limitation of standardized tests is that they may represent an outdated view of reading. Standardized tests divide reading into a series of discrete skills that are often tested in isolation. They do not reflect a current view of reading as a complex interaction between reader and text as the reader seeks to construct meaning.

Most significantly, standardized tests are not effective measures of an individual student's progress in reading development and should not be used in such high-stakes decisions as grade promotion. A student's score on a standardized reading test represents only his or her performance on the specific tasks required of the test on the day of testing. Many conditions contribute to that performance (Gillet, Temple, & Crawford, 2004). Factors within the reader, such as physical condition (including levels of fatigue, hunger, and test anxiety), motivation, prior experience in test-taking, interest and background knowledge in the topic of the passage, and, of course, reading ability, all influence the outcome of the test. In addition to factors within the reader, factors within the reading passages also contribute to the reader's score. Factors such as subject matter, text structure, writing style, vocabulary, grammatical complexity, the amount of information presented, and the size and type of font can all influence the student's score. Added to all these are factors within the testing situation: the lighting in the room, the temperature, the comfort level of the desk, the number of interruptions or other distractions that occur during testing, and the time of day during which the test is given. One or more of these factors can affect the student's score.

Despite their shortcomings, standardized reading tests are generally a part of a school's regular assessment program. Test results can be used effectively by both school administrators and teachers. Administrators use standardized test results as one way to compare classes, schools, school districts, and curriculum effectiveness. For example, if a district wants to determine the effectiveness of the reading program it uses, a standardized test can dependably demonstrate how the reading performance of students in that district compares to that of the norming population. Standardized tests results are presented in numerical reports that are fairly easy to interpret and use for comparisons of this nature.

Standardized tests, which are more cost effective and less time consuming than many informal reading assessments, can be used as screening measures for specialized reading programs and services. Because these tests are designed to test large groups of students, the entire school population can be tested. Test results can be screened to determine those students whose performance falls far enough below average to warrant either additional diagnostic testing or specialized reading services.

For teachers, the results of group tests provide a profile of class achievement. This profile may be helpful in planning the general focus of instruction for the entire class. For example, if the class as a whole performed better in vocabulary than in comprehension, the teacher may conclude that greater attention to comprehension would be an appropriate focus for instruction. The teacher can also use the test results to identify individual students who may not be making satisfactory progress in reading. A student's score in comprehension in the lower stanines, especially in stanines 1 and 2, may indicate that adequate progress is not being made. If the test score is also confirmed by observation and daily performance in the classroom, the student may be a candidate for more in-depth diagnosis and instruction. Standardized, norm-referenced tests are formal assessment measures that can be used in the complex process of assessing reading ability, but the wise teacher and administrator supplement their use with multiple other indicators of reading development.

CRITERION-REFERENCED TESTS

Criterion-referenced tests allow teachers to compare a student's performance to a preset criterion or performance level. Criterion-referenced tests are quite common in education. Spelling tests and math skill mastery tests are examples of criterion-referenced tests. The teacher or the school district determines the level of proficiency that a student must demonstrate to achieve a particular grade. Criterion-referenced tests have potential as diagnostic instruments because they allow the teacher to identify those students whose performance falls below the criterion.

With the current focus on standards-based reading instruction, criterion-referenced testing is becoming more common. Most states have established standards or curricular goals for reading development at each grade level. Although there is some variation in these standards, most are quite similar. Textbook publishers develop their reading programs to meet the state standards. The reading assessments that accompany many reading programs, as well as the state tests that assess a student's progress on those standards, are criterion-referenced tests.

Gillet et al. (2004) describe a three-tiered process for the development of criterion-referenced tests. First, the overall instructional learning goals are determined. These goals are broad, general statements of student proficiencies that are frequently developed at the state level. Examples of state reading program goals might include the ability to recognize high-frequency words in isolation or to read various materials with comprehension and fluency. These goals are known as state learning standards and are often presented as a continuum with benchmarks determined for each grade level.

From the state learning standards, specific program objectives are developed, usually at the district or school level. Program objectives more narrowly define the outcomes of instruction. Examples might include statements like the following:

- Students will demonstrate effective decoding of single-syllable words.
- Students will effectively retell events in sequential order.

Although program objectives are narrower than learning standards, they do not specify the level of proficiency necessary to meet the goal. The third tier of the process accomplishes these tasks. Instructional objectives, sometimes referred to as behavioral objectives, state the specific behaviors the student is to demonstrate after a period of instruction. Good instructional objectives also identify the criterion level of mastery desired for each outcome. For example:

- Given a list of 25 high-frequency words, the 1st-grade student will be able to identify 23 words at sight.
- After the reading of a passage from a 3rd-grade basal reader, the student will be able to list the events in the story with 90 percent accuracy.

Such instructional objectives are sometimes referred to as *benchmarks*. Benchmarks are descriptions of specific tasks students are expected to perform or behaviors students are expected to demonstrate at specific points along the continuum of their educational progress. For example, a benchmark for a student finishing kindergarten may be the ability to identify both upper- and lower-case letters of the alphabet. Benchmarks are behavioral or performance standards.

Rubrics, another term often heard in conjunction with criterion-referenced testing, are instruments designed to assist in the evaluation of behavioral or performance standards. Rubrics feature a rating scale that allows the teacher to determine the level of competency of a specified behavior or performance. For example, some rubrics include such descriptors as outstanding, acceptable, unacceptable or exceeds target, meets target, fails to meet target. Other rubrics include numerical scales of proficiency where, for example, 5 represents outstanding performance and 1 represents little evidence of ability.

Criterion-referenced tests are developed from instructional objectives. Quality criterion-referenced tests have items that are closely aligned with instructional objectives. Test items that "match the learning outcomes and conditions specified in the instructional objectives . . . insure validity" (Gillet et al., 2004, p. 198). Tests that are not closely matched with instructional objectives are of questionable validity. For example, when instructional objectives are developed locally, but a commercially produced test is used, there may be a mismatch. Mismatches can also occur when a school or teacher develops instructional objectives that are not closely aligned to the state standards or when the state standards are not appropriately represented on the state test. Just as with norm-referenced tests, the wise teacher and administrator consider other evidence of students' performance to further validate the scores achieved on a criterion-referenced test. Various kinds of informal assessment serve this purpose.

INFORMAL READING ASSESSMENT

In a position statement, the International Reading Association (2000) notes that students "deserve assessments that map a path toward their continued literacy growth" (p. 7). Informal reading assessments can best provide the kinds of data that help teachers identify an individual student's strengths and needs and that can be used to plan reading instruction that best meets the needs of the students grouped together in a particular classroom. Informal assessments, guided by the expertise of the classroom teacher and characterized by authentic literacy tasks, are more useful for these outcomes. Although there are many types of informal assessment, in this section we discuss only three: the informal reading inventory, running records, and anecdotal notes.

Informal Reading Inventory

An informal reading inventory (IRI) is an individually administered reading test that is considered "one of the best tools for observing and analyzing reading performance and for gathering information about how a student uses a wide range of reading strategies" (Jennings, Caldwell, & Lerner, 2006, p. 83). It is a criterion-referenced assessment that is composed of graded word lists and graded passages that increase in difficulty. The *Basic Reading Inventory* (Johns, 2005), for example, contains words lists and passages that range from pre-primer (beginning reading) through 12th grade. From an IRI, a teacher or reading specialist can learn about the "strengths and weaknesses the student shows during word recognition, oral and silent reading performance, comprehension strengths, and difficulties shown while reading at the independent reading level, instructional reading level, frustration reading level, and listening level" (Norton, 2006, p. 143). Determining a student's three levels is a major function of IRIs and is of great importance to teachers, as knowledge of a student's instructional level allows the teacher to select texts at a level most helpful to advancing reading development through differentiated instruction.

At any time during a student's reading development, there are materials written at levels that are easy, just right, and too hard. Easy materials are at the student's independent level. The student can read materials at this level fluently, with near-perfect word recognition, and without teacher assistance. At the independent level, a student is able to read passages with 99 percent word recognition accuracy and 90 percent comprehension. Materials at this level are useful for pleasure reading; furthermore, any assigned reading that the student is expected to complete on his or her own should be at the independent level.

Materials that are just right for students' instruction are at their instructional level. Texts at this level are challenging for the student but still within his or her comfort zone. A student is able to read passages at the instructional level with 95 percent word recognition accuracy and 75–89 percent comprehension. Students can theoretically make maximum progress in reading when instructional level texts are used in the classroom. Reading materials selected for reading instruction, guided reading, and all content area instruction should be at the student's instructional level.

Materials that are too hard are at the student's frustration level. Texts at this level have no instructional value beyond limited diagnostic purposes. When a student's passage reading demonstrates poor word recognition (at or below 90% accuracy) and poor comprehension (at or below 50% accuracy), the student has reached the frustration level. A serious problem in many classrooms is that a large number of students are asked to read books at their frustration levels. When students are given materials at their frustration levels, they often exhibit behavioral characteristics indicative of the difficulty they are experiencing. Some students simply refuse to read the textbook. Others may exhibit lack of expression in oral reading, lip movement during silent reading, difficulty pronouncing words, word-by-word reading, and/or finger pointing (Johns, 2005). Also, students often become more dependent on the teacher to explain the reading because they are unable to comprehend the text without assistance.

During the administration of the IRI, students initially read words in isolation from the graded word lists and continue by reading graded passages both orally and silently, beginning with levels that are at their independent reading level and continuing until a frustration level has been reached. During the oral reading, the test administrator times the reading and notes all miscues such as mispronunciations, omissions, insertions, repetitions, and substitutions. After the reading of passages, the student is asked to retell what was read and/or to respond to comprehension questions on the reading. When a frustration level has been reached in both oral and silent passages, the test administrator can read additional passages to the student to gain a listening level.

Careful analysis of a student's performance on the various tasks of the IRI yields a great deal of information about the student's reading abilities. From the graded word lists where the student's task is to read words presented in isolation, the test administrator can determine whether the student's word recognition ability can be classified as above, at, or below grade level; can assess the extent of the student's sight vocabulary, including high-frequency words;

can determine some of the student's word identification strategies, such as phonics and structural analysis; and can determine the approximate level at which the student should begin reading graded passages.

Although some initial insights can be gained by analyzing the student's performance on the word lists, much more can be determined from a thorough analysis of the student's performance on the oral and silent reading passages. Successful reading is dependent on two major areas: word recognition and comprehension. The good reader is able to identify words automatically and to construct meaning from the words in the passage. By closely examining the student's performance in both areas, the teacher or test administrator can identify both strengths and needs.

By analyzing the student's oral reading errors or miscues on the graded passages, the administrator can gain greater insight into the student's word identification strategies. Miscue analysis is based on the work of K. Goodman (1967) who believes that reading errors provide insights into the whole reading process. "Such insights reveal not only weaknesses, but strengths as well, because the miscues are not simple errors but the results of the reading process having miscarried in some minor or major ways" (p. 12). There are three basic kinds of miscues: semantic, syntactic, and graphophonic. Semantic miscues make sense in the context in which they are read. The reader is using meaning cues such as illustrations, context clues, or other information from the passage to substitute a word that makes sense in place of an unknown word in the passage. Syntactic miscues make use of the grammatical structure of the language. For example, the student may substitute one noun for another or one adjective for another. In such instances, the student is demonstrating that he or she has internalized the grammatical rules of the language and is using that knowledge in an attempt to recognize unknown words. Graphophonic miscues look similar to the word in the text. For example, if a student reads *sand* for *send,* he or she may be relying on the visual image of the word rather than on the meaning of the context. Much can be learned about the student's reading by a miscue analysis.

Counting the student's total miscues provides a quantitative measure of oral reading that can be used, at least in part, to determine the student's reading level. An in-depth analysis of all significant graphophonemic miscues made during the oral reading will reveal areas of instructional need in decoding. For example, when multiple miscues involve mispronunciation of vowels sounds in consonant-vowel-consonant patterns, the teacher can hypothesize that additional work on vowel sounds is probably needed. Moreover, if the same analysis shows that the student's miscues generally begin with the same sound as the target word, the teacher can determine that the student can successfully decode initial consonants. An analysis of the semantic and syntactic miscues made during oral reading will reveal other strengths and weaknesses in the student's word recognition.

In addition, the student's oral reading can be analyzed for fluency. The student's rate of reading can be compared to norms for his or her grade level, and other components of fluency can be observed and noted by the teacher or test administrator. Fluent readers translate written language into spoken language with automaticity, accuracy, and appropriate expression.

A thorough analysis of all word recognition components will yield much useful information about the student's current level of word knowledge and approaches to unfamiliar words, but word recognition is only one part of the reading process. The IRI is also designed to yield much information about a student's ability to comprehend written text. By analyzing the student's retelling of the passage or the student's responses to comprehension questions, the test administrator can gain useful insights into areas of comprehension that may need additional attention. For example, if a student is able to relate literal information from the passage, but demonstrates a pattern of inappropriate responses to inferential questions, the teacher may hypothesize, based on the evidence provided by the IRI, that the student would benefit from an instructional focus on higher-order comprehension skills such as inferring and drawing conclusions.

Although administration can be time consuming, the IRI is an invaluable assessment instrument for comprehensive diagnosis of student's reading. After the data gathered from the IRI have been carefully analyzed, an instructional plan based on diagnosed needs in reading can be developed. In this way, the information yielded by the IRI informs the subsequent instruction, fulfilling one of the major goals of effective reading assessment.

Running Records

Running records, somewhat similar to the oral reading analysis of the IRI, allow the teacher to closely observe and analyze a student's oral reading. Based on three-quarters of a century of research in reading assessment, including the work of such noted specialists as Donald Durrell (1940), Emmett A. Betts (1946), and Yetta Goodman (1967), Marie Clay (1972) developed running records, a method of assessing oral reading errors or miscues. Conducting running records is "an informal assessment procedure with high reliability . . . that can inform teachers regarding a student's decoding development" (Reutzel & Cooter, 2007, p. 29).

To conduct a running record, the teacher selects a passage that is 100–200 words long. For younger students, shorter passages are acceptable. The reading selection can be from the basal reader or the student's self-selected reading materials. The teacher either stands behind the reader or sits beside the reader and carefully records any miscues made during the reading with a marking code that indicates repetitions, self-corrections, omissions, insertions, and any attempts to pronounce unfamiliar words. Later, the teacher analyzes the miscues to determine the level of the text read and the particular strengths and needs in the student's oral reading.

The percentage of words read correctly indicates the student's reading level on that text. Clay established criteria for oral reading similar to that used in IRIs. According to her criteria, text read with 95–100 percent word recognition accuracy is at the independent level, text read with 90–94 percent word recognition accuracy is at the instructional level, and text read with less than 89 percent accuracy is at the frustration level. Clay's protocol for analyzing the miscues made during the oral reading, very similar to that used in an IRI, is also based on the work of Kenneth Goodman (1967) and allows the teacher to identify three kinds of miscues determined by the cuing system the child was most likely accessing when the miscue was made: meaning, syntactic, and visual. Meaning miscues (semantic) make sense in the context in which they are read. Syntactic miscues make use of the grammatical structure of the language. Visual miscues (graphophonic) look similar to the word in the text. Just as with the IRI, much can be learned about the student's reading by a thorough miscue analysis.

One advantage of running records is that the procedure can be accomplished using classroom materials. In addition, the procedure is not difficult and requires little training. Classroom teachers can easily do initial reading assessments of their students using running records and often find the process efficient because no special materials are required (Strickland & Strickland, 2000). A limitation of running records is that they examine only word recognition.

Anecdotal Records

Anecdotal records, another informal reading assessment, require little training and can be accomplished using classroom materials to assess both word recognition and comprehension. Such records are documentations of student reading behaviors viewed through the classroom teacher's experienced eye. The data gathered "explicitly depends upon the human expert" (Johnston & Rogers, 2002, p. 381), the "connoisseur" (Eisner, 1998, p. 17) of reading behaviors, and the teacher who has spent hours in the classroom, observing students in daily interactions with texts. Anecdotal records are referred to as authentic assessment because the data are gathered in the context of authentic reading tasks. The assessment is ongoing and based on actual literacy experiences that take place within the classroom.

In the simplest form, anecdotal records are documentations of the teacher's observations of students' reading. The teacher creates notes shortly after the observation was made, recording the student's name, the specific reading behavior observed, and the date the observation was made. These observations can include both strengths and needs. For example, the teacher might record a previously taught reading strategy that the student used independently or a reminder to offer the student additional instruction or practice on a specific skill or area of reading that has not yet been mastered.

Successful creation of anecdotal records includes initial planning and preparation. It is important to plan to observe each student. Some students naturally draw more attention from the teacher than others, but to be used as an effective assessment, anecdotal notes must include observations of every student. These observations can be scheduled using a rotation plan. For example, a teacher with 25 students may choose to observe 5 students each day for a minimum of one recorded observation per pupil per week. Intermediate and high school teachers who meet daily with large numbers of students may plan for less frequent observations, focusing on two or three classes per day, for a total of three to five observations per student per marking period.

Another logistic consideration involves preparing a place to record notes before the observation period. Some teachers use an index card for each student; others keep a separate page for each student in a three-ring binder. One common method is to record notes on sheets of blank peel-off address labels. The labels can be prepared ahead of time with the student's name and the date. Later the notes can be transferred to individual student record sheets. Effective planning for who is to be observed and preparation for where the observations are to be recorded allow the teacher to focus on preselected students and to record observations quickly and efficiently.

The final and most important consideration involves what to observe. Throughout the day, teachers are continuously observing and noting their students' behaviors. Recording all behaviors germane to reading would be an impossible task and would offer little assessment value. Therefore a selected focus is required. When anecdotal notes are focused on particular standards-based outcomes, as recommended by Boyd-Batstone (2004), they become "a tool to work common ground across authentic and standardized assessment" (p. 238). When used in this manner, the teacher plans and prepares for observations in much the same manner that he or she plans and prepares for standards-based instruction. The selected standard allows the teacher to focus on particular behaviors; furthermore, the teacher can make use of the verbs in well-written standards to facilitate recording observations. When the standards are written in the language of observable behaviors, such as *identifies, arranges,* or *retells,* the teacher can quite easily record observations using that same language.

Subsequent analysis of anecdotal records provides the teacher with valuable information on the overall progress of students, as well as the overall effectiveness of the instruction given. From an analysis of the records of a particular student, the teacher can easily determine both the student's reading accomplishments and the areas in need of additional instructional support or practice. Such documentation of student progress can become the outline for narrative reports to parents and administrators. From an analysis of all the records on a particular standards-based outcome, the teacher can determine both the progress of students on that standard and the amount of additional work required before all students meet the standard. In addition, such analysis serves as a point of reflection for the teacher who wishes to improve his or her efficacy in reading instruction. When the analysis indicates slow or unacceptable progress on a particular standard, the teacher can re-reevaluate the instructional approach used and plan accordingly for additional instruction. It is in this manner that anecdotal records fulfill the most basic task of informal reading assessment: they inform the instruction that occurs subsequent to the assessment, providing a blueprint for continued reading instruction.

CONCLUSION

Reading assessment is the gathering of data about students' reading for various purposes. Formal, norm-referenced tests compare a student's performance to that of a large representative norm group. Such standardized reading tests are used appropriately to make decisions about programs and groups of students. They are used inappropriately to make decisions, such as grade retention or promotion, about individual students. For such decisions, multiple measures of performance give a more holistic portrait of a student's reading development. Achievement or survey tests identify what the student has already mastered or achieved in reading, whereas diagnostic tests identify those aspects of reading still in need of continued growth. Criterion-referenced tests compare student performance to a preset criterion or performance level. Most state tests for reading proficiency use preestablished outcome standards as the criteria or benchmarks to which student performance is compared.

In addition to methods of formal reading assessment, many opportunities for informal assessment exist. An informal reading inventory can yield a great deal of useful information in the development of an effective instructional plan. Other informal methods such as running records and anecdotal records are examples of more authentic assessments that make use of classroom materials and daily literacy experiences. Whether using formal or informal assessments, questions of reliability and validity must be addressed with all measures of reading development.

There is no one right way or even one best way to effectively measure the complex cognitive process of reading. To ensure that reading assessments are used effectively and ethically, it is important to understand the purpose of the assessment being administered. Whether seeking to understand the efficacy of the reading program at the district level or the reading proficiency of an individual student, we suggest that the best possible use of reading assessment is to improve students' learning. When the data gathered have been thoroughly analyzed with that outcome in mind, teachers, administrators, and parents will be able to determine an instructional program for the continued literacy growth of all students.

REFERENCES

Ayers, W. (1993). *To teach: The journey of a teacher.* New York: Teachers College Press.

Betts, E. A. (1946). *Foundations of reading instruction.* New York: American Book.

Boyd-Batstone, P. (2004). Focused anecdotal records assessment: A tool for standards-based authentic assessment. *The Reading Teacher, 58,* 230–239.

Clay, M. M. (1972). *The early detection of reading difficulties.* Portsmouth, NH: Heinneman.

Criswell, J. R. (2006). *Developing assessment literacy: A guide for elementary and middle school teachers.* Norwood, MA: Christopher-Gordon.

Durrell, D. D. (1940). *Improvement of basic reading abilities.* New York: World Book.

Eisner, E. W. (1998). *The enlightened eye: Qualitative inquiry and the enhancement of educational practice.* Upper Saddle River, NJ: Prentice Hall.

Gillet, J. W., Temple, C., & Crawford, A. N. (2004). *Understanding reading problems: Assessment and instruction* (6th ed.). Boston: Pearson.

Goodman, K. (1967). "Reading": A psycholinguistic guessing game. *Journal of the Reading Specialist, 6,* 126–135.

Goodman, Y. M. (1967). *A phycholinguistic description of observed oral reading phenomena in selected young beginning readers.* Unpublished doctoral dissertation. Wayne State University.

Gunning, T. G. (2006). *Assessing and correcting reading and writing difficulties* (3rd ed.). Boston: Pearson.

International Reading Association. (2000). *Teaching all children to read: The roles of the reading specialist—A position statement of the International Reading Association.* Newark, DE: International Reading Association.

Jennings, J. H., Caldwell, J. S., & Lerner, J. W. (2006). *Reading problems: Assessment and teaching strategies* (5th ed.). Boston: Pearson.

Johns, J. L. (2005). *Basic reading inventory* (9th ed.). Dubuque, IA: Kendall/Hunt.

Johnston, P., & Rogers, R. (2002). Early literacy development: The case for "informed assessment." In S. B. Newman & D. K. Dickenson (Eds.), *Handbook of early literacy research* (pp. 377–389). New York: Guilford.

Norton, D. E. (2006). *Literacy for life.* Boston: Allyn & Bacon.

Reutzel, D. R., & Cooter, R. B., Jr. (2007). *Strategies for reading assessment and instruction: Helping every child succeed* (3rd ed.). Upper Saddle River, NJ: Pearson.

Strickland, K., & Strickland, J. (2000). *Making assessment elementary.* Portsmouth, NH: Heinemann.

Chapter Six

WRITING DEVELOPMENT: CURRICULUM, INSTRUCTION, AND ASSESSMENT

Robert C. Calfee and Kimberly A. Norman

Our purpose in this chapter is to describe strategies that foster writing development between grades 4 and 8. The shift between learning to write and writing to learn, an essential part of development during these years, provides the rationale for deciding which aspects of writing to emphasize and which to background. For example, schools give less attention to spelling, handwriting, and other mechanical features, and instead focus on the generation and organization of ideas, and on the shaping of compositions that have clarity and appeal for the writer's intended audience.

By the upper elementary and middle school levels, students reach a critical stage in their acquisition of literacy. They have moved through a range of experiences, in and out of school, that give them something to talk about. They can now step back and reflect; they can think about something and can think about thinking. Most students have gained some degree of skill in handling print. All are entering a point in the academic curriculum where they are expected to deal with a broad range of substantial topics and concepts, most of which are genuinely new to them. Children still write narratives, but from 4th grade onward, there is a shift toward expositions—informational reports, research papers, persuasive essays, and so on. A book report may begin with a story, but the final product is an analytical work. Personal journaling, show-and-tell, and casual conversations suffice in the primary grades, but by 4th grade, successful students need to demonstrate the ability and motivation to engage in relatively sophisticated writing projects where they assemble material from various sources, develop plans for structuring the information, and add details sufficient to embellish the final product. They confront decisions about the overall organization, the formulation of paragraphs, and the building of coherent sentences. The task may easily span a week or more, during which time students draw continuously on the elements of the writing process: *develop/draft; revise/review; polish/publish.* Accomplishing this task has critical implications for both their academic success and life outside of school. The task is partly about writing, but more important, it is about effective thinking and communicating—the acquisition of *academic language* (Wong-Fillmore & Snow, 2000).

This chapter focuses on *development,* on the movement from the 3rd grader's personalized scribbles to the high schooler's research report. We will use the National Assessment of Educational Progress (NAEP), the "nation's report card," to set the developmental stage. The NAEP illustrates the types of writing assignments that are presented to students in 4th and 8th grades, and reveals how well they perform on these tasks. We then move to the classroom setting, looking in turn at curriculum and instruction, to understand how students' literacy development takes place with support from teachers. Assessment does not appear as a separate category but is woven throughout the paper.

We begin with a review of conventional resources including research reviews, textbooks for students and teachers, and the content standards that now shape the U.S. curriculum. This chapter emerges within the context of the federal No Child Left Behind legislation, which privileges reading and mathematics. Along the way, we encountered a strange finding—from the end of the primary grades to the beginning of high school, the basic advice for writing instruction from all of these sources is "do more of the same, when you have time." Curriculum resources provide little in the way of a systematic progression of skills and knowledge designed to lead the 3rd-grade novice toward the expertise expected of the high school freshman.

After reviewing this situation, we offer suggestions about how to reshape the current state of affairs. Our hope is to persuade our audience of the vital importance of writing development across the content areas during this critical span of years, and of the potential of writing to enhance the full spectrum of students' cognitive, social, and motivational competence. The National Commission on Writing (2003) has called for "doubling the amount of time students spend writing" (p. 3), arguing that "writing today is not a frill for the few, but an essential skill for the many" (p. 3). We agree completely with these recommendations, but we suggest that it is also critically important to define what students are writing about.

BOOKENDS: WRITING ON THE NATION'S REPORT CARD

NAEP is a large-scale assessment regularly administered to 4th-, 8th- and 12th-grade students in several subject areas to track the academic progress of the nation's students. Results are reported as aggregates for various demo-graphic subgroups (e.g., boys and girls, level of parent education) and for state-to-state comparison. The 4th- and 8th-grade writing assessments span the grade range addressed in this chapter. NAEP writing measures students' proficiency in three types or genres of writing: narrative, informative, and per-suasive. The type of writing varies across the grades in response to variations in state standards. In 4th grade, 40 percent of the writing tasks are narrative, 35 percent are informative, and 25 percent are persuasive. By 12th-grade, the emphasis is reversed, with the greatest emphasis placed on the expository or informational writing tasks. In 8th-grade, each genre receives relatively equal attention. Students receive 25 minutes to complete each writing assignment. They are encouraged to draft a plan before beginning the composition and to revise and edit their work.

Each composition is graded as basic, proficient, or advanced. Proficient is defined as "solid academic performance," and basic is the label for "partial mas-tery of prerequisite knowledge and skills that are fundamental for proficient work." The scale is not especially fine grained; basic is considered as "margin-ally passing" at best. The 2002 NAEP results showed that only 28 percent of 4th graders and 31 percent of 8th graders performed at or above the proficient level, which means that the majority of the students were at or below the basic level. Only 1 or 2 percent of the compositions were advanced, which identifies "superior performance." The data showed the usual demographic trends: girls received higher scores than boys, and writing performance varied with family income and education. The report is quite extensive, but the executive sum-mary makes little note of differences among the three genres.

A few released items on the NAEP presented in Table 6.1 give an idea of such factors as familiarity of content, degree of support (e.g., identification of purpose and audience, prompts for details or support), and students' interest. Two of the items are stand-alone and two are text-based (some background material is provided). A couple of the items seem fairly easy, in the sense of familiarity and accessibility of the topic, and a couple are more difficult.

Let's take a look at the writing demands of the 8th-grade prompts. In the easy, text-based prompt, students compose a persuasive text. They read a news-paper article on teenage sleep patterns. The main idea of the article is that because teenagers are at their lowest energy levels in the morning, they should stay up late at night and sleep late in the morning. This topic should appeal to adolescents who are inclined to pull the sheets over their heads in the morn-ing. The article invites the students to ask the principal to think about chang-ing established school routines. The prompt provides useful support. It draws the reader/writer into the situation. The task and audience are clear, and the proposition is authentic. It provides clues to the genre and reminds the writer to support the argument with convincing details.

Table 6.1
Sample Released Items from National Assessment of Educational Progress Writing

	4th Grade	8th Grade
Easy	We all have favorite objects that we care about and would not want to give up. Think of one object that is important or valuable to you. For example, it could be a book, a piece of clothing, a game, or any object you care about. Write about your favorite object. Be sure to describe the object and explain why it is valuable or important to you.	Imagine that the article shown below appeared in your local newspaper. Read the article carefully, then write a letter to your principal arguing for or against the proposition that classes at your school should begin and end much later in the day. Be sure to give detailed reasons to support your argument and make it convincing.

Studies Show Students Need To Sleep Late

Night Owls Versus Early Birds

The *Journal of Medicine* announced today the results of several recent studies on the sleep patterns of teenagers and adults. These studies show that adults and teenagers often have different kinds of sleep patterns because they are at different stages in the human growth cycle.

The study on teenagers' sleep patterns showed that changes in teenagers' growth hormones are related to sleeping patterns. In general, teenagers' energy levels are at their lowest in the morning, between 9 a.m. and 12 noon. To strike the most of students' attention span and ability to learn, the study showed that most teenagers need to stay up late at night and to sleep late in the morning. They

called this pattern "the night owl syndrome."

Studies of adults (over 30 years of age) showed the opposite sleep pattern. On average, adults' energy levels were at their lowest at night between 9 p.m. and 12 midnight and at their highest between 6 and 9 a.m. In addition, a study of adults of different ages revealed that as adults get older they seem to wake up earlier in the morning. Thus, adults need to go to sleep earlier in the evening. Researchers called this sleep pattern "the early bird syndrome."

Researchers claim that these studies should be reviewed by all school systems and appropriate changes should be made to the daily school schedule.

| Difficult (more challenging) | **IMAGINE!**
One morning you wake up and go down to breakfast. This is what you see on the table:

You are surprised. Then when you look out the window, this is what you see:

Write a story called "The Very Unusual Day" about what happens until you go to bed again. | A novel written in the 1950s describes a world where people are not allowed to read books. A small group of people who want to save books memorize them so that the books won't be forgotten. For example, an old man who has memorized the novel *The Call of the Wild* helps a young boy memorize it by reciting the story to him. In this way, the book is saved for the future.

If you were told that you could save just one book for future generations, which book would you choose?

Write an essay in which you discuss which book you would choose to save for future generations and what it is about the book that makes it important to save. Be sure to discuss in detail why the book is important to you and why it would be important to future generations. |

Analysis of the second item reveals more challenges. Students are asked to select a book from the 1950s to guard for future generations. From the outset, students must deal with ancient history (the 1950s) and an unrealistic premise—a world without books. The reference to *The Call of the Wild* is useful only for those students who know the book and who appreciate the influence of books on people's lives. The directions seem straightforward: discuss the book you would save, why it is important, and why the book is important to you and to future generations. One challenge for the writer is to identify a book worth saving for posterity. Actually, the larger puzzle for a 14-year old is to understand what it means to save something for posterity. The audience is unclear; the most likely target of such an essay would probably be the writer of the text, but the implication is that someone else would be interested.

These examples illustrate the challenges and supports that confront students in the NAEP writing tasks. These are tests, and even though the developers encourage planning, drafting, and revising, students are constrained by time and standardization. They must work alone with no opportunities to refine ideas; they receive no feedback and the results do not affect their grade—the tasks have no clear purpose or audience. From one perspective, the results show what students can do under conditions that are not especially supportive. On the other hand, classroom writing is often quite similar, except that the work is graded.

CURRICULUM: WHAT NEEDS TO BE TAUGHT

Writing, like reading, is something of a curiosity. Everyone knows the importance of the "three R's"—readin,' writin,' and 'rithmetic—the curriculum cornerstones for the elementary grades. Unlike the content areas—biology, physics, history, geography, and so on—the three R's do not appear in university catalogues, at least not in a form useful to elementary and middle school teachers. As a result, certification in most states requires relatively little attention to writing instruction.

To be sure, there are *writing standards,* statements about what students should know and do, developed by states as the foundation for tests required by the federal legislation of No Child Left Behind (NCLB). Something strange happened, however, between the creation of standards and development of the tests: the writing "R" disappeared! The Academic Yearly Progress reports mandated by NCLB include reading, math, and science, but not writing. There are several reasons for this decision. It is difficult to prepare valid writing tests that are also cheap, such as those that use multiple-choice formats. NAEP has stayed the course and requires students to actually write something, and some states include actual writing tasks at selected grades, but writing is not on the test. Interestingly, many states include short-answer items in reading, science, and even math, but do not score these as "writing."

For teachers and students in the age-grade range addressed in this chapter, learning to express thinking becomes increasingly critical for success in school. Of course, if students don't have anything to say, they won't have much to write about. *Thinking* is an essential first step, followed by *saying*, and then *writing* (Moffett & Wagner, 1976). In this section, we focus on the writing curriculum, the final stage of the composition process, but we will refer repeatedly to "thinking and saying."

Writing as a Course of Study

What should students be taught about writing during the late elementary and middle school grades? We turned to state and national standards for an answer, and because our assignment was to address development, we also skimmed the earlier and later grades to find out what students should have already learned and what they should prepare for. One set of results, based on a summary analysis of state standards by the Mid-continent Regional Educational Laboratory or McREL (Kendall & Marzano, 2004), is shown in Table 6.2.

Table 6.2
Developmental Spectrum of National Writing Standards by Grade Clusters and Composition Domains After McREL

Domain	K–2	3–5	6–8	9–12
Genre	**Variety of genres**	**Exposition:** Information, cause-effect, chronology	**Exposition:** Common expository structures, compare-contrast, problem solution	**Exposition:** Describes and differentiates; compares-contrasts
Organization	Not clearly specified	**Topic:** Identify, develop, conclude	**Thesis:** Logical organization of detail, intro and conclusion	"Organizes" Develops main idea and details in relative importance
Sources	Picture books, personal experiences, response to literature	"Several sources:" Facts, details, examples, explanations	Knowledge about topic	"First and second-hand:" Books, magazines, computers, community
Presentation and style/ Purpose and audience	Letters, personal stories, entertain, inform		State purpose	Interesting facts, anecdotes, scenario, technical terms, history

The McREL compilation is organized by four grade clusters, the design used by most states, and one that makes considerable sense. We selected elements from several McREL benchmarks and organized them according to four developmental continua: genre (what "kinds" of writing to expect and support), organization (what structural features should be found in student compositions), sources (what should students routinely draw on as a basis for writing), and presentation/style (how to deal with purpose and audience). These categories are admittedly constructed from a complex array of entries, but we think that they capture important features of the McREL summary.

A broad survey of the matrix suggests a few trends. First, the genre category (types of writing) emphasizes exposition from the mid-elementary grades on, with little apparent "development." The same types of writing (e.g., information/description, compare-contrast, persuasion) appear at every grade cluster. Second, organization also seems quite constant; students need to identify a topic (or thesis, which might be an important distinction), and stick with it. The standards from 3rd grade through high school call for compositions with a beginning, middle, and end, as well as reasonable use of details throughout. The standards for sources lay out a progression from familiar and personally relevant items in the primary grades to actively locating and analyzing more abstract and complex information in high school. The nature and progression of this stream are not spelled out. For practical purposes, the standards look the same whether you are teaching 4th or 8th grade.

Why Genre Is Important

What should be changing across the middle elementary grades other than "more of the same?" For both theoretical and practical reasons, we decided to use *genre* as a target for responding to this question. As it turns out, this choice casts a new light on other elements of the developmental curriculum. The genre concept has taken on increasing importance in recent years and ensures a better balance with writing conventions. Proper spelling, correct grammar, and basic organization (beginning, middle, and end) are reasonably easy to identify, assess, and teach. *Genre* includes the other significant aspects of a composition: the choice of a significant topic or thesis, creation of a coherent and appropriate structure, and attention to purpose and audience.

Genre shows up regularly in state standards, but often without clear purpose. Our suggestion is that teachers think about a "genre tool kit" as the foundation for a developmental writing curriculum. Helping students understand when and how to use these tools to construct engaging and informative compositions may be one of the most important developmental tasks during the middle grades.

Genre emphasizes *form*, which implies structure. The definition also mentions criteria calling for the form to fit the topic or function. If your car has a brake problem and the mechanic launches into a long story about how her uncle's car had a similar problem, the genre is wrong for the function. You need information about brake problems and solutions. "Vague" and "no fixed boundaries" might seem troublesome, but they actually invite alternatives to the standard "five-paragraph essay" model—the idea that students should learn to decide on a topic ("peanut butter sandwiches"), sketch three paragraphs with a few details ("type of bread, style of peanut butter, toasted or not"), and finish by composing the introduction and conclusion. Authentic writing surely requires more than this "one size fits all" approach. Writing is partly an artistic activity, whether a novel or the Report of the Iraq Committee. Variations in the patterns are numerous, reflecting the interplay among writing, speaking, and graphic representations. In the midst of this variety, genre can provide a set of constancies that guide the individual from novice through competence to expert.

Table 6.2 shows that students in the primary grades must write in a variety of genres. From the mid-elementary grades onward, the emphasis shifts to *exposition*. Exposition has several meanings but most often contrasts narrative with technical writing, stories with reports, English with the content areas (sciences and social studies), or fact with fiction. None of these comparisons is perfect, but the basic idea is that as students move from the late elementary grades toward high school, academic tasks shift from stories toward reports, narrative toward exposition, for both reading and writing.

One simple approach to the development of genre is that teachers from 4th grade onward should increase writing (and reading) that emphasizes information and sequence—that "expounds." Magazines and newspapers offer examples: what, who, when, where, and so on. Students often read such materials on their own, but are less likely to write academically unless required to do so—text messaging does not count. The five-paragraph essay offers a model to help students compose in a slightly more formal manner, rely less on the first-person pronoun, and pay more attention to the conventions of grammar and spelling. These styles are somewhat rare outside of school; most parents don't "expound" when they take their children to the grocery store, nor do they expect an exposition in response. This image of the developmental course seems simple enough, however, like the shift from crawling to walking.

Why then do so many 8th graders write so poorly? In the McREL summary, genre plays a minor role. Table 6.3 offers a more detailed example from the California Content Standards for "Writing Applications: Genres and their Characteristics."

California requires grade-by-grade standards, and so an explicit progression is laid out. California was late in developing standards, and so this list used

Table 6.3
Developmental Progression of Genre from California State Content Standards
(Cell Entry Indicates Placement in Standards list)

Grade/genre	4	5	6	7	8
Narrative	1	1	1	1	1 (Biography)
Response to literature	2	2	4	2	2
Research report	3	3 (Information report)	3	3	3
Summary	4			5	
Persuasive and argumentation		4 (Letter)	5	4	4
Exposition			2		
Career documents					5
Technical documents					6

many other states for models. Because the standards are grade-by-grade, they are, for practical purposes, scope-and-sequence charts. Between 4th grade and high school entry, California students are expected to make a giant step in the mastery of exposition. The standards are cumulative; writing narratives and responding to literature (book reports) remain at the top of the list. Research reports and persuasive compositions enter at grades 4 and 5, but remain much the same through grade 8. In fact, there is little development along the way. Consider the standards for 4th and 8th grades:

> Fourth Grade: Write information reports that (1) frame a central question about an issue or situation; (2) include facts and details for focus; and (3) draw from more than one source of information (e.g., speakers, books, newspapers, other media sources.
>
> Eighth Grade: Write research reports that (1) define a thesis; (2) record important ideas, concepts, and direct quotations from significant information sources and paraphrase and summarize all perspectives on the topic, as appropriate; (3) use a variety of primary and secondary sources and distinguish the nature and value of each; and (4) organize and display information on charts, maps, and graphs.

The 8th-grade standards are longer, call for more refinement, and add graphs and charts. In 8th grade (but not before), the standards include career documents (business letters and job applications) and technical documents (activities to design a system, operate a tool, or explain the bylaws of an organization). The standards do not seem to require much to be learned, so why do national and international assessments conclude that student writing is not up to par? We believe, as discussed in the next section, that the standards are off the mark because they focus solely on "writing."

A Different Perspective on "What Develops"

We initially assumed that our assignment was quite straightforward. We could refer to various resources—textbooks, research papers, standards documents, and so on—to trace the developmental path of writing from the mid-elementary grades toward entry to high school. We felt reasonably familiar with the practicalities of this age-grade spectrum. As we began our work, however, we encountered much sparser territory than we expected. Summarizing what is known about writing development is easy, but it reveals a large "black hole."

By the end of the primary grades, most students have learned something about writing as a technical activity and can use paper and pencil to express personal experiences—simple stories and brief descriptive pieces. Six years later, when they enter high school, they are expected to compose complex expositions in a variety of disciplines using genres and conventions appropriate to the discipline. Psychologists describe this move as the shift from novice to expert. Much is known about the difference between novices and experts; much less is known about how to help individuals manage the shift. One might expect, for a fundamental task like writing, that the curriculum would provide a road map, standards and scope-and-sequence charts would provide guidelines, and textbooks (for both students and teachers) would fill in the essential details. But much like the situation for reading comprehension, the advice is "practice, practice, practice."

Practice—with feedback—is certainly important in developing expertise. But practice only makes permanent. A great deal depends on what is practiced, as anyone who learned the hunt-and-peck system of typing can testify. As we reviewed standards and textbooks and classroom activities, we experienced an epiphany, centered in part around genre, but also around the "what" question. In previous research (Chambliss & Calfee, 1998), we viewed genre as roughly synonymous with text structure.

In this approach, writing development during the middle grades occurs as students acquire a set of simple structures (e.g., topical net, hierarchy, matrix) and apply these structures to increasingly difficult content, learning along the way the stages of the writing process listed previously. One challenge, well recognized in practice, centers around the question of who is to teach what. By middle school, English teachers handle literature and grammar, content-area teachers deal with content, and nobody really teaches reading and writing.

In the process of constructing this chapter, our conception of writing development during the middle grades turned upside down. Adolescence is a time of considerable change, marked by the emergence of greater self-awareness, greater engagement with peer groups and awareness of others, and the capacity to reflect (Wigfield, Byrnes, & Eccles, 2006). The changes begin in the late elementary grades. Experience shifts even more substantially when the student leaves the elementary grades. Science is no longer a 30-minute session a couple of times a week with the same teacher in the same classroom, but instead becomes 50 minutes crammed into a scattershot daily schedule in different places with different teachers, each dealing with snapshots of 100 to 150 students, and weekly tests that are graded. The same is true for English, mathematics, social studies, physical education, and the occasional elective.

Our reconception, which covers the middle grade span from late elementary through middle school, centers around the development of writing in these subject matters. Why in the world should students learn the Pythagorean theorem, the causes of the Civil War, the structure of the solar system, the different varieties of mammals, *Hamlet* and *Macbeth,* and so on? One answer centers around the traditional notion of the well-educated person—not really at the top of the adolescent agenda. Another approach is more pragmatic; learn these things so students can pass the tests, finish college, get a good job, and make a lot of money. A third response is that the real reason for school is for child care, and the curriculum is a way to keep everyone (students and teachers) busy during these formative but confusing years. To be sure, some teachers manage to find bits and pieces of content that are interesting and engaging: how to measure *pi* with a piece of string, observing a garter snake deal with a cricket, creating a classroom constitution, creating a model moon colony, interviewing your grandparents about the early years of television, and so on.

Each of these approaches appears in practice, but none seems an adequate response to the "why" question. We argue that the situation offers an important developmental opportunity for changing the way that students view the world, and that literacy is an essential ingredient in the process. Our argument builds on two familiar foundations—curriculum integration and literacy across the curriculum.

As noted, the argument contains two essential elements. The first is the potential of the content areas to change the way that individuals view the world. In recent years, psychologists have discovered much about the differences between novices and experts (cf. Bransford, Brown & Cocking, 1999). For example, when the car won't start, the novice opens the hood and sees a tangle of junk, but the expert sees a cable that has come loose from the distributor cap. Most of us, standing on the beach during a brilliant sunset, see the sun sink behind the horizon. The expert experiences the movement of the earth as it rotates away from the sun. The academic disciplines, as recorded in the standards, capture the knowledge accumulated over the ages for changing perspectives, and for building new insights. Standards and books and even five-paragraph essays, however, can amount to little more than "inert knowledge" (Whitehead, 1974). Only as students move from knowledge-telling to knowledge-transforming (Bereiter & Scardamalia, 1987) do the disciplines come alive. The key to knowledge-transforming is composing—taking content from various sources and disciplines and changing it into new constructions, a process in which the genre "tool kit" plays an essential role in assembling, organizing, and constructing projects.

Development is a critical consideration in this argument. The typical 4th grader is just beginning to move beyond the worlds of personal experience, in which the neighborhood sets the limits of space and holidays define the spectrum of time. Friends are important, but the family is still the social centerpiece. Education offers the opportunity for the 8th grader to participate in an entirely new set of possibilities. As noted previously, natural development moves the adolescent into a different world, quite apart from school influences. The challenge is to ensure that educational experiences support and enhance the developmental possibilities. The evidence suggests that schooling in the middle grades actually has a largely negative impact on youngsters (Eccles et al., 1993). To be sure, several case studies offer optimistic views of what is possible (Anders & Guzzetti, 2005; Langer & Applebee, 1987). These studies address questions such as these: What is happening in the best of cases that might inform practice more generally? What are the implications for developmental issues and for writing?

We will use geology to contrast our proposal with present practice. On the surface, the earth looks flat and solid. Geology, we learn in school, presents the earth to be round and dynamic. Of course, most of the time most of us still see the earth as flat and solid; when required, we can "tell" things that we don't fully understand. Geology begins with volcanoes and earthquakes, exciting topics that only a few individuals experience. In the late elementary grades, students learn about three types of volcanoes, and they build models from clay, using baking soda, vinegar, and red food coloring to simulate an eruption. Reading is important; books tell about the three volcanic types and describe how to construct a model. Writing is generally not important; although students may retell what they have read and done, the task does not require any significant amount of thinking. The content is engaging and connects students with experiences that most will not encounter in everyday life. The writing task can provide a foundation for introducing relatively simple genre: comparing and contrasting the three types of volcanic cones, or describing the process of building a vinegar-soda eruption. Students can still see the earth as flat and solid, but they have learned content (sometimes lava erupts from somewhere inside the earth) and process (describing different ways in which eruptions take place) that provides a foundation for the later grades.

By 8th grade, geology presents the globe as a turmoil of dynamic structures and forces: the thin crust on which we live, the molten mantle on which the crust rests, and the dense core that generates the heat that roils the mantle. Describing this system requires of the curriculum designer the skillful interplay of text and graphics, and a constant move between geological concepts and the local environment. Volcanoes and earthquakes now appear as bit players in a much larger drama—the emergence of mountain ranges and the submerging of the Hawaiian Islands, the movement of Los Angeles toward Seattle, the creation of the Grand Canyon. For students to "tell" this knowledge calls for much greater expertise in the use of the structures from the genre tool kit. The telling can be done in a variety of ways, but all require significant decisions about how to reconstruct knowledge. One approach might begin with a description of the structure of the globe, as sketched here, followed by cause-effect segments, using various examples to make the point. A different approach might begin, as many trade books do, with engaging details that are then woven into the larger images of structures and processes. Young children build simple structures with simple blocks; older children still rely on simple blocks, but they build more complex structures. Think about Lego sets, in which simple pieces can be combined into a cube or used to build a model of the Golden Gate Bridge. The move from the cube to the bridge illustrates development.

The preceding example represents more advanced knowledge telling, but we think that knowledge transformation is also an important developmental goal during the middle years. Transformation is partly about transfer, about applying content learned in one setting to a different situation. For instance, a 4th grader uses the compare-contrast structure for different types of volcanoes and then demonstrates understanding of this structure by writing a piece on different types of rocks. Or an 8th grader explains the similarity between the gullies on his family's farm and how the Colorado shaped the Grand Canyon. Both examples demonstrate ways in which students "go beyond the information given" (Bruner, 1957). Transfer depends on an appreciation of similarities, both surface-level and conceptual. Transformation, as we imagine it, occurs when students take information from a variety of sources and create something distinctive, using both content and genre during the construction. For example, the social studies curriculum generally includes investigations of various aspects of a community, both physical and social. Students read about government, the environment, and so on. Transfer happens when, after analyzing one community, students analyze a very different one. For instance, they might study sets of sister cities—San Francisco, Sydney, and Manila. A more challenging and transformative activity would be to design a new community on Mars, considering cities that work and that don't work. In these examples, the content is important, but structuring the task is equally demanding. Writing is part of the building/composing task, but so are graphics and realia.

In summary, as students move from the mid-elementary grades toward high school and beyond, what "develops" in school centers around the various academic disciplines. This development doesn't happen naturally; it is taught. Schooling serves to pass traditions from one generation to another. Youngsters also develop in other ways during this age span, of course, acquiring a variety of informal genres along the way, forms of discourse that often bewilder their parents and other adults. But for schooling, writing is the means by which students demonstrate their acquisition of the various content-area genre—the templates or schemata that academic disciplines have constructed across the years to capture and convey domains of knowledge. From this perspective, the idea of writing (and reading) across the content areas misses the point. Every content area has its own set of structures, and *development* occurs as students acquire the structures that form that discipline. Every teacher, from this perspective, is necessarily involved in teaching reading, writing, and language.

Throughout this section we have focused on curriculum in dealing with development because the two are so tightly related. Educators may see many barriers in the way of practical implementation of the ideas sketched previously, including the daunting pressures of the accountability age—building a Martian community is unlikely to be on the test. On the other hand, we would argue that all of the curriculum "pieces" can be found in the standards, for both content areas and the literacy domain. To be sure, state standards were not constructed with either integration or development as key principles. In addition to curriculum, the teacher has responsibility for instruction and assessment, which are also missing in state standards, but which are essential for implementation of a developmental curriculum.

INSTRUCTION: PROMOTING WRITING DEVELOPMENT

Teachers are central in guiding students' acquisition of the curriculum presented in the previous section. They require knowledge of how students develop in writing from the time they leave 3rd grade to the end of 8th grade. Also, they require the pedagogical knowledge and skills to ensure students leave 8th grade ready to confront the demands of high school writing. From 4th through 8th grade, the teacher's role shifts from generalist to specialist, and as the grades increase, so does the specialization of content knowledge. English teachers still assume the primary responsibility for providing instruction in writing, and teachers of other disciplines assign writing to evaluate student learning. We propose that all teachers provide not only opportunities to write, but also *instruction* that improves students' abilities to compose in a variety of disciplines and to use writing to deepen their content knowledge.

Case studies examining the benefits of integrating literacy and content areas found that when students read and write in science, their thinking and performance were greatly enhanced (Langer & Applebee, 1987). Writing can reveal one's knowledge, but it can also increase learning as students move from knowledge-telling to knowledge-transforming (Bereiter & Scardamalia, 1987). In the next section we present a model that integrates literacy and content areas to advance students' understanding of content and promote literacy development.

The Read-Write Strategy

Historically, reading and writing have been taught separately; in the elementary grades instruction occurs during different times in the day and both have their own curriculum. We recognize that instruction is most effective when the language arts and content are integrated and when students are appropriately scaffolded. The read-write strategy was originally designed as an assessment tool to find out what students can do, when supported, in the area of writing and comprehension. Here we present the model as a framework for instruction: students are guided from the gathering of information (e.g., textual reading) to group discussion to writing. The general strategy is to start with a problem that holds genuine interest and purpose, which requires finding information from a variety of sources, to create a document or presentation for a real audience. The read-write strategy is designed around the CORE framework—connect, organize, reflect, extend. CORE is a conceptual framework that is based on social-cognitive theory as a basis for the acquisition of reading, writing and language. The elements that follow are not discrete stages; they are revisited throughout the learning process.

> *Connect.* Acquiring new knowledge is most effective when it connects to what the student already knows, when it builds on prior knowledge. Teachers facilitate the process by providing experiences and resources, and by clarifying misconceptions. In the Read-Write Strategy the teacher introduces the activity—reading a collection of articles in order to write a position paper. The students might access prior knowledge by generating a semantic map on the primary topic of the text, brainstorming concepts, and organizing them into categories.
>
> *Organize.* We understand and remember information better when it is organized into meaningful chunks. As students think through and organize information, they develop their understanding of the content and the genre appropriate to the discipline. In the read-write strategy, students read and discuss, actively gathering information and generating concepts and vocabulary that will be useful when composing. Teachers scaffold knowledge building along the way by teaching students how to respond to texts—to take notes, ask questions, and seek additional resources. Ideas are organized using graphic structures such as webs and matrices.

Reflect. Learning is most effective and long lasting when students step back from the task and reflect on the process, the learning, and the next steps. In the read-write strategy, students confer with peers about their reactions to the readings and other information, and develop plans for writing by considering the purpose, audience, structure and content. In a persuasive piece, students consider the available evidence to support their claims. Do I have enough support to help the reader understand my points and to be convinced? Feedback from others is critical; small-group discussions help students clarify their thinking and deepen understanding.

Extend. Students apply their new learning and continue to develop their understanding as they compose using their prewriting notes, discussion notes, and graphic structures as resources. They use the writing process—*develop/draft, review/revise, polish/publish*—to construct the text. Peer interactions and self-monitoring continue, and students receive feedback, revisit their organizational schemes, and revise accordingly. In this context, students are likely to be more motivated, and the quality of their work is likely to increase.

In this section we have focused on instruction that supports students' writing development across the curriculum. Further, we laid out a model for integrating writing (and the other language arts) and curriculum. The model provides the structure for students to acquire content knowledge and the ways of thinking and organizing information in discipline-specific ways.

CONCLUSION

We have focused on curriculum in dealing with development because the two are so tightly related. Educators may see many barriers in the way of practical implementation of the ideas sketched previously, including the daunting pressures of the accountability age—building a Martian community is unlikely to be on the test. On the other hand, we would argue that all of the curriculum "pieces" can be found in the standards, for both content areas and the literacy domain. To be sure, state standards were not constructed with either integration or development as key principles.

Instructional practice and assessment techniques are also barriers. The proposal sketched in this chapter assumes substantial student engagement around group tasks, with authentic performances as the primary outcomes. We briefly reviewed both of these matters in the final section of the chapter, but the territory has actually been well traveled during past decades. The most significant hurdles center around teacher knowledge and autonomy, a point of continuing controversy. For those who are convinced that teachers are incapable of making principled decisions in adapting the curriculum to local contexts and opportunities, the proposal may seem unrealistic. Some teachers and some students might be able to handle the demanding tasks entailed in this proposal, but most teachers and most students need to follow a more prescribed and routinized path. We agree with the basic theme that "no child should be left behind," but we think it important to consider "behind what?"

REFERENCES

Anders, P. L., & Guzzetti, B. J. (2005). *Literacy instruction in the content areas* (2nd ed.). Mahwah, NJ: Lawrence Erlbaum.

Bereiter, C., & Scardamalia, M. (1987). *The psychology of written communication.* Mahwah, NJ: Lawrence Erlbaum Associates.

Bransford, J. D., Brown, A. L., & Cocking, R. R. (Eds.). (1999). *How people learn: Brain, mind, experience, and school.* Washington, DC: National Academy Press.

Bruner, J. S. (1957). Going beyond the information given. In H. E. Gruber, K. R. Hammond, & R. Jessor (Eds.), *Contemporary approaches to cognition* (pp. 41–69). Cambridge, MA: Harvard University Press.

Chambliss, M. J., & Calfee, R. C. (1998). *Textbooks for learning: Nurturing children's minds.* Malden, MA: Blackwell.

Eccles, J. S., Midgley, C., Wigfield, A., Buchanan, C. M., Reuman, D., Flanagan, C., & Mac Iver, D. (1993). Development during adolescence: The impact of stage-environment fit on young adolescents' experiences in schools and in families. *American Psychologist, 48*(2), 90–101.

Kendall, J. S., & Marzano, R J. (2004). *Content knowledge: A compendium of standards and benchmarks for K-12 education.* Aurora, CO: Mid-continent Research for Education and Learning. Online database: http://www.mcrel.org/standards-benchmarks/

Langer, J. A., & Applebee, A. N. (1987). How writing shapes thinking: A study of teaching and *learning* (Research Report No. 22). Urbana, IL: National Council of Teachers of English.

Moffett, J., & Wagner, B. J. (1976). Student centered language arts and reading, K-13: A handbook for teachers (2nd ed.). Boston: Houghton Mifflin.

National Commission on Writing in America's Schools and Colleges. (2003). *The neglected "R": The need for a writing revolution.* New York: College Entrance Examination Board.

Whitehead, A. N. (1974). *The organization of thought.* Westport, CT: Greenwood Press.

Wigfield, A., Byrnes, J. P., & Eccles, J. S. (2006). Development during early and middle adolescence. In P. A. Alexander & P. H. Winne (Eds.), *Handbook of educational psychology* (2nd. ed., pp. 87–113). Mahwah, NJ: Lawrence Erlbaum.

Wong-Fillmore, L., & Snow, C. (2000). *What reading teachers need to know about the English language.* Georgetown DC: Center for Applied Linguistics.

Chapter Seven

CHILDREN'S LITERATURE: CONNECTING AND TRANSFORMING CHILDREN'S WORLDS

Kathy G. Short

Children's literature can be defined in many different ways, but the most essential criterion is that children view these books as reflecting their life experiences, understandings, and emotions. A children's book is one that occupies a child's attention. The uniqueness of children's literature is the audience that it addresses, both in terms of whom the author focuses on as readers and which books children claim as their own. In general, children's literature is considered to be books written expressly for children from birth through age 12. There are books, however, that children reject as nostalgic or sentimental because they reflect adult perspectives of looking back on childhood or portray adult emotions of cynicism and despair. At the same time, there are books written for adults, such as the classic tale of Robinson Crusoe, that children adopt as their own.

Children's books, first and foremost, are literature and constitute the imaginative shaping of experience and thought into the forms and structures of language (Kiefer, 2007). These structures include narratives, poetry, exposition, and descriptive texts that can be presented as fiction or nonfiction. Children's literature has the same standards of quality as any other form of literature. The difference is one of audience, not the quality of the literature itself. These books include a range of topics and themes in the form of chapter books or picture books that span the genres of realistic fiction, historical fiction, folklore, fantasy, science fiction, poetry, biography, and nonfiction.

Children's literature and textbooks are both written for children, but they differ in purpose. Textbooks, by design and content, are for the purpose of instruction. Examples include basal readers, collections of abridged or short stories used for reading instruction, and the textbooks used in schools to teach subjects such as science and social studies. Children's literature, also called trade books or library books, are written for the purposes of entertainment and information. Children read literature to experience and learn about life.

Literature offers children experiences that go beyond entertainment. One of the most critical experiences literature has to offer is the potential to transform children's lives through connecting their hearts and their minds, bringing together feeling and thought. Children find themselves reflected in stories and so make connections to literature that transform their understandings of themselves. This potential for transformation is also apparent in informational books that are written from the perspective of one enthusiast sharing with another to "light fires" in children's minds. Literature expands children's life spaces by taking them outside the boundaries of their lives to other places, times, and ways of living to see that there are alternative ways to live their lives and to think about the world. Literature also stretches their imaginations and encourages them to go beyond "what is" to "what might be." For generations, hope and imagination have made it possible for children to be resilient and to rise above their circumstances. Transformation occurs as children carry their experiences through literature back into their worlds and view their lives differently.

Rosenblatt (1938) defined reading as a transactional process in which each reader brings his or her personal and cultural experiences, beliefs, and values to the reading of a text so that both the reader and the text are transformed. Although a text has particular potential meanings, readers construct their own understandings and interpretations as they engage in "lived through experiences" with that text. Readers construct these understandings in light of their experiences and rethink their experiences in light of the text, thus bringing meaning to and take meaning from a text. A consideration of children's literature therefore must include both an examination of the texts and of the ways in which children as readers engage with these texts. The texts that constitute children's literature can be evaluated from a range of perspectives, including the literary and the content qualities of each book. The literary and aesthetic qualities include consideration of the literary elements, such as plot, setting, theme, character, style, and format, as well as visual elements and literary genre. The content qualities that are significant focus on multicultural and international issues, including the cultural authenticity of the books. Children bring their life experiences to construct interpretations of these texts as they read for pleasure and understanding and to develop reading strategies.

THE ROLE OF LITERARY AND VISUAL ELEMENTS IN CREATING EXCELLENCE IN LITERATURE

The elements that work together to create a story determine the potential of a text to invite readers' responses and constructions of meaning. Lynch-Brown and Tomlinson (2005) point out that children are particularly drawn to stories in which something happens. They want a plot that is fast moving, with conflict to build the excitement and suspense to keep them engaged. Long after the plot is forgotten, however, readers remember the characters that they have come to know through that story. The characters involved in the plot events must matter to the reader to make the reading relevant, so authors find ways to help readers know a character through actions, dialogue, description, and interactions with other characters. The events and characters occur within a particular setting, a time and a place that sometimes is specific and well developed, as in historical fiction, and other times is more vague and general, as in folktales.

Plot, character, and setting are connected by theme, the underlying meaning or significance of a story. A theme is not the message or moral, but the larger meaning beneath the surface of a story that goes beyond the plot action and reveals something of the author's purpose in writing a particular story. Sometimes, adults write stories to teach morality lessons, leading to a didactic or "preachy" story that children resist, instead of telling the story in such a way that the messages evolve for readers. Style refers to the way in which the author tells the story and includes the word choice, the flow of language, the organization of the book, the point of view from which the story is told, and the use of symbolism to suggest meanings by analogy. The author's goal is to tell a story that integrates all of these elements into a compelling whole.

Many children's books use both written language and illustrations to tell the story. In picture books, the illustrations are essential to the telling of the story. Other books use illustrations to help the reader visualize the physical setting and the characters' appearance and actions, as well as to provide visual appeal. The visual elements of line, color, shape, and texture are arranged within an illustration to create relationships and an overall composition. Illustrators make decisions about proportion, balance, and harmony within the various elements to provide a visual impact that extends and enriches the meaning and mood of the text.

Illustrators use a range of artistic media, materials, and techniques to create pictures, including drawing, collage, printmaking, photography, and painting. The media and visual elements are used in distinctive ways by each illustrator to create an individual artistic style. These artistic styles can also be grouped by general characteristics to reflect realistic, impressionistic, expressionistic, abstract, surrealistic, folk, and cartoon art. Effective illustrations combine the elements, style, and media to reflect, extend, and enrich the text without contradicting its message.

The written language and visual images in children's books are organized within a book format to create the final product—a book. This format includes the external dust jacket, the book cover, the endpapers inside the front and back covers, the title page and other front matter that proceed the beginning of the story, and any additional back matter, such as glossaries or author notes.

The size, shape, and darkness of the print type also vary from book to book as does the page layout or placement of illustrations and print on each page. Other factors include the type of paper, the size of the book, and the book-binding.

THE RANGE OF GENRES AVAILABLE TO CHILDREN

These visual and literary elements interact in varying degrees of significance within the various genres that constitute the broader body of children's literature. Typically within children's literature, the genres include poetry, traditional literature, fantasy, realistic fiction, historical fiction, biography, and informational books. All literature is either poetry or prose that can then be divided into fiction (fantasy and realism) and nonfiction (biography and informational). In addition, each of these genres can be found within two different formats, picture books and chapter books. An in-depth examination of genres is the most typical approach to organizing and understanding the field of children's literature for adults, although the lines between genres often blur. These genre categories are less important to children than theme and topic, but adults use genre to understand the broader field and to develop evaluation criteria and balance in their collections and use of books with children.

Picture books are a genre based on format rather than content in which the illustrations are of equal or greater importance as the written language in creating meaning. A majority of picture books are for younger readers, with some geared to older readers, even adults. Books with occasional illustrations that break up or decorate the text or add interest are known as illustrated texts. The illustrations are incidental to the content and are in contrast to picture books in which pictures or illustrations are essential to the telling of the story.

Children's first experiences with books must be enjoyable to encourage their involvement with reading, so picture books play a critical role for young children. The category of picture books contains books ranging from fiction to nonfiction and from fantasy to realism and includes special types such as baby board books, pop-up books, wordless books, alphabet books, counting books, concept books, and pattern books. Baby board books are simply designed, brightly illustrated, durable picture books in which the illustrations dominate to focus on a particular concept or story. Wordless books use only illustrations to convey a story or information, whereas concept books explore or explain an idea or concept rather than tell a story.

Many picture books are intended to be read aloud to young children, but some are created to be read by children themselves. Pattern books, for example, use a repetitive pattern or refrain and predictable sentence and story structures to invite young children to participate in the reading of the book. The books intended to be read by young children usually include fewer words and highly predictable sentence structures and rely more heavily on illustrations to convey a story.

The most prestigious award for children's picture books in the United States is the Caldecott Award, given annually by the American Library Association to the illustrator of the most distinguished American picture book for children during a particular year. The text should be worthy of the illustrations, but the award is made primarily for the artwork. Other comparable awards are given in other countries, such as the Kate Greenaway Medal in the United Kingdom and the Vivian Wilkes Award in South Africa.

The Newbery Medal, given annually by the American Library Association, is awarded to the author of the most distinguished contribution to American literature for children published in a particular year. Similar awards in other countries include the Carnegie Medal in the United Kingdom and the Australian Book of the Year Award. Although the Newbery Medal has sometimes gone to writers of picture books, poets, and biographers, it is typically awarded to writers of chapter books of realistic fiction, historical fiction, and fantasy.

Realistic fiction, which reflects the actual world that children live in today, remains very popular and includes books on animals, adventures, mysteries, sports, humor, family and peer relationships, and growing up. These books increasingly portray the harsh realities of life and current societal issues such as racism and poverty, which are part of many children's lives. This genre also includes many popular series books that focus on a particular character or group of characters across a number of books.

Historical fiction brings history to life by placing children in accurately described historical settings. Through the stories of characters' everyday lives, young readers explore the human side of history, making it more real and memorable, and indicating how their lives were influenced by a particular historical time period. The settings are typically presented in great detail to make the content more believable and interesting.

Fantasy refers to stories in which the events, settings, or characters are outside the realm of possibility. The story needs an original setting and an internal consistency and logic to persuade readers to open themselves to the strange, whimsical, or magical. Fantasies that have long been popular include animal fantasies in which animals behave as human beings, stories in which beloved toys are brought to life, and worlds inhabited by miniature people. Other fantasies include time travel, modern variants of traditional folklore, and science fiction. Quest stories have recently gained general popularity as a result of the enormous success of the Harry Potter books and movies about C. S. Lewis's Narnia and Tolkien's world of Hobbits. These stories, also known as high fantasies, reflect the struggle between good and evil through the quest of a character on a journey of self-discovery and personal growth.

Other genres include traditional literature or folklore, poetry, and nonfiction. Traditional literature is the body of ancient stories and poems that grew out of the oral tradition of storytelling. These stories reflect cultural "truths" for a particular group of people and remain popular with children because of their strong emphasis on action plots, rhythmic language, familiar stylistic features, and beautifully illustrated interpretations. Poetry is the expression of ideas and feelings through a rhythmical composition of imaginative and carefully selected words that range from simple lullabies to complex metaphoric explorations of life. This genre is often a natural beginning to literature for young children because of the musicality of nursery rhymes. The National Council of Teachers of English sponsors an award every three years to an outstanding poet for children in honor of that poet's work.

Nonfiction includes biographies giving factual information about the lives of actual people and informational books about features of the biological, social, or physical world. These books highlight expository writing whose purpose is to inform and explain in contrast to fiction or narrative writing where the purpose is to tell a story. This genre includes topics that span a large range of information in which the author has shaped the content to reach a particular audience of children. The quality of writing and illustration and use of organizational features in nonfiction have increased substantially, with recognition being given by several awards. The National Council of Teachers gives the Orbis Pictus award to an author for excellence in the writing of nonfiction and the American Library Association gives the Robert F. Sibert Informational Book Medal to the author of the most distinguished informational book.

LITERATURE THAT IS MULTICULTURAL AND INTERNATIONAL

A literary perspective on children's literature is the one traditionally taken by most educators and librarians and has allowed particular insights about the literary elements and structures that authors and illustrators use to construct meaning. Readers, however, engage with literature not only because of the literary qualities of a well-told story, but also because the content connects and transforms their understandings of themselves and the world. One of the ways in which this content focus has been frequently explored within children's literature is through exploring multicultural and global issues and how they play out in determining the cultural authenticity of the literature that children read. Concerns about multicultural literature grow out of research showing that people of color have been consistently underrepresented and stereotyped in North American children's books. The more recent interest in international literature has come in response to the increasingly global nature of society, the mobility of people within the world, and the growing availability of books from other countries.

Fifty years ago, children's books reflected the culture of those in power—white, middle class, male, suburban/small town, and North American. Publishers believed that children's books should reflect the dominant society and focus on "universal" experiences that cut across all children. The result was many bland books that did not reflect the lives of real children, even those children who were supposedly the focus of those books. This emphasis on the universal gave way to a focus on children as individuals, highlighting books connected to children's personal interests.

Eventually, educators and publishers began to focus on children as members of communities and cultural groups that influence their thinking, values, and ways of living. This realization led to ethnic studies where children's books were organized by specific ethnic groups and countries, particularly focusing on books about people of color who have been excluded or negatively stereotyped in children's literature. Over time, this definition of culture has expanded to include many aspects of cultural identity, including but going beyond ethnicity and race. Geertz (1973) defines culture as "the shared patterns that set the tone, character and quality of people's lives" (p. 216). These patterns include language, religion, gender, relationships, class, ethnicity, race, disability, age, sexual orientation, family structures, nationality, geographical regions, and rural/suburban/urban communities. At the same time, international books originating in a particular country became a stronger focus, in contrast to "travel" books written by Americans who visit a country for a short period of time.

Sleeter and Grant (1987) state that multicultural perspectives should be part of all education and literature, not just a special book or curriculum unit. They argue for the term *an education that is multicultural* to indicate that multiculturalism is an orientation that pervades the curriculum. A literature that is multicultural and international includes a broadened definition of culture as a perspective that cuts across children's books to highlight the many different cultural identities that children bring to their reading experiences. Children need to find their specific cultural experiences within their reading, as well as to connect to the universal experiences and needs they share with children around the world.

This expanded understanding of culture needs to be balanced by the recognition that people of color and other groups who have not historically been in positions of power in society have largely been absent from children's literature. The tremendous discrepancy in the amount of quality literature reflecting the experiences of people of color indicates the need for a continued emphasis on publishing books that focus on the experiences of those who have been the most excluded and marginalized. These same issues of marginalization and exclusion are present in international literature, which has been dominated by

Western perspectives through books from English-speaking countries, especially the United States and United Kingdom.

The number of high-quality books reflecting the cultural diversity of society has also been affected by the changing nature of the publishing industry in children's literature. The majority of publishing houses have been acquired by large entertainment conglomerates, leading to less diversity in what and who are being published. The increasing commercialization of children's books has resulted in a focus on how much money a book and its products can make, rather than whether the book tells a worthwhile, compelling story.

THE COMPLEXITY OF CULTURAL AUTHENTICITY

One of the major issues related to a literature that is multicultural and international is that of cultural authenticity. This issue seems to continuously resurface, eliciting strong emotions and a wide range of perspectives. Authors, illustrators, editors, publishers, educators, librarians, theorists, and researchers have different points of view that they each feel strongly about based on their sociocultural experiences and philosophical perspectives. Arguments about cultural authenticity in literature for children are not just academic in nature; the voices in these debates are passionate and strong, reflecting deeply held beliefs at the heart of each person's work in creating or using books with children.

Even defining cultural authenticity is difficult. Many authors and educators discuss the complexity of cultural authenticity rather than define it, often arguing that "you know it when you see it" as an insider reading a book about your own culture. The reader's sense of truth in how a specific cultural experience is represented within a book, particularly when the reader is an insider to the culture in that book, is the most common understanding of cultural authenticity. Insiders know a book is "true" because they feel it, deep down, saying, "Yes, that's how it is."

Howard (1991) states that an authentic book is one in which a universality of experience permeates a story that is set within the particularity of characters and setting. The universal and specific come together to create a book in which "readers from the culture will know that it is true, will identify, and be affirmed, and readers from another culture will feel that it is true, will identify, and learn something of value about both similarities and differences among us" (p. 92). Given that each reading of a book is a unique transaction that results in different interpretations (Rosenblatt, 1938), and given the range of experiences within any cultural group, this definition indicates why there are so many debates about the authenticity of a particular book.

The outside/insider distinction is the most frequently debated issue within cultural authenticity. The question of whether outsiders can write authentically about another culture is often asked and answered from oppositional positions, with both sides vehemently arguing their perspective. Some see this question as a form of censorship and an attempt to restrict an author's freedom to write. Others argue that the question reflects larger issues of power structures and a history of misrepresentations of particular groups of people and countries. Most see the question as simplistic, setting up a dichotomy that overlooks the broader sociopolitical issues and that can potentially narrow the discussion to pretentious jargon and an emphasis on conformity.

This debate can be viewed as revolving around an author's social responsibility, rather than the freedom of authors to use their creative imaginations and literary skills to tell a powerful story. Authors have a social and artistic responsibility to be thoughtful and cautious when they write about characters, plots, and themes related to specific cultural groups, whether they are insiders or outsiders to that culture. Although authors need freedom to determine their own writing, their work has social origins and effects that need to be examined and critiqued.

Harris (1996) argues that the real issue is the contrast of authorial freedom with authorial arrogance, the belief that authors should be able to write without subjecting their work to critical scrutiny. Authorial arrogance connects to white privilege in that whites, specifically whites in Western countries, have been socialized into a racialized society that gives them particular privileges and status that are not available to people of color and to developing countries and that are not acknowledged but taken for granted as the way life is for everyone. Without critical scrutiny, white authors are often unable to transcend their positions of privilege when writing books about people from marginalized cultures and so continue subtle forms of racism, even when the more blatant racism and misrepresentations of the past have been eliminated from their writing. This cultural arrogance is based in the unconscious assumption by many members of mainstream society that what they value is universally valued by other cultures. An additional consideration is that members of a particular culture want to tell their own stories as a way to pass on their culture.

Both literary excellence and cultural authenticity should be used as criteria for evaluating children's books when the book reflects the experiences of a specific cultural group. A book is always evaluated for both content and writing style. Cultural authenticity focuses on content, whereas literary criteria focus on writing, so there is no dichotomy between a good and an authentic story. Thus the debate is not whether or not cultural authenticity should be part of the criteria for evaluating a book, but what kind of criteria and understandings should be used, particularly when the book is created by outsiders.

The question of what counts as experience and the kinds of experiences needed to write with truth as an outsider of a specific culture is often debated. Cai (1995) addresses this issue as the relationship between imagination and experience, noting that imagination is needed for a book to have literary excellence but that too much imagination without experience leads to inaccuracies and bias and defeats the purpose of literature to liberate readers from stereotypes. Specific authors, such as Katherine Paterson and Paul Goble, have successfully crossed cultural gaps to write outside their own experiences; crossing cultural gaps is difficult, however, and requires extreme diligence by authors to gain the experiences necessary to write authentically within another culture. There is disagreement on what counts as the experience needed to cross a cultural gap as an outsider, particularly whether direct personal experiences are essential or if those experiences can be gained through careful research. Most authors who successfully write outside their own culture have had significant in-depth experiences within that culture over many years, and have engaged in careful and thorough research.

One question that authors can ask themselves is *why* they want to write a particular book. Not only does making an author's intentions and beliefs explicit influence the criteria for evaluating a book, but this process also engages an author in the critical self-examination necessary to choosing whether or not to write outside one's culture and to clarify the kind of story that the author is seeking to write. Bishop (2003) points out that authors who write within their own culture usually have the intention of enhancing the self-concept of children from that culture and of challenging existing stereotypes and dominant culture assumptions, as well as of passing on the central values and stories of their culture to children. Authors writing outside their own cultures often write from the intention to build awareness of cultural differences and improve intercultural relationships. These differing intentions result in different stories for different audiences and different evaluations of authenticity.

Criteria that are typically considered in evaluating the content of a book are the accuracy of the details and the lack of stereotyping and misrepresentation. Authors cannot ignore cultural facts, and so both the visible facts of daily life and the invisible facts of values and beliefs must be accurately represented. Cultural sensitivity refers to whether a book is sensitive to the concerns of the culture that is portrayed. Cai (1995) refers to this cultural sensitivity as an ethnic perspective, the worldview of a specific cultural group that has been shaped by an ideological difference with the majority view. It is the existence of this ethnic perspective that he believes authors who write outside their own culture often do not take on; instead they may unconsciously impose their own perspective onto that culture.

Authenticity goes beyond accuracy or the avoidance of stereotyping to include the cultural values and practices that are accepted as norms within that social group. Accuracy focuses on cultural facts; authenticity focuses on cultural values. Evaluations of accuracy can indicate whether the facts in the story believably exist in a culture, but not whether those facts actually represent the values held by most of the people in that group. Mo and Shen (2003) state that a story can be accurate but not authentic by portraying cultural practices that exist but are not part of the central code of a culture. This central code is the range of values acceptable within a social group and recognition of the conflicts and changes in beliefs within a culture.

Authenticity of illustrations is based on whether the art form serves its purpose in relation to the story. An authentic art form does not have to be rigidly interpreted as a typical or traditional style for a particular social group. The creative process leads to art that is part of the story to create an authentic whole. The role of art, however, differs across cultures, and mainstream traditions of experimentation with art elements to enhance meaning can change or confuse meanings for members of particular cultural groups when that experimentation contradicts cultural traditions.

Another aspect of authenticity is the use of particular words and phrases from a specific culture within an English-language book. Barrera and Quiroa (2003) note that the issue is not just accurate translations, but how the words are used, particularly whether the words are added for cultural flavor and result in stereotypes. These elements have to be used strategically and skillfully with cultural sensitivity to create powerful multilingual images of characters, settings, and themes. These phrases and words must not only enhance the literary merits of the book but also make the story comprehensible and engaging to both monolingual and bilingual readers without slighting the language or literary experience of either. The tendency to stay with formulaic and safe uses of Spanish, for example, and to translate these words literally to cater to the needs of monolingual readers often results in culturally inauthentic texts for bilingual readers and poor literary quality for all readers.

Another complicating factor is that there is no one insider perspective that can be used to evaluate cultural authenticity. Opposing evaluations of the authenticity of a book can be made by different groups of insiders because of variations within that culture. Insiders can also inadvertently perpetuate stereotypes of their own culture. Recognizing the complexity of both insider and outsider perspectives adds another layer to the issues that have been previously raised about cultural facts and values and what is considered "truth" about a particular cultural experience. Bishop (2003) argues that because variance always exists within a specific culture, no one set of definitive criteria can ever be created to evaluate books about that culture. She also notes, however, that scholars can create criteria to show the range of themes and ideologies at the core of a particular culture through a serious scholarly study of the books published by insiders.

All children have the right to see themselves within a book, that is, to find within a book the truth of their own experiences instead of stereotypes and misrepresentations. Culturally authentic books are more engaging for children from that culture and are a source of intercultural understandings for children from other cultures. These books provide children with insights into power and social and political issues while also serving to challenge the monocultural perspective of dominant society that characterizes most schooling. In addition, authors have the right to tell stories that are used within their own particular cultural group to pass on their cultural identity to children. Literature is one of the significant ways that children learn about themselves and others; therefore those images should not be distorted.

A number of awards recognize excellence in authenticity and literary qualities for a literature that is multicultural and international. For example, the American Library Association gives the Batchelder Award for the most outstanding book published in another country and translated into English. This same association gives the Coretta Scott King Award to African American illustrators and authors and the Pura Belpré Award to honor Latino authors and illustrators. The International Board of Books for Young People gives the Hans Christian Anderson Award to an illustrator and an author whose complete works have made important international contributions to children's literature. This organization also publishes the IBBYP Honor List of top books from countries all over the world.

Evaluations of the literary excellence and cultural authenticity of a book are not designed to lead to censorship, but rather to engage children in critical readings of these books to question the meanings embedded in texts from dominant cultural perspectives. Children need to be able to tackle issues of literary quality and cultural difference, equity, and assumptions about race, class, and gender as they read literature. Thus criteria for evaluating literary excellence and cultural authenticity are not just issues about creating or choosing books for children; they are also criteria that children themselves need to understand and use as critical readers. Children need regular engagements with quality children's books that are culturally authentic and accurate.

CHILDREN'S ENGAGEMENTS WITH LITERATURE

A book has the potential to engage children when it captures children's attention and invites their participation in the story world of that text. This intense experience with literature goes far beyond extracting information from the text. Engagement with literature connects children to the pleasures of reading and encourages lifelong reading. Reading is devalued if the books children read are not worth the effort of reading—when what they read adds nothing of significance to their lives. Reading fiction and nonfiction literature with authentic, rich language and convincing narratives is the first step to engagement, but this literature must be supported by effective experiences that powerfully bring children and books together.

These experiences include reading for enjoyment, reading to think about oneself and the world, and reading to learn about literacy. Balancing these experiences supports the child's development as a reader and as a person, although the emphasis may shift as children become proficient readers and gain life experiences. Older readers may primarily focus on using reading to think, whereas young children focus more on reading for enjoyment and to learn about reading strategies. This shift in emphasis does not exclude the other types; all three should be integrated into the experiences offered to children, no matter what their age, because each serves a different purpose and highlights different books and roles for adults and children.

Reading literature for enjoyment involves reading for pleasure from a wide range of reading materials. The focus is on choice and the extensive reading of many books for personal purposes. Often these books are predictable materials where readers can easily follow the plot and language, such as patterned language books for young children and series books for older children. Extensive reading provides children with a broad background of literature from which to develop comprehension and interpretation, promotes positive attitudes about reading, and encourages the development of lifelong reading habits. In addition, reading many materials with ease increases fluency and the integration of reading strategies.

Experiences that encourage reading for pleasure include independent reading and read alouds. The role of adults is to provide a regularly scheduled time and a variety of reading materials and to read alongside the child. For preschool children, this reading often involves "telling" the story as they hold a book. Many children prefer nonfiction materials and computer-related reading, and so they resist an overemphasis on fiction. Reading for personal purposes increases the likelihood that children will continue to read as adults and is correlated with gains in fluency, vocabulary, and comprehension. Research indicates that many adults stop engaging with books once they leave school and view reading as boring school work because of the lack of choice in reading materials in schools (Gambrell, 2000).

Reading aloud to children is another means of inviting children to engage with literature through a pleasurable experience. Research indicates that there is a high correlation between parents reading aloud frequently to young children and later reading achievement in school (Galda & Cullinan, 2000). Reading aloud introduces concepts of print, book language, and story structures, as well as encourages positive attitudes. Children from cultures with strong oral traditions often enter school with a background in oral literature and storytelling, rather than in written literature. In addition, children from families living in poverty frequently have many experiences with functional everyday print. The success of these children depends on whether teachers build from children's strengths in oral stories and functional materials.

Reading literature to think about oneself and the world involves reading to consider issues in children's lives and in the broader society. These experiences support children in becoming critical and knowledgeable readers and thinkers. Readers are encouraged to engage deeply with the story world of a text and then to step back to share their personal connections and to reflect critically with others about the text and their responses.

This focus on the intensive reading of a few books to think deeply and critically balances the extensive reading of many books. Because the books chosen for intensive reading have multiple layers of meaning, they are challenging for readers and invite social interaction and discussion. Children share their connections and move into dialogue around particular issues. Because the focus is on children's thinking, the literature may be beyond their reading ability, so the text is read aloud to them, particularly in the case of young children and struggling readers. In addition, children may engage with literature as part of a thematic study or inquiry within content areas such as math, science, and social studies. They read critically to compare information and issues across these books and to learn facts about the topic, as well as to consider conceptual issues. Literature becomes a tool for understanding the world and considering broader social and scientific issues, as well as a means of facilitating children's interest in a topic. Children are challenged not only to think about *what is* from a critical perspective, but also to ask *why* things are the way they are and to consider *what if* in order to imagine new possibilities.

Reading literature to learn about literacy creates strategic readers who reflect on their reading processes and text knowledge. These engagements highlight instruction by adults to help children develop a repertoire of strategies to use when they encounter difficulty, either in figuring out words or in comprehending, and to gain knowledge of text structures and literary elements. Readers who have a range of effective reading strategies and text knowledge can problem-solve when encountering difficulty and thus develop reading proficiency. Adults take the role of guiding children's reflections on their reading processes and teaching lessons on strategies and text structures. Adults choose literature to highlight particular reading strategies based on their knowledge of children's needs.

Many schools use commercial materials for reading instruction, rather than literature. Research has indicated that, although children are taught how to read through these materials, they sometimes do not develop the desire or habit of reading (Gambrell, 2000). They are capable of reading but are not engaged readers who are motivated, knowledgeable, and strategic.

Most cultures view reading as necessary to a well-ordered society and to the moral well-being of the individual. Engagement with literature invites children to make meaning of texts in personally significant ways to facilitate learning and to develop lifelong reading attitudes and habits. In addition, children gain a sense of possibility for their lives and that of the society in which they live along with the ability to consider others' perspectives and needs. Engagement with literature thus allows them to develop their own voices and, at the same time, go beyond self-interest to an awareness of broader human consequences.

CONCLUSION

Rosenblatt (1938) reminds us that children's engagements with literature matter not only as ways to learn and think about self and the world, but also as tools for democracy. If democracy is the negotiation between individual diversity and community needs, then each child needs to have faith in his or her own judgments and beliefs, as well as to consider the consequences of those values on others and maintain an open mind to alternative perspectives. Literature encourages imagination, supporting children in considering other possibilities and putting themselves in the place of others in order to go beyond self-interest to broader human consequences. Children's talk about literature opens up space for readers to share their individual voices and engage in dialogue about other points of view. Literature can thus play a key role in how children transform themselves as human beings and in how they think about and act on the world.

REFERENCES

Barrera, R., & Quiroa, R. (2003). The use of Spanish in Latino children's literature in English: What makes for cultural authenticity? In D.L Fox & K.G Short (Eds.), *Stories matter: The complexity of cultural authenticity in children's literature* (pp. 247–267). Urbana, IL: National Council of Teachers of English.

Bishop, R. S. (2003). Reframing the debate about cultural authenticity. In D.L. Fox & K.G. Short (Eds.), *Stories matter: The complexity of cultural authenticity in children's literature* (pp. 25–37). Urbana, IL: National Council of Teachers of English.

Cai, M. (1995). Can we fly across cultural gaps on the wings of imagination? Ethnicity, experience, and cultural authenticity. *The New Advocate, 8*(1), 1–16.

Galda, L., & Cullinan, B. (2000). Children's literature. In M. Kamil, P. Mosenthal, D. Pearson, & R. Barr (Eds.), *Handbook of reading research, Vol. III* (pp. 361–379). Mahwah, NJ: Erlbaum.

Gambrell, L. (2000). Literature-based reading instruction. In M. Kamil, P. Mosenthal, D. Pearson, & R. Barr (Eds.), *Handbook of reading research, Vol. III* (pp. 563–607). Mahwah, NJ: Erlbaum.

Geertz, C. (1973). *The interpretation of cultures.* New York: Basic Books.

Harris, V. (1996). Continuing dilemmas, debates, and delights in multicultural literature. *The New Advocate, 9*(2), 107–122.

Howard, E. F. (1991). Authentic multicultural literature for children: An author's perspective. In M. Lindgren, *Cultural substance in literature for children and young adults* (pp. 91–99). Fort Atkinson, WI: Highsmith.

Kiefer, B. (2007). *Charlotte Huck's children's literature* (9th ed.). Boston: McGraw Hill.

Lynch-Brown, C., & Tomlinson, C. (2005). *Essentials of children's literature* (5th ed.). Boston: Pearson.

Mo, W., & Shen, W. (2003). Accuracy is not enough: The role of cultural values in the authenticity of picture books. In D. L. Fox & K. G. Short (Eds.), *Stories matter: The complexity of cultural authenticity in children's literature* (pp. 198–212). Urbana, IL: National Council of Teachers of English.

Rosenblatt, L. (1938). *Literature as exploration.* Chicago: Modern Language Association.

Sleeter, C., & Grant, C. (1987). An analysis of multicultural education in the United States. *Harvard Education Review, 57,* 421–444.

Chapter Eight

THE NATURE AND DEVELOPMENT OF SPELLING

Shane Templeton and Bob Ives

As a topic, *spelling* is far broader than traditionally conceived; it is more than merely a skill for writing. When students spell words, they give insight into their underlying word knowledge—the knowledge that underlies their ability to *read* words as well as their ability to *spell* words (Perfetti, 1997). Learning to spell is a process of *conceptual* development and not merely a process of memorization. In this chapter, we explore this broader conception of spelling, or *orthography*, through an examination of the nature of the spelling system, the developmental phases through which students move in acquiring knowledge of the spelling system, and implications from research for how teachers may best guide this development in typically developing students, English learners, and students who are struggling.

THE NATURE OF SPELLING AND OF SPELLING DEVELOPMENT

The spelling or orthographic system of English makes far more sense than most people think—we just have to know where to look. It is a system that represents information about the meaning and history of words, as well as information about sound. These types of information interact to result in an "intricate simplicity" (Cummings, 1988, p. 461). The intricacies lie in the different levels on which spelling represents information about language, from sound through meaning. The simplicity lies in the design and consistency with which it represents this information at the level of sound and of meaning. Unlike some spelling systems that have a consistent letter-sound correspondence, English spelling uses 26 letters and letter combinations to represent approximately 44 sounds. These letter and letter combinations, although not representing sound perfectly, do a better job than often believed. For the vast majority of English words, however, these letter combinations correspond more directly to *meaning*.

Three fundamental principles determine the spelling of words in English: the *alphabetic* principle, the *pattern* principle, and the *meaning* principle (Henderson, 1990). The alphabetic principle—that speech can be segmented into sounds that may in turn be represented by individual letters—is acquired during the kindergarten and 1st grade years. The pattern principle applies both within and between syllables. How groups or clusters of letters *within* single syllables correspond to sound—the within-syllable *pattern* principle—develops later in the 1st grade and continues through 2nd and in many instances 3rd grade. The between-syllable pattern principle develops from late 2nd grade on through the intermediate grades. The *meaning* principle, interestingly, begins to apply when students are learning about within-syllable spelling patterns. Selecting the appropriate spelling for /brāk/ is not a matter of flipping a coin to decide between *break* or *brake:* The correct spelling depends on the *meaning* that is intended. If one is writing about what happens to a bone the spelling is *break;* if writing about a bone, the spelling is *brake.* As students move through the grades—particularly in the intermediate grades and beyond—they learn about the broader application of the meaning principle: words and word parts that are similar in meaning are spelled similarly. This applies to prefixes and suffixes, base words to which prefixes and suffixes have been added, and to Latin and Greek stems—parts of words to which prefixes and suffixes attach but that cannot stand alone as words. An interesting corollary to the meaning principle is that, when meaning is visually represented in a consistent fashion, sound is not represented as consistently. This is the trade-off between sound and spelling, and for most words in English, representing meaning consistently trumps representing sound consistently. This is an advantage for readers; as Venezky explained, "Visual identity of word parts takes precedence over letter-sound simplicity" (1999, p. 197). For example, note how the spelling of the base word remains constant in the words *similar/similar*ity and *condemn/ condemn*ation, even though the pronunciation changes. Words that are related in meaning are often related in spelling as well, despite changes in sound. Table 8.1 presents the significant spelling categories that characterize alphabet, pattern, and meaning principles.

Learners acquire knowledge of the system as they move through a developmental sequence that reflects these sound, pattern, and meaning principles. Young children attempt to spell by matching letters they are learning to features of speech. The criteria they use to establish this relationship have been studied by a number of researchers over the years. For example, younger children often match up letters with syllables, as in this five-year-old's spelling: BBCUS ("Bye bye, see you soon"). When children are fully phonemically aware—explicitly

Table 8.1
Common Spelling Features: Alphabet, Pattern, and Meaning

Alphabet	Pattern: Within Syllables	Pattern: Between Syllables	Meaning
Beginning single consonants	Common long vowel patterns	Inflectional suffixes –ed, –ing	Simple homophones: *sail/sale beat/beet*
Consonant digraphs	r- and l-influenced vowels	Plural endings Changing final *y* to *i*	Simple homographs: *dove* (N) / *dove* (V) *tear* (N) / *tear* (V)
Consonant blends	Three-letter consonant blends	Syllable patterns: VC/CV	Compound words
Short vowel patterns	Complex consonants: Final sound of /k/ Final /ch/: *cb tcb* /j/: *dge Vge*	*bas/ket rab/bit* V/CV open: *bu/man* VC/V closed: *cab/in*	2-syllable homophones: *peddle/pedal dual/duel* 2-syllable homographs: *present* (N) / *present* (V) *record* (N) / *record* (V)
	Common spelling for diphthongs /ow/, /oi/ Less-frequent vowel patterns	Vowel patterns in accented and unaccented syllables	Spelling/Meaning Connection: *sign music signal musician ignite reside ignition resident mental mentality*
			Greek and Latin stems –*therm*– –*spect*– –*pboto*– –*dic*–
			Assimilated/Absorbed Prefixes: *in*- + *mobile* = *immobile ad*- + *tract* = *attract*

aware of consonant and vowel sounds within single syllables—they may learn how the sounds of many words in English are spelled quite straightforwardly. At first, their spelling attempts reflect the sound and articulatory characteristics of letter names: I LIK SETG INDR MY FAVRT CHRE ("I like sitting under my favorite tree"). They match letters and sounds in a consistent left-to-right manner. We know that beginning readers and writers, in fact, expect the spelling system to work this way: They hear a sound, and they search to find a letter that matches that sound. Many of the simple words with short vowel sounds that children learn to read and spell in first grade—*Sam, cat, fan, go, we*—certainly work this way. Children also apply this level of analysis, however, to words that have a long vowel sound in them: *tape* and *rain* may be spelled TAP and RAN, respectively. With continued exposure to words through reading, writing, and phonics/spelling instruction, learners will come to understand how spelling *patterns* work. Although children first approached spelling from a one-letter/one-sound perspective, they now learn that groups or chunks of letters—*patterns*—work together to represent sound. So, for example, students learn about the vowel-consonant-silent *e* pattern: When they see a word that has this spelling pattern in it, odds are that the vowel will be long, not short, as in *tame* and *bike*. Although the letter *e* in this vowel-consonant-silent *e* does not itself stand for a sound, it provides information about how *other* sounds in the pattern are to be pronounced. Most children learn about these spelling patterns in the primary grades and apply this knowledge when they spell words and when they read words. Pattern knowledge develops first *within* single-syllable words.

Two broad types of information help to determine how sounds are spelled within a word, and knowledgeable teachers guide students' learning, over time, to an understanding of these types: first, is the word a *homophone*—a word that has different spellings but the same pronunciation? Rather than bemoaning the fact that the word /māl/ may be spelled two different ways, for example, students should attend to the *meaning* as they are learning the spelling: When children are writing about sending and receiving letters, /māl/ will *always* be spelled *m-a-i-l;* when writing about boys or men, /māl/ will *always* be spelled *m-a-l-e.* Second, how sounds are spelled usually depends on their *position* within a word (Venezky, 1999). Does the sound occur at the beginning, the middle, or the end of the word? What other sounds and spellings occur before and/or after it? For example, although there are different spellings for the /ch/ sound, as in the word *chip,* when the /ch/ sound comes at the beginning of a word, it is almost always spelled *ch;* hardly ever will you see the spelling *tch* at the beginning of a word. On the other hand, both the *ch* and the *tch* spelling of the /ch/ sound occur at the *end* of a word: The appropriate spelling usually depends on the sound that precedes /ch/. If it is a long vowel sound, as in *coach,* use *ch;* if it is a short vowel sound, as in *catch* and *snitch,* use *tch.* Yes, there are exceptions on occasion (*rich, such*), but the number of words that follow the pattern far outnumber those that do not. A bit later, students learn how spelling patterns apply *between* syllables within words. For example, compare *bitter* and *biter:* In the first word, the *t* is doubled to indicate that the vowel in the first syllable is short; in the second word, the *t* is not doubled, and this indicates that the vowel in the first syllable is long. These two patterns are widespread in the spelling system: Where syllables come together, two consonants indicate the vowel preceding them is short, and one consonant indicates the preceding vowel is long. Do these syllable patterns *always* work? For most two-syllable words, yes. For many other polysyllabic words, particularly those with more than two syllables, no. This is because the *meaning* principle takes precedence. For example, when a task is completed it is *finished.* Because there is an /i/ in the first syllable; why isn't the *n* doubled? The *n* is not doubled because it shares a meaning relationship with the word *final,* and a meaning relationship will usually override a rule based on sound—in this case, the "double the consonant when preceded by a short vowel" rule. The common spelling of *fin* occurs across the spelling-meaning family that includes *fin*ish, *fin*al, *fin*ite, in*fin*ite. This common spelling reflects the Latin stem, *-fin-* (meaning "end"), from which all of these words came.

As shown in Table 8.1, students' understanding of how the meaning principle operates begins with simple homophones; develops later in the elementary grades with the spelling-meaning connection in which the combination of base words, prefixes, and suffixes is explored; and then moves to an exploration of the more abstract function of Greek and Latin stems. Linguists refer to prefixes, suffixes, base words, and Greek and Latin stems as *morphemes,* or the smallest units of meaning in the language. It is important to emphasize that students' awareness of many of these morphemic elements begins to develop through teachers' vocabulary instruction *before* students are expected to consistently spell words containing these elements.

IMPLICATIONS OF RESEARCH FOR SPELLING INSTRUCTION

Most researchers agree that students do not learn the underlying principles of English spelling simply through immersion in reading and in writing; nor do they learn by memorizing and applying spelling rules. Rather, most learners need guidance by knowledgeable teachers in exploring the spelling system and learning how the principles of alphabet, pattern, and meaning function. As we noted at the beginning of this chapter, effective instruction supports students' *reading* as well. Perfetti (1997) observed that practice in spelling helps reading more than practice in reading helps spelling. "Practice," however, does not include repetitive, low-level activities such as writing words several times each. Rather, effective activities should include reading and writing words in contexts that engage students in comparing and contrasting words in an active exploration for patterns. Given that a common underlying core of word knowledge supports both the encoding and the decoding of words, a number of researchers and educators are reframing the traditional perspective on spelling, using the term *word study* (Invernizzi & Hayes, 2004). Word study is defined as a developmental approach to phonics and spelling instruction, and the term has also been applied to a developmental approach to spelling and vocabulary. In general, what are the implications of the recent research into the development and instruction of spelling or orthographic knowledge?

First, it is critical that teachers encourage emergent and beginning readers and writers to apply their knowledge of letter names and their developing phonic knowledge as they write. For emergent learners particularly, this contributes to the development of phonemic awareness, a critical understanding in the development of literacy. For beginning and transitional readers and writers, this encouragement accelerates the acquisition of conventional spelling (Snow, Burns, & Griffin, 1998) provided that developmentally appropriate word study is also ongoing. At all developmental levels, not surprisingly, frequent opportunities to write should be provided so that students are able to apply and exercise their developing spelling knowledge.

Second, effective instruction is based on determining students' appropriate developmental or spelling instructional level. The appropriate instructional level may be determined by administering a qualitative inventory of spelling knowledge. Such an inventory will usually reveal a range of spelling instructional levels within the same classroom, just as there is a range of reading levels. Within one 4th-grade class, for example, it is not uncommon to find the following range and types of spelling errors,: SHEP for *ship;* WHAN for *when;* HURY for *hurry,* ALOW for *allow,* STRIPPED for *striped;* IR-RELEVENT for *irrelevant,* CONFRENCE for *conference,* COMPISITION for *composition.* Clearly, these errors reflect the different levels of spelling knowledge across several students.

Third, at all developmental or instructional levels, *comparing* and *contrasting* words in the active search for pattern is very effective (Bear et al., 2004). This approach to examining words involves students in making categorical decisions about the spelling patterns that they are examining while reading and writing the words. These activities strengthen connections among pronunciation, spelling, and meaning. These connections, in turn, facilitate the identification of words in reading and the more automatic spelling of words in writing.

Following are examples of the types of comparison/contrast word sort or categorization activities that would be appropriate at each developmental phase of spelling and literacy: Beginning readers and writers would compare and contrast words such as *rag, map, sip, slip, flag,* and *flap,* attending to the differences in sound and spelling at the beginning, middle, and end of the words. Transitional readers and writers would compare and contrast words such as *show, know, roast,* and *coach* and *sock, bike, pack,* and *take,* noting the effects of position and adjacent sounds on the spelling of vowels and consonants. Intermediate readers and writers would explore words such as *super/supper, later/latter,* and *tiger/Tigger,* noting the interaction of vowel sound and consonant doubling. Later, intermediate readers and writers would explore, for example, how to determine the spelling of the *–ion* suffix (*-sion, -ssion, -tion, -ation, -ition*) by comparing and contrasting words such as *subtract/subtraction, discuss/discussion, digest/digestion, ignite/ignition,* and *inflate/inflation,* learning that the spelling of the base word provides the clue to the spelling of the related suffixed word. More advanced readers and writers would explore words such as *custody/custodian, conspire/conspiracy,* and *impede/impediment,* examining the sound changes and spelling consistency that derivationally related words share. The systematic exploration of Latin and Greek stems is also underway at this level; for example, students examine words that are derived from the Latin stem *spect,* meaning "to look," in the words *inspect, introspect, spectator, perspective, circumspect,* and *spectrum,* as well as words derived from the stem *tract,* meaning "pull," in the words *attractive, traction, distract, protract, abstract,* and *extraction.* Not only is the relationship between the spelling of such words and their meanings reinforced through students' examination of these stems and their combination with prefixes and suffixes but the intersection of vocabulary development with spelling is most pronounced at this level as well (Carlisle & Stone, 2005). A number of studies suggest that awareness of these morphological or word-formation processes in English may be facilitated by attending to the spelling of these morphological elements. For example, Leong (2000) pointed out that "there is a need for systematic and explicit teaching of word knowledge and spelling, based on morphemic structure and origin of words and their productive rules, from elementary grades onwards" (p. 298).

Teachers are addressing the challenges and opportunities presented by students speaking a broad array of languages other than English. It is not realistic, of course, to expect classroom teachers to become competent in all the conversational registers of the home languages spoken by the students in their classrooms, but the following three types of knowledge will help teachers better support their English language learners' understanding of English orthography: first, their own awareness of the principles that govern English spelling; second, a familiarity with the types of activities that that best support knowledge about English spelling; and third, their awareness of the degree to which their students' spoken and written home language corresponds to the sounds of English—where is there overlap, and where is there divergence?

The first two of these guidelines are appropriate, of course, for teaching native English speakers; the third will require additional effort. It is important to know that, for most languages that have a written script, learners approach the script expecting a correspondence to sound; they then attend to pattern and meaning. How much attention is given sound, pattern, and meaning depends on the degree to which the writing system reflects that type of information. When first approaching English spelling, English language learners who are literate to some degree in their home language will apply what they know about the relationship between sound and print in their home language to their learning of English. For example, when native Spanish speakers initially approach the exploration of English orthography, their perspective is more alphabetic than pattern-based. Spanish orthography represents the alphabetic principle more consistently than does English, which represents pattern and meaning more frequently. When reading words such as *break* and *couch,* native Spanish speakers who are beginning readers and writers in English will attempt to sound out each vowel; when spelling, they will often elongate the pronunciation of English words in their attempts to represent the sounds, with the effect of adding additional sounds. *Blade,* for example, may be spelled BLEAD; *ripen* may be spelled WAIPEN (the *w* is often used in place of initial /r/). The initial /s/ in blends does not occur in Spanish, so *snake* may be spelled ESNAK; native Spanish speakers who are transitional readers and writers in English may spell *spoil* as ESPOLLO. Students who are not literate in a home language will depend on the sound features of their home language in attempting to spell English words. A seven-year-old Korean student, for example, spelled *top* as TO, because there is no syllable-final /p/ sound in Korean. She did, however, attend to the final /t/ sound in *bat,* spelling it BT. She spelled *wag* WC; she chose the letter *c* because she had learned it can stand for the /k/ sound, and /k/ is the closest sound to /g/, a sound that does not occur in Korean.

English language learners who are intermediate or advanced readers and writers benefit from the examination of *cognates* shared by English and other languages. Cognates are words whose spellings and meanings are similar in different languages. With respect to Spanish and English, some cognates are straightforward, such as *tecnología/technology, teléfono/telephone,* and *aeropuerto/ airport;* others are close but not exact, such as *enfermo/infirm.* This second category, incidentally, provides an opportunity for native English speakers to expand their vocabulary in English while acquiring a bit of Spanish vocabulary as well. In English, *enfermo* means "sick" but the corresponding cognate, *infirm,* does not occur nearly as often in the language as the word *sick,* so by attending to the Spanish word *enfermo,* native English speakers may become aware of the word *infirm.*

SPELLING INSTRUCTION FOR STRUGGLING STUDENTS

There is far less research on spelling instruction for students who struggle than there is for typically developing students. Many of the studies in this area actually look at instruction intended to improve reading skills rather than spelling skills specifically. In these cases, spelling is an additional outcome measure. At the same time, students who struggle may struggle for a wide range of reasons. The relative scarcity of research and the diversity of struggling students make it difficult to reach any general conclusions about instruction for these students, but it does appear that a majority of these students follow the same developmental continuum as do typically developing students (Ehri & McCormick, 1998). We focus here specifically on instruction for students with literacy-related learning disabilities (LD) and young students at risk for future difficulties with spelling within the context of the alphabetic, pattern, and meaning levels of spelling principles. Students with LD have average range or better intelligence, but they are achieving well below average in one or more academic areas. Research has led to a widely held consensus that these students benefit from direct, explicit, supplementary instruction that is intense and of extended duration; and these approaches to instruction are reflected in studies on spelling instruction.

Some of these studies of spelling instruction for students with LD have focused primarily on the alphabetic level of spelling. Jitendra et al. (2004) provided supplementary reading instruction consisting of phonemic aware-ness, phonics, reading fluency, vocabulary, and reading comprehension to a group of 1st- to 3rd-grade students with LD, as well as attention disorders and to students who were English language learners. All of the students were poor readers. These instructional components focus on the alphabetic level of reading and other reading skills, which was appropriate given the spelling developmental level of these students. At the end of 16 weeks of this supple-mentary instruction, the students showed significant gains in basic reading, reading comprehension, and spelling. Joseph (1998–1999) also demonstrated significant improvement in spelling in elementary school students with LD. Word boxes were used to conduct word study activities that focused on the alphabetic level of spelling. Joseph and McCachran (2003) have found similar results when applying word study, including word sorting activities, at this level to students with mild to moderate mental retardation (MR), and stu-dents reading in the bottom 20th percentile. Maki, Vauras, and Vainio (2002) worked with a small number of 3rd- and 4th-grade students with writing dif-ficulties, and whose spelling knowledge reflected alphabetic and within-word pattern principles. The instruction was carried out for approximately 20 weeks for 90 minutes per week and involved developing self-regulating strategies with a focus on phonetic knowledge, and a small number of orthographic pat-terns. Here again, the students' spelling improved, as did their ability to correct spelling errors.

Some studies have taken a more balanced approach to teaching at both the alphabetic and pattern levels of spelling. Graham, Harris, and Chorzempa (2002) worked with 60 students in the 2nd grade whose spelling was at least two-thirds of a standard deviation below average. The students received supplemental word study instruction for six months that addressed high-frequency words through letter-sound association, patterns, and rime. Spelling improved significantly for the group and the spelling gains were maintained for at least six months after the supplementary instruction ended. Vadasy, Sanders, and Peyton (2005) provided word study tutoring with and without reading practice to 1st graders in the bottom quartile for reading. The word study addressed letter-sound associations, two-vowel combinations and digraphs, and onset-rime patterns. Some word endings were also taught as patterns, but not for meaning. Both groups in this study made significant spelling gains compared to peers who did not receive the additional tutoring. Hatcher (2000) compared spelling outcomes for a group of students with dyslexia, a group with mild to moderate MR, and a group of younger students matched for literacy level to the group with dyslexia. All three groups participated in 12 weeks of multisensory training focusing on grapheme-sound linkage and onset-rime patterns. The two groups with disabilities made comparable gains in spelling, but those gains were less than the gains made by the younger group without disabilities.

Students who are considered at risk for future problems with literacy skills are typically 1st grade or younger students who score low on assessments of skills and abilities that are foundational to literacy skills. Examples of these foundational skills and abilities include auditory processing, phonemic awareness, and letter naming; however, these students have not been identified with specific disabilities. Sustained, systematic, direct, explicit instruction has been recommended for these students, but relatively few studies have looked at instruction for these students. Poskiparta, Niemi, and Vauras (1999) identified 1st-grade students at risk because of low phonemic awareness. These students participated in a linguistic awareness program that included instruction on rhyme, phonemic awareness, and word and syllable awareness. Interestingly, the instruction led to improved spelling skills. Schneider, Ennemoser, Roth, and Kuspert (1999) provided phonemic awareness instruction to at-risk kindergarten students. These students showed improved spelling at 1st- and 2nd-grade follow-up assessments. Vadasy, Jenkins, and Pool (2000) provided supplementary tutoring to at-risk students that addressed both the alphabetic level and the pattern level. These students were in the 1st grade and had been identified by teachers as at risk for LD. Instruction in this study focused on letter-sound association. The students showed significant gains in spelling after one year of 30-minute sessions four times per week. These gains were diminished at a one-year follow-up assessment; however, this may have been a result of the pattern-level instruction being at a level above the students' actual developmental level, which was alphabetic. Morris, Tyner, and Perney's (2000) reading intervention with 1st-grade, at-risk students also targeted spelling, including word-sort activities in the context of a systematic word study component.

Recent research into struggling students' spelling development confirms that more supportive and direct instruction does produce spelling gains for students with LD and students at risk for future difficulties with literacy skills. More specifically, instruction that addresses the alphabetic level of spelling, or both the alphabetic and pattern levels, improves these students' spelling skills. Opportunities to explore consistency of spellings at the alphabetic level and at the pattern level help students integrate their spelling knowledge with reading and with the development of a sight vocabulary. The answer to the following question is somewhat ambiguous: "Can teachers provide spelling instruction to struggling students that will have lasting effects?" Graham, Harris, and Chorzempa (2002) and Vadasy, Jenkins, and Pool (2000) have conflicting answers to this question; research reviewed by Ehri and McCormick (1998) strongly suggests that instruction that is developmentally based is more effective than instruction that is not.

SUMMARY

The spelling system of English is more logical than often assumed. Acquiring knowledge about the types of information it represents, however, is a process that continues over many years. Learning to spell is a conceptual process, and spelling knowledge underlies the ability to read as well as spell. It is not simply a skill for writing. By determining where students fall along a developmental continuum of spelling knowledge, teachers are able to provide more appropriate word study that resonates with students' focus on the alphabetic, pattern, or meaning principles of the English spelling system.

REFERENCES

Bear, D. R., Invernizzi, M., Templeton, S., & Johnston, F. (2004). *Words their way: Word study for phonics, vocabulary, and spelling instruction* (3rd ed.). Upper Saddle River, NJ: Merrill/Prentice-Hall.

Carlisle, J. F., & Stone, C. A. (2005). Exploring the role of morphemes in word reading. *Reading Research Quarterly, 40,* 428–449.

Cummings, D. W. (1988). *American English spelling.* Baltimore: Johns Hopkins University Press.

Ehri, L. C., & McCormick, S. (1998). Phases of word learning: Implications for instruction with delayed and disabled readers. *Reading & Writing Quarterly, 14,* 135–163.

Graham, S., Harris, K. R., & Chorzempa, B. F. (2002). Contribution of spelling instruction to the spelling, writing, and reading of poor spellers. *Journal of Educational Psychology, 94,* 669–686.

Hatcher, P. J. (2000). Sound links in reading and spelling with discrepancy-defined dyslexics and children with moderate learning difficulties. *Reading and Writing: An Interdisciplinary Journal, 13,* 257–272.

Henderson, E. H. (1990). *Teaching spelling* (2nd ed.). Boston: Houghton Mifflin.

Invernizzi, M., & Hayes, L. (2004). Developmental-spelling research: A systematic imperative. *Reading Research Quarterly, 39,* 216–228.

Jitendra, A. K., Edwards, L. L., Starosta, K., Sacks, G., Jacobson, L. A., & Choutka, C. M. (2004). Early reading instruction for children with reading difficulties: Meeting the needs of diverse learners. *Journal of Learning Disabilities, 37,* 421–439.

Joseph, L. M. (1998–1999). Word boxes help children with learning disabilities identify and spell words. *Reading Teacher, 52,* 348–356.

Joseph, L. M., & McCachran, M. (2003). Comparison of a word study phonics technique between students with moderate to mild mental retardation and struggling readers without disabilities. *Education and Training in Developmental Disabilities, 38,* 192–199.

Leong, C. K. (2000). Rapid processing of base and derived forms of words and grades 4, 5 and 6 children's spelling. *Reading and Writing: An Interdisciplinary Journal, 12,* 277–302.

Maki, H. S., Vauras, M. M. S., & Vainio, S. (2002). Reflective spelling strategies for elementary school students with severe writing difficulties: A case study. *Learning Disability Quarterly, 25,* 189–207.

Morris, D., Tyner, B., & Perney, J. (2000). Early steps: Replicating the effects of a first-grade reading intervention program. *Journal of Educational Psychology, 92,* 681–693.

Perfetti, C. A. (1997). The psycholinguistics of spelling and reading. In C. A. Perfetti, L. Rieben, & M. Fayol (Eds.), *Learning to spell: Research, theory, and practice across languages* (pp. 21–38). Mawah, NJ: Lawrence Erlbaum Associates.

Poskiparta, E., Niemi, P., & Vauras, M. (1999). Who benefits from training in linguistic awareness in the first grade, and what components show training effects? *Journal of Learning Disabilities, 32,* 437–446, 456.

Schneider, W., Ennemoser, M., Roth, E., & Kuspert, P. (1999). Kindergarten prevention of dyslexia: Does training in phonological awareness work for everybody? *Journal of Learning Disabilities, 32,* 429–436.

Snow, C., Burns, M. S., & Griffin, P. (Eds.) (1998). *Preventing reading difficulties in young children.* Washington, DC: National Academy of Sciences.

Vadasy, P. F., Jenkins, J. R., & Pool, K. (2000). Effects of tutoring in phonological and early reading skills on students at risk for reading disabilities. *Journal of Learning Disabilities, 33,* 579–590.

Vadasy, P. F., Sanders, E. A., & Peyton, J. A. (2005). Relative effectiveness of reading practice or word-level instruction in supplemental tutoring: How text matters. *Journal of Learning Disabilities, 38,* 364–380.

Venezky, R. L. (1999). *The American way of spelling: The structure and origins of American English orthography.* New York: Guilford Press.

Chapter Nine

TEACHING LITERACY FOR SOCIAL JUSTICE

Rachelle D. Washington, John Bishop, Emma Bailey,
and JoBeth Allen

> One of the most difficult tasks we face as human beings is communicating
> meaning across our individual differences, a task confounded immeasurably
> when we attempt to communicate across social lines, racial lines, cultural
> lines, or lines of unequal power.
> —Lisa Delpit, *Other People's Children* (p. 66)

After a packed summer of graduate school, curriculum planning meetings, and
a too-short vacation on Edisto Island reading nothing but children's books,
Megan was eager to meet her new students. She imagined the blank canvas of
walls filled with personal narratives, poetry, letters, and the science and history
projects her new class of 28 diverse 3rd graders would create. She imagined
the tables around the room filled with the buzz of children's voices with their
rich linguistic heritages of Spanish, African American vernacular, and other
English dialects, and perhaps other languages. Megan began filling the tables
with her favorite children's literature, a mix of beautiful picture books, short
chapter books, intriguing informational texts, poetry collections, and texts her
previous students had written.

Last year, Megan started the first day with "business"—class rules, textbooks, procedures, and information forms. It had been a negative experience
for both her and her students. This year, she wanted her students to fall in love
the very first day—with a book, with writing and sharing something of their
own, with their new school family. She wanted them to fill the blank bulletin
boards with their lives.

Just then, Frank Jenkins stepped into Megan's doorway. A veteran 3rd-grade teacher, Frank often called impromptu meetings, "Just wanted to let you know all the 3rd-grade teachers are meeting in the library in 15 minutes to go over the student files. Let's get a feel for this new bunch of kids."

Last year, Megan dutifully attended this meeting where teachers read comments from previous teachers and swapped stories about the children. The comments tended to focus on behaviors: "He can't sit still for a single minute," and "Bless her heart, she doesn't get any discipline at home"; academic ability: "We need to get him another segment of special ed—he just can't do 3rd grade math" and "He was in the lowest reading group all year;" and families: "Watch out for that one—I had his brother." So many negatives remarks, and so many of them were about African American boys.

"Frank, I'm not coming to the meeting," Megan said with more confidence than she felt. "I hope nobody gets offended. I want to get to know my students before I read their test profiles—and by then, maybe I won't even want to read them. I want to learn what they are interested in reading before I look at what level they were reading on last year." She'd been thinking about this annual ritual ever since she read *Ways with Words* (Heath, 1983) in her language, literacy, and culture class that summer. Heath's research in South Carolina had convinced her that African American students who had rich home language abilities and knowledge often shut down in school settings because of the mismatch with school tasks. She had been very uncomfortable reading about teachers who judged poor students, both white and black, as less intelligent based on their language, where they lived, or what their parents did. "I know I've done that," she thought to herself. "And I know where it started—in that very first preplanning meeting."

A DUAL FOCUS ON SOCIAL JUSTICE

Megan had survived the first two years of teaching, gaining confidence in planning curriculum and managing the classroom; however, she felt she had not done nearly enough to meet the needs of her culturally and linguistically diverse students. Megan was determined this year to focus on two aspects of teaching for social justice. The first was educational equity, ensuring that all her students had an equal opportunity to learn and succeed. The commitment to increased equity grew out of her sense of failure with several students in the past. She had stopped ability grouping last year, when her principal had shared research by Richard Allington (2000); Megan realized that her "low group" suffered the stigma of being "poor readers" and were being short-changed with a focus on word recognition at the expense of meaning. There were so many areas in which she felt her teaching could be more equitable: better support for English language learners, teaching students living in poverty, and looking critically at special education placements, especially for her African American males who were, as educational consultant Jawanza Kunjufu (2005) had pointed out, overrepresented in classes for students with "behavioral disorders" and underrepresented in gifted classes. She decided to focus on a process that had potential impact across many areas of concern, learning more about students' home cultures to make learning more relevant.

The second aspect of teaching for social justice was involving her students in issues that affected their lives. In terms of making social issues central to her curriculum, Megan had written in her journal over the summer:

> It doesn't seem that there is ANY room in our schools for addressing social issues that have deeply affected our society for hundreds of years. My kids so desperately need to talk about these issues and learn how to positively deal with them. I wish I could teach reading and writing, social studies, and science *through* addressing social justice issues.

Megan had been inspired by teachers who somehow had found a way to do just that. Could she do something like Maria Sweeney (1997), who asked her 4th-grade students to question what they read constantly: "Is this fair? Is this right? Does this hurt anyone? Is this the whole story? Who benefits and who suffers?" (p. 279). Sweeney's students studied the end of apartheid and the elections in South Africa and wrote a play, "No Easy Road to Freedom." They performed it for the rest of the school and community, and urged the audience to get involved with fighting racism by actions such as giving money to the Africa Fund and joining antiracist groups.

Maybe she'd encourage her students to explore a topic closer to home. She was often disturbed by the way students talked to each other, using words like "fag," "retard," and racial slurs. Could she get her students to examine their own prejudices, like 4th grade teacher Barbara Michalove had? Disturbed by the intolerance her students displayed toward Hispanic classmates and those with hearing impairments, Michalove (1999) created an interdisciplinary immersion into discrimination. Through biographies, fiction, a video on the history of intolerance in America, interviews with family members, and shared stories, her students learned not only about the various groups who have been the brunt of discrimination in the United States, but also about themselves. It took time to "circle in" on their own prejudice, but once they did, students were honest in their recognition of intolerance and decisive in their actions. They created rules for their own conduct as they successfully changed their classroom.

To learn more about what other teachers were doing and gather resources, Megan started by entering "teaching for social justice" in her computer's search engine. She subscribed to *Rethinking Schools* and *Teaching Tolerance,* journals and Web sites with a wealth of teaching materials and detailed classroom examples. Megan also joined the National Council of Teachers of English

(NCTE) and began receiving their elementary journal, *Language Arts*. Finally, she spread the word among colleagues; several people slipped articles into her mailbox or e-mailed resources to her all year.

Everything she read emphasized the importance of multicultural literature, including books that explored social issues in her community such as racism, gender stereotypes, attitudes about immigrations, and name-calling. She asked the media specialist to order books she'd identified and also checked out armloads from the public library. Megan wanted books that the kids could relate to and that would encourage critical thinking. She had read an intriguing article by Karla Möller (2002) who led literature discussions of books about social issues, like *Heart of a Chief* (Bruchac, 1998) about preserving Native American culture as well as the ravages of poverty, and *Run Away Home* (McKissack, 1997) on difficulties experiences by southern African American and Native Americans in the late 1800s. Maybe like the students of 2nd-grade teacher Andrew Allen (1997), whose antiracist/antibias approach helped them identify omission and stereotyping in children's literature, her students would learn to name instances of race, class, and gender oppression and even rewrite problematic texts.

Megan had so many questions. What was her role—should she introduce issues or wait for them to come up naturally? What if they didn't? Could her students handle these topics? Would they engage her students who seemed so turned off to reading? She was determined to find out.

CONNECTING HOME CULTURES AND SCHOOL LEARNING

The first month of school, Megan concentrated on initial connections with her students' families. She had been thinking all summer about how to more effectively incorporate home-school reading journals in which she, the students, and their parents wrote about the literature they were reading. Her home-school journals last year had been disappointing. How did those teachers in *Engaging Families* (Shockley, Michalove, & Allen, 1995) find the time to respond every day to the journals? Shockley and Michalove's students had taken library books and their reading journals home three to four nights a week, and families read with their students and then wrote in the journals about the books. The teachers had written back in each journal every day, and formed a close relationship with the parents, grandparents, older siblings—whoever wrote back. The neat thing to Megan was that it wasn't about behavior or signing a "My child read xx minutes" log; it was about the books the children were reading. "This kind of home reading connection could really make a difference for all my students, and especially my struggling readers," Megan thought. "And it's a way of involving parents who can't or don't feel comfortable coming to school for PTA and workshops."

This year, Megan explained the journals and invited family members to participate during home visits. She also asked each family, "Tell me about your child" to get insights on how to connect her curriculum to the students' home lives. She talked with parents, grandparents, and guardians, some in their homes, some at a local restaurant, a few by phone, and three at the community housing center. She thought of Heath's (1983) time in the homes of children, of getting to know what was important to them, what they "bragged on" about their kids, and what they confessed as worries.

Megan had her own worries. As a white, well-educated woman, she was just beginning to question her own biases. When she had visited the homes of children who lived in the nearby housing project last week, she had been unsure what to expect. Would she be looked at with suspicion? What could she learn that would help her teach each child and connect with each family? After one visit she wrote in her journal:

> What I can't get out of my head are my unconscious expectations. I realize that because Stan is poor and African American and has some behavioral and academic issues, I assumed certain things about him and his family. What I found was a mother who obviously cared deeply about her son. I found a simple but neat apartment where Stan had a room with a bunk bed that he was extremely proud of. I saw a note on the refrigerator from his 2nd-grade teacher praising him for getting 100 percent on a spelling test. But I am wrestling with other things. I saw a lot of adults sitting outside in the middle of the day. I heard yelling, cursing, and threatening within earshot of young children. Now I understand why some of my students told me that their parents don't let them play outside.

The home visits made Megan more determined than ever to stay in touch with parents throughout the year and to enlist their help through the home reading journals. She had to learn more about her students' home lives from them and from their families to create an equitable classroom where learning was meaningful and all her students grew as literacy learners.

BUILDING ON STUDENT STRENGTHS AND INTERESTS

At the same time she was getting to know the children and their families outside of school, Megan was learning their strengths and needs as learners. She held individual conferences with each student to listen to them read, find out about their interests, and match children and books. Students tried out all the learning centers and recorded their discoveries, giving Megan valuable information about both content knowledge and informational writing abilities. Students interviewed their family members with questions they generated, such as "What was school like when you were in 3rd grade? What did you like to read? What was your favorite game at recess?" They created pie graphs of major findings and a Venn diagram of "School Then/School Now";

Megan learned a great deal about the children's literacy, as well as about their families.

Megan was eager to move into books about social issues, but she knew she needed to start with the children's own experiences. She read aloud Patricia Polacco's *My Rotten Red Headed Older Brother* (1994). "Do you know why I chose this book?" she asked. "Because I really do have a rotten red-headed older brother!"

"Is he mean?" Donedra asked.

"Does he look like a weasel?" asked Jordan, referring to a description in the book.

Megan laughed, "Well, he's not so bad now, but he used to give me "the tickle torture" until I yelled for Mom to make him stop. It was not fair—I was the one who got in trouble!" Megan was working harder this year to help students find connections between their lives and their learning. She began with a favorite 3rd-grade topic, fairness. She planned to build on the topic throughout the year, reading books like *Fly Away Home* (Bunting, 1993) about a boy and his father who didn't have a home, and *The Faithful Elephants* (Tsuchiya, 1999) about how even animals suffer in times of war. But she had to begin with the students' own experiences. "Sometimes we don't feel like everything is fair in our families. Can you think of a time when you think you were treated unfairly?"

Students eagerly recounted injustices in their own families. Megan encouraged them to write the stories they had just told. She conferred quickly with those who had trouble getting started, encouraging some to start with a picture of a family member and then write a description; some to write letters to family members in Juárez, Dominica, and New York City; and some to write a "cartoon," illustrating sequenced panels with short captions.

Megan sat down next to Michael, and asked, "What are you writing about?"

Michael answered, "My cousin Julian."

"Would you read it to me?" Megan asked.

Michael read slowly from his text: "Julian my cuzin he ride a 4 wheelr. He don't let me driv."

Megan nodded and asked, "Why wouldn't he let you drive?"

"He said I'm too little, but he's only 10," Michael replied angrily.

"Tell me more—why do you want to drive a four wheeler?" Megan encouraged. Michael's eyes lit up and he talked more in the next three minutes than he had in three days. He told her about the machine, his cousin, and the trails around their house.

"Wow! You've got so much to write. I think everyone is going to want to hear all about what you just told me," Megan said, handing Michael a sticky-note with several phrases he had mentioned to prompt his memory. She noticed several possible mechanical topics she could focus on—spelling, run-on sentences, and subject-verb agreement—but she would save those for an editing conference.

She moved around the table to Santiago. A recent immigrant from Juárez, Mexico, Santiago spoke softly and infrequently. Megan had teamed him with Lilia, who spoke fluent English and Spanish. Santiago had drawn a detailed picture of a woman driving a bright yellow car with purple fire on the hood. Santiago covered everything with penciled illustrations, from his writing journal to the fact sheet in the science center. His passion was drawing hot rods, '68 Mustangs and '71 Cobras. He rarely wrote, however.

Megan's conference with Santiago was less successful. When she asked questions about the drawing, praising its color, precision, and sense of motion, Santiago shrugged. When she pressed him about the woman in the picture, he said softly "Tía," one of the 20 or so words Megan knew in Spanish. She helped him sound it out, and asked Lilia if she would help him write other words. She readily agreed, then asked if she could share first.

Nestled in the Storyteller's Chair, Lilia read, "My Beautiful Black Haired Young Mamá. My mamá is the bravest person I know. She crossed the Rio Grande when she was just 16 years old. I was not even born yet because I was in her belly. I was born in Houston and I am American citizen." Lilia read with her head high to this point, but dropped her chin before going on. "She is brave and beautiful, but she is scared and so am I. There might be a new law that makes her go back to Mexico. It is not fair." The other children had many questions, and Megan let the discussion go on longer than usual. This was the kind of issue she wanted at the center of her curriculum, issues that affected children and their families. She need not have worried that her students might not identify important issues. The next day she read aloud *How Many Days to America* (Bunting, 1990), a story of a harrowing boat journey to the United States. After a heated discussion about issues of fairness (why some people have to flee their countries, why some are turned away from the United States, how those who immigrate are treated), the students generated a chart to guide their inquiry: What do we know about immigrants to the United States? What do we want to learn? How can we find out? By the next week they had 13 books, 8 Web sites, and 3 community members—including Lilia's mother.

RESPECTING AND STUDYING LANGUAGE DIVERSITY

As the children became more engaged throughout the fall by investigating, reading, and writing about "fairness," Megan began to focus in individual conferences on specific literacy strategies for reading fluency, word analysis, comprehension, vocabulary, grammar, and spelling. She was uncertain whether she should push her Spanish speakers like Santiago to write in English, and she really struggled with what to do about dialect variations. She kept thinking about a passage she read during her summer course:

> [Teachers] should recognize that the linguistic form a student brings to school is intimately connected with loved ones, community, and personal identity. To suggest that this form is "wrong" or, even worse, ignorant, is to suggest that something is wrong with the student and his or her family. On the other hand, it is equally important to understand that students who do not have access to the politically popular dialect form in this country, that is, Standard English, are less likely to succeed economically than their peers who do. How can both realities be embraced? (Delpit, 1995, p. 53)

That was her dilemma. According to Delpit, correcting children's oral speech was both ineffective and damaging. How would they learn standard English then? Delpit suggested that writing conferences were a logical time to discuss language choices. Megan tried to find the balance by honoring their home languages, whether that was Spanish or an English dialect, and also by teaching the politically powerful dialect.

During her daily read aloud, Megan focused on language: learning new words, learning nuance to familiar works, studying the author's sentence structures, and talking about language choices. Megan was reading Jacqueline Woodson's (2003) book, *Locomotion*, a poetic novel, when the perfect occasion arose. The main character Lonnie writes in his poetry journal, "Not a whole lot of people be saying *Good, Lonnie* to me."

Jordan's hand flew up, "Ms. Megan, is Lonnie a black kid?"

"What makes you think he's black, Jordan?" Megan questioned.

"He talks like a black person," he answered. Many heads nodded.

"How so?" Megan asked.

"He said *people be saying,* and white folks don't talk like that." More nods.

"Why do you say that?" Megan asked.

Jordan paused and then said, "You're white. You don't talk that way."

"That's true," Megan thought for a minute, "but Ms. Teish is a black teacher and she and I talk in a similar way."

"That's because she teaches school."

"So you think we're supposed to talk a certain way at school?"

More vigorous nodding. Megan seized the opportunity to introduce some of the language about language—dialects, code switching, and different registers. "How could we study this?" Megan asked when the children were reluctant to end the discussion. Ten minutes later, they had given themselves an assignment: in the next week, keep a log with examples of different languages, dialects, and registers on their favorite TV show. "Pretty sneaky of us, isn't it Ms. Daniels," Amanda concluded in delight, "TV for homework!"

The language study, which seemed like a natural extension of their study on immigration, extended several weeks. The students, who fell in love with Lonnie in *Locomotion,* decided to study their classroom library for decisions authors made about language. They were disappointed. "We don't have any books in Spanish," Lilia moped.

"Lilia, I have an idea. Why don't you talk with Ms. Órea today when you go to her class? Ask her if she has any books written in Spanish," Megan suggested.

"Guess what!" Lilia announced when she returned from her class for English language learners. "Ms. Órea has lots of bilingual books and she's going to come talk with us tomorrow!" The class language study became a full-blown inquiry. Students posed questions, with help from Megan and Ms. Órea: Which children's authors use black dialect in their books? How did English become the national language? What is the English-only law in our state, and how did it come about? Why do people get so mad about Spanish and dialects? And of course, can English speakers learn Spanish from watching Spanish-language TV shows, and vice versa for Spanish speakers?

CONNECTING AND DISCONNECTING WITH FAMILIES

The empty classroom canvas of August was awash in texts by December. There were student drawings; Santiago's "muscle cars" had generated a study of transportation and an illustrated, annotated travel timeline. Student writing covered the walls—science observations, math estimations, language comparison charts, and immigration stories the students had gathered from their families. There were books in every center, on every ledge. Megan introduced new books, music, poetry, and magazines each week with a "book tease" connecting with their home cultures, expanding the science and social studies curriculum, and introducing new "mentor" authors. Students began to do their own book teases, following Megan's dramatic techniques like dimming the lights, displaying a quote with the LCD projector, even shouting "Lights, Camera, Action!" before reading just enough to pique interest. Megan introduced poetry by Maya Angelou, Gary Soto, and Nikki Giovanni; the students brought in the poetry of their favorite music, including country, Christian, and rap and spoken-word poets like Floetry and Common.

With the music they loved opening the door, Megan's students often wrote poetry. Some of her students who usually stared in dismay at the blank page excelled at writing poems, raps, even TV advertising jingles. At the end of the semester they invited family and friends to a Coffee House Poetry Reading.

The night of the event, parents, grandparents, and neighbors filled the classroom, many dressed up for the gala social occasion. Students were at stations serving hot chocolate, playing CDs of their favorite artists (they had engaged in heated debate to establish the play list), leading a "gallery walk" of their artistically displayed poetry, and seating guests at tables festooned with candles and class poetry albums.

The students had practiced until most were able to perform the pieces, not just recitethem, using a karaoke microphone. Lilia and Santiago alternated voices on a poem they had written in both Spanish and English; Michael wore a motorcycle helmet and read his four-wheeler poem, an extension of his first writing piece; and Stan shared a moving tribute to his uncle who had died of AIDS. Megan was thrilled as she circled the room after the last performance, accepting the praise of grownups, relishing the pride her students showed. Then Michael's mother approached Megan. She was not smiling.

"Why did you let Michael read that piece before correcting it?" she asked.

"What do you mean?" Megan answered, caught off guard.

"Well, for starters, he said, 'Julian ride his four-wheeler' instead of 'Julian *rides* his four-wheeler.' Isn't subject-verb agreement on the 3rd-grade test?"

Megan answered, "Yes, and we're working on subject-verb agreement. We've been investigating when authors use formal and less formal language styles. Michael said that's the way he and his buddies talk about four wheelers."

Michael's mother responded, "I want my son passing 3rd grade. I'm not interested in him learning a 'less formal style.' You make him sound stupid by not correcting him."

Megan was stunned. She had been working so hard to honor students' language, and now she found her philosophy in direct conflict with at least one of her student's parents. Did others feel the same way? The evening was further dampened when Stan's aunt left early, saying angrily, "Stan knows better than to be telling things like that about his family. And you should know better too." Megan went home in tears.

RECONNECTING WITH FAMILIES

The comments troubled Megan throughout the winter holidays. Was the intense language study a waste of time—should she have been teaching formal English exclusively? Should she have discouraged topics that were too personal? In trying to make her classroom more equitable, she had made assumptions about what families valued rather than learning first hand. Her home visits and the home-school reading journals had been a starting point, but they were not enough.

That afternoon, she and her students drafted a letter to their families: "Dear _____, We are starting our home reading journals again after the break. We want to know your opinion. Do you like to read with us? Do you like to write in the journals? Do you like it when Ms. Daniels writes back? What would make the journals special to you? Please write back. Love, _____"

Students personalized the letters in their journals. Megan emphasized their most readable handwriting; she also worked in explicit instruction on letter writing and subject-verb agreement. ("Is it 'When Ms. Daniels *write* back or *writes* back'? Why?") By Friday, they had 12 responses. Several parents said they thought reading at home helped their children, and they appreciated it when Megan wrote back. But they also wanted to know how their children were doing, what they were studying, and what they could help with at home. Megan eagerly agreed to extend the written dialogue; she could share curriculum (like their language study), enlist family participation, and let parents (and students) know what each child needed to be working on.

During independent reading later that week, Megan pulled her chair beside Santiago. After he told her about his book, she asked casually, "Santiago, is there someone at home you like to read to? I notice you've been checking out many books from Ms. Órea's room. Do you read them in English or Spanish—or both?"

"Mostly I read them to myself. Ms. Órea said to read both languages, so I could be bi- bi-. . ." he looked up for help.

"Bilingual—no, biliterate! She talked with our class about that. I wish I could read and write in two languages! So maybe you could read to someone at home and they could write in the journal—what do you think?" Megan queried.

After a long silence, Megan put her hand gently on Santiago's arm. Finally he said softly, "They don't write, my family." Megan had assumed that Santiago's family wrote in Spanish. What was that book they had read last summer— *Con Respeto?* The researcher, Guadalupe Valdés (1996), had documented many miscommunications between Mexican immigrant families and their teachers, and now Megan was guilty herself. She had gotten the letter translated inviting parents to participate in the journals, but had never thought about families who might not have the literacy levels or family networks to read the Spanish version. No wonder they had not been participating.

"Santiago, let's try an experiment. I think your mamá might enjoy hearing this book you are reading. She mentioned several times when she drops you off in our classroom that she wants to help you be a good reader. After you read, could you write down one thing that you say, and one thing that your mamá says about the book? " Megan almost held her breath. She felt like she was asking a lot, but also that she had been asking too little for too long. Santiago shrugged, noncommittal. When he left that afternoon, however, the book was tucked in his backpack.

FAILING

Megan had been assessing her students' reading through a variety of formal and informal strategies throughout the year. She celebrated the progress most of the children were making, but worried about several children who were not making enough progress.

One of those students, Bobby, stumbled over many words in a 1st-grade level book and wasn't able to talk about the text after he finished. Several other children in the class had begun the year with similar difficulties. Knowing that all children had to pass the state reading test to pass the 3rd grade, Megan was beginning to panic.

She had what she considered to be a balanced reading program: each day children read self-selected books independently or with a partner; participated in the shared reading where the whole class read together a newspaper article or something from the class set of 3rd-grade reading books; read in a small guided reading group a book carefully selected by Megan to be at their instructional reading level; wrote on topics of their own choice or topics related to what they were learning in science or social studies; and studied the way language works—phonics, spelling, and other word analysis strategies. Still, six students were reading below grade level by district standards. They had made progress, they were becoming more confident, but they would not pass the standardized tests. Should she abandon her balanced literacy program? What was more "just": to focus only on skills that were tested and have her students say they hated reading, as several had done last year, or to focus on what she considered meaningful reading and writing and risk students flunking 3rd grade? With the state test pressure building, she asked more experienced teachers for advice.

"I focus on phonics, vocabulary, and test-taking skills. We do daily drills and practice tests every week," Frank Jenkins told her when she brought the topic up in the teachers lounge. "Third grade is do or die. If they fail, they don't go to 4th grade. I spend most of the year getting kids ready for the test—they hate it, I hate it, but that's what we are being forced to do. It is no kindness to your students to ignore high-stakes tests."

"But if they hate the drills, don't they start to hate reading?" Megan asked.

"For the short term. I hope Linda, Barb, and Lois can help them regain that love in 4th grade. I just know I have to get them there. We can see what happens when they flunk; I'm sure Bobby came into your class hating reading, because that's why he is in 3rd grade again," Frank pointed out.

Megan's mentor teacher Janice Teish arched her soda can into the trash and said pointedly, "I'm sure you have noticed which kids are struggling Megan."

She did. Five of the six students she was worried about received federal lunch assistance. How could this be? Surely being poor didn't mean these children couldn't read as well as more economically advantaged peers. Surely it didn't mean she couldn't teach Bobby to read. She walked out of the lounge with Janice, asking confidentially, "Do you agree with Frank, that from now until March 14 we just do test prep?"

"Yes. But Frank and I have a little different approach. I show them how the test is going to try to trick them. Then I show them how smart they are, and how they are going to do well on that test. I take books we are reading, stories that they are writing, science notebooks they've been writing observations in, and help them translate what they know into what they'll be asked to demonstrate. I start using test language, and I point it out to them. Our genre study in March is 'Reading Test Genre.' Once they get the hang of reading those weird little passages and those trivial questions, they can tell you exactly how "reading-test reading" is different. We act out stories and then I ask them comprehension questions—once they've acted them out, they can infer so much better!"

Megan was taking furious notes. Kids were coming back from lunch.

"One more pearl of wisdom," Janice offered. "Pull that little group of six you are most worried about and work directly with them on the particular skills they need."

"But that's ability grouping—I can't . . ." Megan sputtered.

"No, it's sitting down with the kids who need the most help, not for the whole year but right now so they can succeed on the test, and saying, 'This is what you need to know and I'm here to teach it to you!'" Janice said convincingly.

Megan hurried through her door to see almost everyone with a book. "They know the routines so well," she thought. "I hope I can teach them this test routine without wrecking our learning community."

For their first step, Megan went back to books they had read earlier about families and fairness: *Grandfather's Journey* (Say, 1993) about Japanese immigrants and their longing for home; *Oliver Button is a Sissy* (dePaola, 1979) about a boy who countered name calling and gender stereotypes; *Tar Beach* (Ringgold, 1996) about life in Harlem in the 1930s; and *Fly Away Home* (Bunting, 1993), which they had read in their first inquiry into fairness. In these rereadings, Megan incorporated strategies Janice had suggested to help students focus on vocabulary and drawing inferences, two areas in which her students had underperformed in previous years.

Megan's next move was to restructure her literature discussion. The students loved choosing their own books, especially ones related to their inquiries on immigration and language, but they struggled at times in their student-led discussions. Her less-proficient readers needed more support, her shy students needed her encouragement, and almost all of them had trouble asking what they called Really Important Questions. Janice Teisch encouraged her to read *Literature Study Circles in Multicultural Classrooms* (Samway & Whang, 1995), which detailed a more teacher-directed approach that some of her students needed.

For these literature discussions, students began identifying books for their next inquiry, sparked by Megan's rereading of *Fly Away Home*. After the students had gotten beyond their initial reaction—that it would be cool to live in an airport—they decided to study homelessness and how it affected children. Megan told them about how teacher Mary Cowhey (2006) collaborated with her primary-grade students and their families. They not only baked pies and cookies for a Thanksgiving dinner for the homeless, they studied the complex causes of poverty, challenged stereotypes of "poor people," and learned how local activists fight poverty. Megan's students selected *Bud, Not Buddy* (Curtis, 1999), about an orphan on the run from abusive foster homes in 1930s; *Maniac Magee* (Spinelli, 1999), about a homeless boy and the racism he encountered; and *Lucy's Wish* (Nixon, 1999) and other books in the Orphan Train Children series, as well as nonfiction books like *Orphan Train: One Boy's True Story* (Warren, 1996). Homelessness and affordable housing were issues the community was focusing on, which made it especially timely. Several of the books dealt with difficult subjects, however, including child neglect and abuse. Megan sent a note to parents in the reading journals telling them about the books and the inquiry; she followed up with a phone call to each family to see if they had concerns or suggestions.

Megan worked especially hard with the children she was most worried about failing the state test. She helped them select a book on their reading level, taped the book herself so they could listen as they read along, and worked on specific skills they would be tested on. She was determined to keep her dual focus on a social justice curriculum *and* on social justice for her students.

She failed.

Bobby, Marcus, and Santiago failed the test. Bobby and Marcus's parents appealed retention, but Santiago failed 3rd grade. Megan was outraged that a child who entered her class speaking little English had been failed by an English-only test.

RENEWING RESOURCES FOR TEACHING FOR SOCIAL JUSTICE

It had been an exhausting and exhilarating year. School was barely out for the children when Megan returned to her studies. At Janice's urging, Megan had applied for the local chapter of the National Writing Project (http://www.writingproject.org/). The two friends attended the month-long, all-day institute together. Megan soon realized many teachers in the institute were asking social justice questions similar to hers: What can I do to make students' out-of-school lives central in my curriculum? How do I turn racist, sexist, and homophobic comments into learning situations? How can I teach writing through new technologies in an equitable way? Megan's question, sharply focused by her experience the previous year, was how can I create a social justice curriculum that also prepares students for standardized tests?

Throughout the summer, Megan renewed the emotional, intellectual, and relational resources she needed to begin thinking about her next year of teaching. She took to heart suggestions by Herbert Kohl (Ayers, Hunt, & Quinn, 1998); he had been teaching for social justice for more than 30 years! Kohl encouraged Megan, "Watch your students ... listen to them, observe how they learn, and then, based on your experience and their responses, figure out how to practice social justice in your classroom." Kohl reminded her of Paulo Freire (1998), whom she'd read in the writing institute. This Brazilian educator and champion of social justice encouraged teachers, "And as we dream about democracy, let us fight, day and night, for a school in which we talk to and with the learners so that, hearing them, we can be heard by them as well" (p. 68).

Kohl's (2000) final suggestion was "protect and nurture yourself. . . . Don't turn teaching for social justice into a grim responsibility, but take it for the moral and social necessity that it is." Megan wrote in her journal the day before she left for Edisto Island:

> My head is spinning—so much to think about. I think I'll have a meeting with parents and students to plan the home-school journals, and maybe talk about issues that students want to study and parents could get involved with too. I can't wait to sit by the ocean and read the new multicultural children's literature I'm taking. I've packed *Open Minds to Equality* by Schniedewind and Davidson—it's supposed to be a great resource for helping students address issues of race, gender, class, language, sexual orientation, physical and mental ability, and even religion. Anna loaned me *Writing Sense* by Kendall and Khuon; she said it has practical ideas for teaching writing to English language learners. Note to self: order Allen's new book, *Diverse Families, Welcoming Schools* when I get back from Edisto. It's all about forming partnerships with families that support kids' learning. I think that's my next step—parents as partners in creating a social justice curriculum!

REFERENCES

Allen, A. (1997). Creating space for discussions about social justice and equity in an elementary classroom. *Language Arts, 74*(7), 518–524.

Allen, J. (in press). *Diverse families and welcoming schools: Partnerships that support student learning.* New York: Teachers College Press.

Allington, R. (2000). *What really matters for struggling readers: Designing research-based programs.* Boston: Allyn & Bacon.

Ayers, W., Hunt, J., & Quinn, T. (1998). *Teaching for social justice.* New York: Teachers College Press.

Bruchac, J. (1998). *The heart of a chief.* New York: Dial.

Bunting, E. (1990). *How many days to America?* New York: Clarion Books.

Bunting, E. (1993). *Fly away home.* New York: Clarion Books.

Cowhey, M. (2006). *Black ants and Buddhists.* Portland, ME: Stenhouse.

Curtis, C. (1999). *Bud, not Buddy.* New York: Delacorte.

Delpit, L. (1995). *Other people's children.* New York: New Press.

dePaola, T. (1979), *Oliver Button is a sissy.* Voyager Books.

Freire, P. (1998). *Teachers as cultural workers: Letters to those who dare teach*. Boulder, CO: Westview Press.

Heath, S. (1983). *Ways with words*. Cambridge: Cambridge University Press.

Kendall, J., & Khuon, O., (2006). *Writing sense: Integrated reading and writing lessons for English language learners*. Portland, ME: Stenhouse.

Kohl, H. (2000/01). Teaching for social justice: A veteran educator offers pedagogical and personal suggestions learned over 30 years experience. *Rethinking schools online*, 15(2). http://www.rethinkingschools.org/archive/15–02/Just152.shtml, retrieved 12/4/06

Kunjufu, J. (2005). *Keeping black boys out of special education*. Chicago: African American Images.

McKissack, P. C. (1997). *Run away home*. New York: Scholastic Press.

Michalove, B. (1999). Examining prejudice in history and in ourselves. In J. Allen (Ed.), *Class actions: Teaching for social justice in elementary and middle school*. New York: Teachers College Press.

Möller, K. J. (2002). Providing support for dialogue in literature discussions about social justice. *Language Arts, 79*, 467–477.

Nixon, J. (1999). *Lucy's wish*. New York: Yearling. *Rethinking Schools*. Available: http://www.rethinkingschools.org/

Polacco, P. (1994). *My rotten redheaded older brother*. New York: Aladdin.

Ringgold, F. (1996). *Tar Beach*. New York: Crown.

Samway, K., Whang, G. (1995) *Literature study circles in multicultural classrooms*. Portland, ME: Stenhouse.

Say, A. *Grandfather's journey*. (1993). New York: Houghton Mifflin (1993).

Schniedewind, N., & Davidson, E. (2006). *Open minds to equality* (3rd ed.). Milwaukee: Rethinking Schools.

Shockley, B., Michalove, B., & Allen, J. (1995). *Engaging families: Connecting home and school literacy communities*. Portsmouth, NH: Heinemann.

Spinelli, J. (1999). *Maniac Magee*. New York: Little, Brown Young Readers

Sweeney, M. (1997). "No easy road to freedom": Critical literacy in a fourth-grade classroom. *Reading & Writing Quarterly, 13*, 279–290.

Teaching Tolerance. Available: http://www.splcenter.org/teachingtolerance/tt-index.html.

Tsuchiya, Y. (1999). *Faithful elephants: A true story of animals, people, and war*. Boston: Houghton Mifflin.

Valdés, Guadalupe (1996). *Con respeto: Bridging the distances between culturally diverse families and schools: An Ethnographic portrait*. New York: Teachers College Press.

Warren, A. (1996) *Orphan train: One boy's true story*. Boston: Houghton Mifflin.

Woodson, J. (2003). *Locomotion*. New York: Putnam.

Chapter Ten

ACCOMMODATING DIGITAL LITERACIES WITHIN CONCEPTIONS OF LITERACY INSTRUCTION FOR A NEW CENTURY

David Reinking and Amy Carter

It is difficult to overstate how much reading and writing have changed between the beginnings of our respective careers as classroom teachers. The first author of this chapter began his career as an elementary and middle-grade teacher during the early 1970s; the second author began her teaching career at the turn of the new millennium. The older first author began teaching in a world that included the clacking of the keys on a typewriter, often after writing a handwritten draft, searching for books in the library using a card catalogue, completing virtually all school assignments on paper with a pen or pencil, and writing a research paper by taking handwritten notes on 3 × 5 index cards that were then scattered on the living room floor to experiment with different organizational schemes. There were no cell phones, FAX machines, or home and office printers, and making copies of a map for a social studies lesson meant learning how to use a ditto or mimeograph machine (and learning which cleaners best removed the inevitable smudges and stains on hands and clothes). The most advanced technologies for teaching were the movie, film-strip, or the overhead projector, although personal computers were just beginning to attract some attention.

On the other hand, the younger second author began teaching at a time when handwritten drafts were often a last resort after a laptop battery expired and the clacking keys of a typewriter were a distant childhood memory. She was required by state teaching standards to instruct her students on how to conduct research on the Internet and to teach them about the differences between print and electronic sources. In her 3rd-grade classroom, students' presentations were created with the assistance of widely used software for displaying digital slide shows on a large screen. The accompanying artwork was often created by using a computer program that allowed digital painting on a computer screen, not the paint in the art supply cabinet. Even among her 3rd-grade students, it was not uncommon to hear a cell phone ring during instruction. The scope and sophistication of digital technologies available for her to integrate into her teaching were almost overwhelming and made it difficult to keep abreast of them or to decide which ones to use.

As this contrast suggests, the most prominent and consequential change in the lives of students and teachers spanning the years between the beginnings of our respective careers is that written communication has become increasingly digital and decreasingly handwritten or printed. Both acknowledging and understanding that change are critical for educators because of the implications with regard to how they conceptualize and approach virtually every aspect of literacy instruction in schools today and for the foreseeable future. Because literacy is foundational to formal schooling, a shift to digital forms of reading and writing also has important implications for other subjects. It should also be relevant to parents, policy makers, and others who have a vested interest in preparing students to be literate in the twenty-first century.

In this chapter, we provide background pertaining to these changes in relation to what they imply for literacy instruction in schools. Our intent is to highlight the importance of accommodating digital technologies into conceptions of literacy instruction and to highlight the challenges that have worked against achieving that accommodation. We begin by tracing the roots of the digital revolution and how it gave rise to a shift from an essentially monolithic view of literacy based on printed materials to one based on diverse electronic forms of reading and writing that have been referred to collectively as digital literacies. Then, we summarize how educators and researchers have responded to the increasing prominence of digital literacies and what factors have limited their response. We also provide a few examples of how digital literacies are modifying or might modify conventional print-based understandings of literacy instruction. Throughout the chapter, we cite additional sources of information for those who wish to delve more deeply into this topic.

THE DIGITAL REVOLUTION AND THE RISE OF DIGITAL LITERACIES

The shift to digital forms of reading and writing is a prominent part of a larger digital revolution, which might arguably be dated from an event in 1983. In that year, *Time* magazine did not select a man or woman in its annual issue highlighting the person of the year. Instead, it named the computer "machine of the year," citing how advances in technology made computers small, powerful, and affordable enough to be within the reach of people in all walks of life, not just computer scientists. At the same time, two software applications, word processing and the electronic spreadsheet, represented powerful tools readily applicable to tasks in the home and in the workplace. Computers, *Time* argued, were poised to make a tremendous difference in the lives of people in the future.

In retrospect, *Time*'s decision in 1983 seems clearly justified and prescient. Computers, or more generally an array of digital technologies, affect almost every aspect of our daily lives. Perhaps none of the applications of digital technologies affect us so pervasively today as those we use to communicate and to search for information. E-mail is ubiquitous. Today, not having an e-mail address to list on a form requesting personal information is almost as anomalous as not being able to list a phone number or credit card. Cell phones, another prominent example, not only enable voice communication, but also allow a vast textual world, including e-mail, the Internet, and text messaging to be available 24 hours a day and 7 days a week, and is as convenient as reaching into a pocket or a purse. The Internet today, arguably the most culturally and globally significant technology of the new century, is increasingly the first source to which people, including students at all grade levels, turn when they need information.

These and other digital forms of communication fundamentally change the nature of reading, writing, and texts. For example, a host of new forms of digital reading and writing have raised interesting and sometimes controversial issues. There is instant messaging, with its possibilities for creating and exploiting false identities. Like e-mail, it also promotes a conversational informality in writing that is at odds with the more formal conventions of spelling, grammar, and usage associated with printed texts. There is Wikipedia (www.wikipedia.org), the online, open-access encyclopedia that permits virtually any reader to edit its content, which raises issues about the reliability of information, how it is determined and by whom, not to mention the questions it raises about traditional understandings of authorship. The blog (short for web log) is a new genre of writing that allows anyone with Internet access to claim a public writing space for sharing his or her thoughts and musings. The far-reaching implications of such open forums are suggested by at least one notable occasion when bloggers scooped professional journalists in exposing a national hoax (http://news.com.com/Bloggers+drive+hoax+probe+into+Bush+memos/2100–1028_3–5362393.html). Presentations to audiences today, whether in person or on a Web site, often involve using digital tools to create multimedia texts that may come into conflict with conventional understandings of intellectual property and with copyright laws that evolved mainly in a typographic world.

Young people particularly have claimed their own niches in the digital world of communication, which has implications for fully understanding their literate lives. Instant messaging is one example. *Zines,* which are an on-line outgrowth of independently published fanzines (i.e., small independent fan magazines), frequently developed by and for young people, represent another example. These forms suggest how personally engaging digital forms of writing may be, because they allow students to access a potentially large and diverse audience and because they have an aura of subversion as underground publications that allow adolescents to explore their own identities beyond the control of adults.

Clearly, every aspect of people's literate lives, young and old, has become more digital, a trend that has been documented and written about for at least a decade. That trend is indisputable and irreversible. An abundance of statistical information substantiates that conclusion. An excellent source of such information is the Pew Internet and American Life project (http://www.pewinter net.org/), which systematically tracks Internet use and trends in the United States. For example, several of that project's reports issued during 2006 reveal the following: 39 percent of Internet users have gone online to find a place to live; on a typical day in August 2006, 26 million Americans were online to seek information and news pertaining to the forthcoming mid-term elections (in 2005, an estimated 50 million people got their news daily from the Internet). High-speed Internet connections increased twice as fast in 2006 as in 2005, particularly among middle-class Americans, and 87 percent of online users reported using the Internet at least one time to research a scientific topic or concept. At the same time, newspaper subscriptions continue a 20-year decline (see http://www.washingtonpost.com/wp-dyn/content/article/2005/05/02/AR2005050201457.html), particularly between 1994 and 2006, when the percentage of Americans reporting that they had read a newspaper the previous day dropped from 58 to 40 percent.

Paralleling these societal trends, the National Center for Educational Statistics of the U.S. Department of Education has provided data substantiating that schools are increasingly equipped to gain access to the Internet and to the diverse sources of information and forms of communication that it provides. One report (U.S. Department of Education, 2006) indicates an increase from 4 to 94 percent in the percentage of instructional rooms in public schools with Internet access between 1994 and 2005. That increase is matched during the same period by a decrease in the ratio of students to computers with Internet access from 12.1 students per computer in 1994 to 3.8 students per computer in 2005.

The status of printed texts in what defines daily literacy in the twenty-first century might be compared to the status of currency in our financial transactions. Cash still plays a role in everyday financial transactions, particularly in certain circumstances, but it is a diminishing and increasingly secondary role. Just as daily commerce, ranging from personal transactions, such as swiping a debit or credit card at a gas pump, to corporate bookkeeping, is increasingly electronic, so too is our reading and writing and our access to information. That unrelenting shift toward digital forms and processes in every aspect of our daily lives creates and defines digital literacies and consequently establishes the clear need to incorporate digital literacies into schools.

The rise of digital literacies has far-reaching societal and global implications. If schools are to be at all relevant to the world as it is, and if they are to prepare informed, productive, and democratic citizens for the future, it is clear that they must weave digital literacies into the fabric of their curricula and instruction. How have literacy educators and researchers responded to the rise of these digital literacies beyond bringing the necessary technologies into the schools? What issues and challenges do they face, particularly in the language arts curriculum?

THE RESPONSE OF LITERACY EDUCATORS AND RESEARCHERS

It would be shortsighted and foolish, if not unethical, for educators to ignore this shift from printed to digital forms of communication or to ignore the Internet as a means to access information digitally. For example, who today would congratulate a teacher for an innovative and skillfully delivered lesson on how to use a card catalogue in a library, especially if that teacher never engaged students in activities that helped them become proficient in locating information in electronic databases? Is it acceptable for a teacher to teach students the conventions of writing a business letter without addressing the conventions of e-mail communication? Likewise, is it acceptable to teach students how to use an index in a book without teaching strategies for using a search engine on the Internet? Such questions are becoming harder for educators to avoid and more anachronistic when they do fail to address them.

Yet, there is general agreement that the overall response of educators to the revolutionary changes in reading and writing has not been timely or adequate. Many observers who are interested in how digital technologies alter conventional conceptions of literacy have lamented the slow pace at which educators and policy makers have responded. For example, Leu (2006) pointed out that as recently as 2005, not a single state in the United States had made provision for students to use word processing when taking mandated, and often high-stakes, state writing assessments. This example is representative of many other points of divergence that often exist between the availability and use of digital literacies in everyday life and the print-based literacy instruction that remains entrenched in many schools.

From the outset of the digital revolution, education has lagged behind the increasingly widespread adoption of digital technologies for reading and writing in society at large. Historically, that lag is typical as evidenced by other new technologies that have crept only slowly into schools. To illustrate, there is a well-known story about an educator who many years ago observed out of frustration that he was hoping to get an overhead projector in his classroom now that he saw them in bowling alleys. Schools are typically conservative institutions that are rarely in the vanguard of adopting new technologies, especially when, as is the case with digital technologies, they require essentially new ways of thinking about teaching, learning, and literacy. One writer (Papert, 1993) argued that schools treat computers like the human body's white blood cells treat an invading virus. Even in California's Silicon Valley, the Mecca of the digital revolution, populated by some of the most tech-savvy individuals in the United States, Cuban (2001) found that the integration of digital technologies into curriculum and instruction was meager and perfunctory. Conservative attitudes, benign neglect, or active resistance to new technologies in schools may mean only a frustrating delay in incorporating a technology like the overhead projector, but it may be a much greater concern when it means that schools are no longer in touch with the literate demands of society at large.

Furthermore, when schools do embrace digital technologies, they often do so tangentially in ways that preserve conventional print-based literacy as the center of the curriculum. Taking students to a computer lab once a week to engage in activities involving word processing, e-mail, or the Internet hardly seems to be an appropriate and authentic response to the revolutionary changes in reading and writing occurring outside of the classroom. We find it useful to characterize such relatively superficial responses by borrowing the term *assimilation* from Piaget, the famous child psychologist, who applied it to children at a stage of development during which they tried to make new, anomalous observations fit into their existing internal schemes for understanding the external world. In a similar way, educators *assimilate* digital technologies when they squeeze them into existing curriculum and into conventional modes of teaching that remain essentially unchanged. As Piaget pointed out, however, when children mature cognitively, they come to *accommodate* new information that conflicts with their existing internal schemes by creating new and fundamentally different internal representations. Likewise, in light of the fundamental changes in reading and writing that digital technologies have brought about, it may be necessary for educators to reorient and to reframe fundamentally what is taught in the name of literacy.

It is important not to underestimate the difficulties and challenges that schools, teachers, and students face when literacy instruction moves from assimilating digital technologies into existing curriculum and instruction. It is understandable why this shift has been slow to occur. Many teachers, particularly more experienced teachers whose formative years preceded the digital revolution, are themselves on the trailing edge of digital forms of reading and writing. They rarely use the Internet or e-mail, and may have only a vague notion of newer genres and forms, such as instant messaging, blogs, and wikis (evolving texts created on the Internet by groups of individuals over time where no one person maintains control of a text). Hence, they may feel incompetent or insecure about engaging their students in activities where the students are more expert. Some are novices who would like to know more, but who may not have the time or the professional support they need. Others are so invested in conventional printed forms that they actively resist engaging students in digital forms, and sometimes they may romanticize about how printed forms are an inherently superior or more valid technology for reading and writing.

The slow pace of movement toward accommodating digital technologies is also understandable because literacy educators must contend with a host of potentially challenging financial, technological, logistical, curricular, pedagogical, political, and other factors. These factors have a local dimension, such as the need for teachers to upgrade their skills and be provided an opportunity to do so, to feel confident in managing fast-changing technological developments. Other challenges, however, are the result of larger systemic factors. For example, there are substantial pressures on policy makers, administrators, and teachers to raise achievement on conventional basic literacy skills as mandated by the federal No Child Left Behind (NCLB) legislation in the United States (P.L. 107–110, 2002). Attempts to introduce digital technologies into classrooms may be significantly curtailed if they are perceived as distracting attention from that more pressing and immediately consequential concern. It is difficult for schools and teachers to become fully engaged in promoting and developing digital literacies when doing so may risk that they do not meet the annual yearly progress in conventional reading achievement as mandated by that legislation, particularly when failure to perform adequately may have dire consequences. The irony is that the need for global competitiveness often cited as a rationale for NCLB is more likely to be achieved through the development of knowledge and skills directly related to digital literacies, not to mention the higher purpose of maintaining an informed democratic citizenry in an age of digital information.

Even if a strong commitment is made to integrating digital technologies into curricula and instruction, it is not always clear what agendas should dominate such efforts. Should there be a focus on ensuring that adequate hardware and software are available, on using digital technologies innovatively to accomplish more conventional goals of reading instruction, on exploiting digital technologies to transform literacy instruction, preparing students for the literacy of the future, or empowering students in ways not possible or typically explored with more conventional technologies (e.g., engaging students in a critical literacy that entails community involvement, social critique, and social activism)? Or, should all of these as well as other agendas be addressed to some degree?

These are curricular issues that have not been resolved and about which there is little focused dialogue, let alone consensus. A related challenge is that digital technologies have implications for almost every aspect of language arts instruction including topics as diverse as assessment, vocabulary development, spelling, writing, comprehension, second language development, and readers with special needs.

Another challenge is that digital forms of reading and writing are continuously and rapidly evolving and each evolution typically requires logistical and conceptual accommodations. On the technological side new applications and new versions of existing applications often appear monthly, weekly, and even daily, not slowly across years or decades (Leu, 2006). For example, since the earliest days of classroom computing, each new and engaging application often required expanded memory, a peripheral device (e.g., a CD drive), a new or upgraded operating system, or an updated version of a software application that had to be purchased separately and installed. Advances in technology during the past few years have mitigated these difficulties, however. Many applications are web-based, and software applications and operating systems are upgraded through automatic downloads. Newer computers are ready to use out of the package and are equipped with built-in features that eliminate the need for elaborate setups with separate, external devices.

Conceptually, too, it is a challenge for educators to stay abreast of these developments and to accommodate such rapid change. Authentically accommodating digital technologies into education in general and into literacy education in particular involves major conceptual, physical, logistical, curricular, and pedagogical changes (e.g., see the technology standards created by the International Society for Technology in Education, 2002) that may call into question many longstanding assumptions and practices of traditional schooling. For example, a teacher may no longer be viewed as a font of knowledge. Instead, learning activities may more naturally be student centered, spontaneous, unpredictable, and open ended when multiple sources of online information are readily available. Textbooks are no longer likely to be at the center of instruction. These and similarly fundamental changes are implied by digital technologies and the literacies that they naturally promote.

Accompanying these technological and conceptual changes, the logistics for engaging in activities aimed at promoting digital literacies are remarkably more complex. A teacher who plans activities around a textbook, for example, faces few of the issues faced by teachers who wish to engage students with online activities. That complexity, however, is reduced somewhat by those teachers who are fortunate enough to participate in wireless laptop initiatives where all students have laptops with wireless connections to the Internet. Nonetheless, a teacher using conventional materials will not likely face difficulties such as a computer server that goes down in the middle of a lesson, or a school firewall that is indiscriminate in denying access to benign and useful sites for the sake of guarding against the possibility of accessing inappropriate sites.

Younger teachers who may be more familiar and more comfortable with digital forms of reading and writing may be less resistant to, and more adept at, accommodating digital literacies into their teaching. Yet they may be hampered in doing so by their general inexperience in teaching and by a lack of support or understanding from their more senior colleagues and supervisors. They may have received relatively little guidance during their preservice preparation for how to accommodate digital literacies into their instruction, which may be explained in part by the fact that methods courses are often taught by instructors who are heavily invested in printed materials and who have little interest or background in teaching with digital materials. In our experience, few programs of teacher education include methods courses that help preservice teachers understand or cope with reading and language arts instruction devoted to addressing digital forms of reading and writing. The contrasting concepts of assimilation and accommodation that we introduced earlier in this section are no less applicable to teacher preparation programs than they are to elementary and middle-school classrooms.

Lest we paint too dismal a portrait, we wish to note that there are encouraging exceptions to our overall assessment that educators' response to the rise of digital literacies has been inadequate. There are indications that the tide is slowly turning. For example, some popular reading methods texts are beginning to go beyond the now obligatory section or chapter on technology. Those texts are beginning to suggest materials and activities that teachers might use to move beyond using digital technologies only to further the goals of conventional print-based instruction in reading and writing. For example, rather than providing examples of how digital technologies might be used to teach the conventional skills of reading and comprehending printed texts, such as finding or writing the main idea of paragraph, these texts may include ideas for engaging students in locating information on the Internet and creating multimedia presentations.

An increasing number of books and Web sites (e.g., www.reading.org/resources/community/links_rumphius_info.html) highlight innovative approaches and projects developed by teachers committed to integrating digital literacies and the Internet into their teaching, especially for teachers who have the motivation and wherewithal to face the challenges of doing so. Nonetheless, overall, a wide chasm still exists between the digital literacies that are continuously evolving in daily life outside of schools and the literacy instruction in the majority of classrooms. Education has not yet reached the point where digital literacies are fully incorporated or accommodated into literacy instruction and where the respective emphases on digital and print-based literacies reflect the shifting balance of those literacies outside schools and classrooms. This lack of progress is not surprising given the many challenges and obstacles that stand in the way of educators moving from assimilation to accommodation of digital literacies. We are also impressed with the many creative, dedicated, and skilled teachers and administrators who are willing to face those formidable challenges and obstacles. There is much potential progress on the horizon with the Internet poised to become a mainstream instructional tool, as well as an object of study in its own right as it becomes more firmly entrenched as an inescapable artifact of the new century. The accommodation of digital literacies is likely to leap forward as laptops and wireless connections become more prevalent.

THE CONTRIBUTION AND ROLE OF PROFESSIONAL ORGANIZATIONS

The field's leading professional organizations have also responded to the awareness that digital literacies need to be accommodated within conceptions of literacy instruction. The International Reading Association (IRA; www.reading.org) is a prominent example. In 2002, IRA paired with the National Council of Teachers of English (NCTE) to create ReadWriteThink.org, a freely accessible Web site that includes peer-reviewed lesson plans for reading and language arts teachers, Web resources, and a plethora of interactive teaching tools, many of which related to digital literacies. In addition, in 1997, IRA launched *Reading Online* (www.readingonline.org), a free online-only publication to offer peer-reviewed articles on literacy practice and research. At its Web site, IRA also makes available a position statement articulating the importance of integrating technology into the literacy curriculum, the necessity of equal access to technology for students, and the need to provide students with technologically literate teachers. To provide literacy educators with a way to interact with each other about common problems and issues related to digital literacies, IRA also supports RTEACHER, an online forum for discussing instructional practice, research, theory, and policy. Members of RTEACHER also select teachers who develop outstanding Internet resources to receive IRA's Miss Rumphius Award, given to teachers each year who have developed innovative units, projects, and activities involving digital technologies.

THE STATUS AND ROLE OF RESEARCH AND SCHOLARSHIP

A consideration of how digital technologies connect to literacy instruction has attracted the interest of a relatively small group of scholars and researchers since the earliest stages of instructional computing. As early as the mid-1960s, a large federal grant to Stanford University included a project to create a computer-based reading curriculum that would teach children to read independent of a human teacher. A historically noteworthy publication was a book entitled *Computer Applications in Reading* (Mason, Blanchard, & Daniel 1983), published by the International Reading Association. That book, which went into its 3rd edition in 1987, provided an exhaustive annotated summary of the many diverse research and development projects that incorporated digital technologies into the teaching of reading and writing. Its status as a best seller among literacy educators was an early indication of the interest and excitement generated by computers among literacy researchers and educators. Nonetheless, these early projects were often aimed at using a computer to enhance the goals of conventional, print-based reading instruction, and they provided little specific guidance about how educators might integrate applications into instruction. Understandably at this early stage, almost no attention was given to how digital technologies might completely reframe the experience of reading and writing, to how the computer might create new textual genres, or how schools might accommodate expanding definitions of literacy into their thinking.

Beginning in the early 1990s, however, there was considerable interest in hypertext, a nonlinear form of writing and reading, but it attracted mainly writers interested in its literary and historical implications. Literacy scholars and researchers were being confronted with the idea that broader definitions of literacy were necessary in an increasingly multimedia world (e.g., Flood & Lapp, 1995). That period, which saw significant technological advances and increases in computing speed and memory (e.g., the Compact Disk), also saw the first serious serous questioning of the centrality and future viability of the book as the dominant technology of written communication. The seeds for a more mainstream interest in new digital forms of reading and writing also arose at that time, however. The use of e-mail as a form of communication became almost a necessity, at least in the academic and business worlds (following its first use in the military) and for almost all sectors of society soon after. Also, early versions of the Internet appeared and rapidly precipitated the dot-com boom that solidified the Internet as a major cultural phenomenon.

As we moved into the new millennium, it became increasingly clear that the conservative walls erected by schools were unlikely to resist the juggernaut of digital forms of reading and writing growing outside those walls. Despite many calls for action among scholars and researchers committed to promoting the integration of digital technologies into curriculum and classroom instruction, other than the acquisition of hardware, the pace of change in schools has been relatively slow.

Given the revolutionary changes that digital forms of reading and writing imply for schooling, relatively little research has been conducted to guide educators in their efforts to accommodate digital literacies into curriculum and instruction. For example, Kamil, Kim, and Intrator, (2000) documented the miniscule proportion of articles devoted to digital literacies in the field's leading research journals. The influential, yet controversial, National Reading Panel report (2000) commissioned by the U.S. Congress found only 21 studies published in technology and reading instruction that met their criteria for rigor, which was too few for the panel to draw conclusions. Reviews of the research literature related to digital technologies and literacy and published periodically since the early 1990s invariably conclude that the research base includes many studies of questionable conceptual or methodological rigor. There have also been calls for different research questions and methodologies that might more directly inform practitioners.

When compared to the small number of research studies, the scholarly literature related to digital literacies is dominated by reflections and commentary on the changing landscape of literacy (e.g., Bruce, 2003), theoretical perspectives on what those changes mean and how they can be interpreted (e.g., Alvermann, 2002), calls for more research (e.g., Kamil et al., 2000), and admonitions to the field stating that the interest in and response to digital literacies has been inadequate (e.g., Leu, 2006). That literature is supplemented by many books, articles, and Web sites offering innovative approaches and activities for using digital technologies in literacy instruction. This more practitioner-oriented literature rarely springs from, or is supported by, rigorously conducted research, nor is it often conceptualized in terms of accommodating new conceptions of literacy.

SOME ILLUSTRATIVE EXAMPLES OF ACCOMMODATION

In this section, we briefly highlight a few examples of how digital literacies might be accommodated into new conceptions of literacy instruction and of the type of issues that result in doing so. We first give examples drawn from traditional areas of reading instruction followed by examples from a more contemporary view that integrates reading and writing instruction. For readers who wish to become familiar with the full range of topics, issues, and research concerning how digital technologies have been integrated into literacy instruction, we recommend the following sources: (1) the *International Handbook of Literacy and Technology Volume 2* (McKenna, Labbo, Kieffer, & Reinking, 2006), (2) two comprehensive reviews of the literature pertaining to digital technologies and literacy for young children (Blok, Oostdam, Otter, & Overmaat, 2002; Labbo & Reinking, 2003; see also Labbo, this volume), and (3) the chapter on learning to read in the *Cambridge Handbook of Multimedia Learning* (Reinking, 2005).

TRADITIONAL READING INSTRUCTION

Traditional reading instruction can be divided roughly into three fundamental areas: decoding texts (automatically identifying words for fluent reading), comprehending texts, and instilling an enjoyment of reading. Instructional applications involving digital technologies have been used and studied in each of these areas, and each area illustrates the potential to accommodate, rather than to more superficially assimilate, digital literacies into conceptions of literacy instruction. Each of the examples illustrates the following characteristic, which we selected from among the many potential attributes and characteristics of digital texts that have implications for accommodating digital literacies: digital technologies permit reading to be an interactive and multimedia experience that respond to the needs of an individual learner.

Decoding. Using digital technologies for decoding has been exploited in many ways in literacy instruction. Digital texts have been created to provide various types of assistance and instruction aimed at helping beginning readers identify difficult or unfamiliar words in ways aimed ultimately at creating more independent readers. For example, a beginning reader might, under certain circumstances, be given the option of clicking on an unfamiliar word to hear it pronounced. Several commercial software programs have these capabilities and many studies document the conditions under which these capabilities might be used effectively, often focusing on students who are having difficulty learning to read (Olson & Wise, 2006). These applications may reshape, if not undermine, some conventional notions about reading texts and teaching beginning reading. For example, what defines a text's difficulty when these supports are available? How does it reshape fundamental pedagogical concepts such as matching a reader's ability to the difficulty of the text?

Comprehending. How would a view of vocabulary development, a dimension of comprehending texts change if a reader can click to see a context-specific definition that goes far beyond a standard dictionary, perhaps including a video illustrating the word's meaning? The availability of such a capability has long been shown to have positive benefits for vocabulary development and comprehension of texts, and much more sophisticated approaches are becoming part of online reading. For example, a new extension can be added to one of the popular Internet browsers that provides automatic links to hundreds of authoritative sources defining terms and concepts when a reader clicks on any word in any text displayed by the browser. Having that capability makes the meanings of new vocabulary automatically more contextual, more incidental, less intrusive, and potentially more effective than the way vocabulary is typically taught in conventional reading instruction.

How might those possibilities lead us to rethink vocabulary instruction and its relation to comprehending a text? That is, how would this application be accommodated within our conception of literacy instruction? Other applications have similarly interesting and important implications for reading instruction in the area of comprehension. For example, could the Internet more readily facilitate critical reading when texts from different sources on the same topic can easily be compared and contrasted and a variety of new possibilities exist for determining veracity and reliability? More generally, should our definitions of comprehension or our instructional emphases be modified in light of online reading and sources such as the Internet provides?

Instilling enjoyment in reading. Texts displayed digitally can be presented in multimedia formats that are dynamic rather than static, and they can be interactive and supportive of an individual reader's needs. Thus they are likely to be more inherently interesting and motivating to students than conventional printed texts. That view has been the underlying assumption for several commercial programs offering digital versions of popular children's books, which have also been the object of considerable research. Children who read these digital books can receive various types of assistance during reading, see clever animations related to or sometimes tangential to the story, select alternative routes through the story, and so forth. The research on these books is somewhat mixed, but overall it suggests that digital stories are highly motivating and under the right conditions are otherwise beneficial to children's developing literacy skills (e.g., see DeJong & Bus, 2004). Clearly, there are some playful and enjoyable aspects of digital reading and writing that not only initiate children into digital literacies but may also increase their overall motivation to read and their engagement in reading (Labbo, 1996). As this example illustrates, accommodating digital literacies into our conceptions of reading instruction may mean recognizing that digital texts have some advantages over printed texts, which is a possibility not readily embraced by many literacy educators.

CONTEMPORARY LITERACY INSTRUCTION

For many educators and scholars, separating reading and writing instruction into two distinct curricular areas is unnatural and inappropriate. They consider reading and writing to be essentially complementary, inseparable forms of communication that should be merged seamlessly into the curriculum. They also elevate the value of literacy as it occurs in everyday life (as opposed to a narrower academic view of literacy), and similarly they incorporate a wider range of purposes and media into their conceptions of literacy.

Accommodating digital literacies within conceptions of literacy instruction reinforces and fits well with that view. Reading and writing are clearly more closely connected in digital environments and more often involve authentic purposes for communication. E-mail is a prime example. Likewise, emerging genres of online collaborative writing (e.g., wikis) means reading closely what other authors have written before adding one's own modifications to the text. Seeking information on the Internet may entail e-mailing an individual for more information or responding directly to an author to express an opinion, to point out erroneous information, and so forth. Constructing a Web page or developing an informative slide show for a presentation means mastering multiple modes of expression using various multimedia effects and genres. Thus adopting more contemporary views of literacy instruction opens up a natural space for accommodating digital literacies into conceptualizations of literacy instruction.

HOW WILL DIGITAL LITERACIES ULTIMATELY BE ACCOMMODATED?

In this chapter, we highlighted the need for a new conception of literacy instruction that accommodates digital literacies. We pointed out that despite the increasingly wide use of digital technologies outside of school and the increasing access to necessary technologies in schools, digital literacies have not been fully accommodated into conceptions of literacy instruction. Consequently, there is a widening gap between inside-of-school and outside-of-school literacies, in part because conceptions of literacy instruction in schools remain largely associated with the technologies of print. We also outlined some of the difficulties and challenges that explain the relatively meager and perfunctory response of educators and researchers to the imperatives of digital literacies, despite the calls for more attention to that issue in the literature and the resources made available by the field's largest professional organizations. Finally, we gave some examples of how digital literacies have been or might be accommodated into literacy instruction in terms of traditional reading instruction, and how adopting a more contemporary view of literacy instruction is more accommodating to digital literacies.

In closing, we draw attention to what is arguably the most important factor that might stem or turn the tide toward accommodating digital literacies into literacy instruction. It is based on one of the most robust findings in the literature related to integrating technology into instruction. In a word, it is *beliefs*. That is, the most important factor in determining how digital technologies are used in literacy instruction are the beliefs of educators, researchers, and policy makers about the essential goals of literacy instruction and the role of digital technologies in helping to achieve the goals that they value. If they believe that the longstanding conventional goals of literacy instruction rooted in print are essential, they are likely to conceptualize digital technologies as merely intriguing tools in service of those conventional goals. In short, they will assimilate digital literacies into curriculum and instruction. If they open themselves up to new conceptions of literacy consistent with the existing digital world, and they reformulate their beliefs accordingly, they are more likely to genuinely accommodate digital literacies into instruction. We hope this chapter makes a substantive contribution toward the latter transformation.

REFERENCES

Alvermann, D. E. (Ed.). (2002). *Adolescents and literacies in a digital world.* New York: Peter Lang.

Blok, H., Oostdam, R., Otter, M. E., & Overmaat, M. (2002). Computer-assisted instruction in support of beginning reading instruction: A review. *Review of Educational Research, 72,* 101–130.

Bruce, C. (Ed.). (2003). *Literacy in the information age: Inquiries into meaning making with new technologies.* Newark, DE: International Reading Association.

Cuban, L. (2001). *Oversold & underused: Computers in the classroom.* Cambridge, Mass.: Harvard University Press.

DeJong, M. T., & Bus, A. G. (2004). The efficacy of electronic books in fostering kindergarten children's emergent story understanding. *Reading Research Quarterly, 39,* 378–393.

Flood, J., & Lapp, D. (1995). Broadening the lens: Toward an expanded conceptualization of literacy. In K. A. Hinchman, D. J. Leu, & C. K. Kinzer (Eds.), *Perspectives on literacy research and practice: The 44th Yearbook of the National Reading Conference* (pp. 1–16). Chicago, IL: National Reading Conference.

Guzzetti, B. J., & Gamboa, M. (2004). Zines for social justice: Adolescent girls writing on their own. *Reading Research Quarterly, 39,* 404–436.

International Society for Technology in Education. (2002). *The National Educational Technology Standards* (NETS) Project is an ongoing initiative of the International Society for Technology in Education. Available online: http://cnets.iste.org/

Kamil, M. L., Kim, H., & Intrator, S. (2000). Effects of other technologies on literacy and literacy learning. In M. L. Kamil, P. B. Mosenthal , P. D. Pearson, & R. Barr (Eds.), *Handbook of reading research* (Vol. 3, pp. 773–791). Mahwah, NJ: Lawrence Erlbaum Associates.

Labbo, L. D. (1996). A semiotic analysis of young children's symbol making in a classroom computer center. *Reading Research Quarterly, 31,* 356–385.

Labbo, L., & Reinking, D. (2003). Computers and early literacy education. In N. Hall, J. Larson, & J. Marsh (Eds.), *Handbook of early childhood literacy* (338–354). London, UK: Sage.

Leu, D. J. (2006). New literacies, reading research, and the challenges of change: A deictic perspective. In J. Hoffman, D. L. Schallert, C. M. Fairbanks, J. Worthy, & B. Maloch (Eds.), *55th yearbook of the National Reading Conference.* Oak Creek, WI: National Reading Conference.

Mason, G., Blanchard, J., & Daniel, D. (1983). *Computer applications in reading.* Newark, DE: International Reading Association.

McKenna, M. C., Labbo, L. D., Kieffer, R. D., & Reinking, D. (Eds.). (2006). *International handbook of literacy and technology* (Vol. II). Mahwah, NJ: Erlbaum.

National Reading Panel. (2000). *Teaching Children to Read: Summary Report.* Retrieved from the National Reading panel website: http//www.nationalreadingpanel.org/

Olson, R. K., & Wise, B. (2006). Computer-based remediation for reading and related phonological disabilities. In M. C. McKenna, L. D., Labbo, R. D. Kieffer, & D. Reinking (Eds.), *International handbook of literacy and technology* (Vol. II, pp. 57–74). Mahwah, NJ: Erlbaum.

Papert, S. (1993). *The children's machine: Rethinking school in the age of the computer.* New York: Basic Books.

P. L. 107–110. (2002). *No Child Left Behind Act of 2001.* [WWW document]. URL http://www.nclb.gov/

Reinking, D. (2005). Multimedia learning of reading. In R. E. Mayer (Ed.), *Cambridge handbook of multimedia learning* (pp. 355–374). New York: Cambridge University Press.

U.S. Department of Education. Institute for Education Sciences. National Center for Education Statistics. (2006). *Internet access in U.S. public schools and classrooms: 1994–2005.* (NCES 2007–020). Washington, DC: U.S. Government Printing Office.

Part Three

CHILDHOOD LITERACY BEYOND THE CLASSROOM

Chapter Eleven

CHILD CULTURE AND POPULAR CULTURE

Thomas Newkirk

McGuffey's Fifth Eclectic Reader, published in 1879, begins with a story called "The Good Reader." In the story, a young farm girl, Ernestine, skilled in oral reading from her many experiences reading letters for her neighbors, is in the court of Frederick the Great, who is tired from hunting and becomes frustrated when neither of his pages can successfully read a letter from a poor widow petitioning that her son be excused from military service. Ernestine steps forward and successfully conveys the emotion of the letter—and from that one piece of successful reading comes an avalanche of positive results. The petition is granted, and Ernestine's father gets a position in the king's court. Even the two pages, remanded by the king to develop their reading skills, become successful professionals "chiefly due to their good elocution" (p. 42). Literacy as presented here is not a neutral "skill," but a mode of socialization; the reader takes on the role of responsible, empathetic adult. As in many of the *McGuffey* stories, the moral is hardly subtle—reading is a practical skill that is linked to moral behavior and can lead to social advancement.

This moral dimension has been part of reading instruction in schools since the early *New England Primer* with its simplified religious lessons. The *McGuffey Readers* were full of moral uplift. For example, William Ellery Channing's sermon warned, "Erase all thought and fear of God from a community, and selfishness and sensuality would absorb the whole man" (p. 285). By contrast, there was deep suspicion of novels during this period because they were so focused on entertainment that did not pretend to be self-improving—romance, adventure, even the macabre. They had no place in formal school instruction and were seen as particularly corrupting to women. Booth Tarkington, one of the most popular authors of the early twentieth century, recalled the way that he would read dime novels, tucked inside the official classroom textbook, a practice that continues to the present day as the official literacy of the school competes with (and loses to) unofficial literacy written (and often drawn) for popular consumption. Even in the twentieth century, as novels began to assume a central place in a reading curriculum, the case for reading them was often a moral one. The reading of quality literature was not a mere escape and not a cheap form of pleasure. It was a way to confront profound human dilemmas, to enter the experience of others, and, in doing so, gain greater sensitivity and empathy. As Matthew Arnold predicted at the end of the nineteenth century, literature would begin to take on the civilizing function of religion.

As print literacy faced competition from the visual media, even the act of reading itself came to be seen as a positive form of self-control. Reading is a skill that must be taught and learned, unlike the watching of television. It typically moves at a slower pace, requiring that the reader postpone the need for quick gratification. Reading requires the reader to operate actively as co-producer of the text, transforming written words into internalized images and action. For many parents and educators, silent sustained reading (of just about anything) is a deeply reassuring practice; it is a sign that the child can assume the role of student who can control inclinations to move about and to socialize. He or she can assume the particularized identity of a reader, making a personal transaction with the text, in sharp contrast to a homogenizing mass culture in which the individual participates in a more collective way (as at football game), submerging oneself in the group. School literacy often tends to define itself against visually mediated popular culture—it doesn't draw on that culture; it resists it. This chapter focuses on the wisdom of this opposition.

MEDIA HABITS OF U.S. CHILDREN

If popular visual media *are* in competition with school literacy, there is no question which side is winning. The most thorough study of media habits of U.S. children and young adults was conducted by the Kaiser Family Foundation and published as *Generation M: Media in the Lives of 8–18 Year Olds* (Roberts, Foehr, & Rideout, 2005). The authors of the study concluded the children they studied were "media-saturated"—often exposed to a seemingly improbable 9 to 10 hours of media per day. It seemed that the limit had been reached in terms of possible exposure (they estimate 6 to 6.5 hours a day), but *Generation M* documents an increase in multitasking, such as playing video games while listening to music on an iPod. Multitasking was particularly common among African American children who were engaged with two or more media 31 percent of the time in which they were involved with media.

The study both reinforces and challenges common assumptions about media use. Among the findings are these:

- *There are major gender differences in media use.* Girls spend more time listening to music and using Instant Messenger. Boys spend more time playing video games—38 percent as opposed to 31 percent for girls who report playing one in the last 24 hours. Although neither gender spends a great of time reading, girls spend more time reading books than boys (29 minutes compared to 19 minutes for boys).
- *There are major racial differences in media use.* African American children watch far more television than white children, with Hispanic children falling in the middle. White children watch an average of 2 hours 45 minutes per day; African American children watch 4 hours 5 minutes per day—a difference of 1 hour 20 minutes per day. Hispanic children watch 3 hours 23 minutes per day. The report also found that African American families were more likely to have television on during meal times, although this is a common practice among all racial groups.
- *Family education does not significantly affect TV watching.* Surprisingly, the study found that children of college-educated parents watched 3 hours 3 minutes per day; children of parents with a high school education watched 3 hours 12 minutes per day. Family education, however, does correlate with somewhat more self-chosen reading.
- *Comedy is the favorite TV genre across gender and racial groups.* If combined with reality shows (often watched as comedies), these two types account for more than 50 percent of the preferences. Paradoxically, the shows watched by the grandparents of the children studied would be more likely to feature guns and shooting, particularly in westerns like *Gunsmoke, The Rifleman, The Life and Legend of Wyatt Earp,* and *Wanted: Dead or Alive.* This finding corresponds with the general perception that young adults get much of their political commentary as satire—on shows like *The Daily Show with John Stewart* or *The Colbert Report.*
- *Reading is a small part of the media diet.* An average of 45 minutes per day is spent with print media. For boys, less than half of this time (19 minutes) is spent with books. Reading books declines after age 10; the authors speculate this occurs because this activity is associated with schoolwork, and children choose to spend their leisure time doing something else.
- *Heavy video game players tend to read more than light video game users.* One of the most counterintuitive findings of the study focused on the habits of heavy media users (e.g., those who watch more than five hours a day of television or spend more than one hour a day playing video games). One would expect that heavy use of video games would occur at the expense of reading (or even other media use). But the study found that children who were active in any media use tended to be active in all media use. Active video game players tended to be heavy TV watchers and even more active readers than light users (by 14 minutes per day). They even reported more physical activity by a statistically significant margin.
- Although the media use might suggest a "crisis" in reading achievement, there is no evidence for a decline in reading scores during the last 35 years. In fact, there is some evidence of slight improvement. According to the National Assessment for Educational Progress ("National Trends," 2006), reading scores have been stable since 1971, particularly at the upper grades, with a modest improvement in the

4th-grade assessment. To put this trend another way, children today read as well, if not better, than their parents did when they were in school. Is there cause for alarm?

The virtually constant exposure to mass entertainment is a source of concern to almost everyone involved in child care and education—parents, educators, psychologists, social workers, pediatricians, and even those involved in the more traditional forms of family entertainment. For example, the National Park Service recently reported a steep drop in park attendance in the Northeast, about 20 percent at Acadia National Park and the Cape Cod National Seashore (MacQuarrie, 2006). The Nature Conservancy, a nonprofit conservation and advocacy group, attributed this decline to changing patterns of family entertainment. People, particularly children, are spending more time on the Internet, often playing video games, and less with their families in natural park settings.

Anecdotal reports from educators suggest that children spend less time with board games and for some middle-class children, a great proportion of play time is structured. Even school recesses are less frequent and more tightly regulated. These restrictions—combined with the dominance of mass media—may also lead to the extinguishment of traditional forms of child play. Opie and Opie (1969) catalogued children's games in post–World War II England and published their findings in their classic text, *Children's Games in Street and Playground: Chasing, Catching, Seeking, Hunting, Racing, Duelling, Exerting, Daring, Guessing, Acting, Pretending.* This title alone suggests the rich lore of children that may be lost as "the street" becomes perceived as too dangerous and the playground too regulated, and as the television becomes a substitute for play.

This general pattern of family change has been analyzed by sociologist Robert Putnam (2000) in his book, *Bowling Alone: The Collapse and Revival of American Community.* According to Putnam, the members of the post–World War II generation were joiners; popular culture was often a *local* form of association—bowling leagues, bridge clubs, piano recitals, PTA meetings, company picnics. Putnam demonstrated that this high level of involvement is closely associated with a number of social and personal benefits such as higher voting rates, more charitable giving, and even better personal health. For a variety of reasons (time spent driving, two-earner households, more time with home entertainment media), subsequent generations have fallen away from community involvement. A recent study of friendship in this country supports that the number of close friends or confidants has dropped in the past 20 years from an average of 2.94 to 2.08 per person, with respondents less likely to name individuals outside the immediate family (McPherson, Smith-Lovin, & Brashears, 2006). From this perspective, children's media exposure is part of a wider social problem of isolation.

Another concern about the influence of popular culture is the way in which mass media target young children as consumers, almost from the time of their birth, and justify the process in the name of "empowering" children. Schor (2004) in her study, *Born to Buy*, describes the ways in which advertising is not limited to commercials; many cartoons for young children serve as promotions to buy products depicted in the animation. Advertisers target the sugar craving of children to sell profoundly unhealthy products, and they offer guidance to children in how to "nag" parents to make the purchase. They also market an unhealthy vision of preadolescent sexual attractiveness with seven- and eight-year-old girls wearing tight tank tops that expose their midsections. Increasingly, advertisers are bypassing traditional commercials (which kids can flip away from) in favor of product placement in movies and television shows, so the dividing line between advertisement and entertainment is blurred. Even functional items like Band-Aids are designed and marketed as a form of toy. These marketing techniques, critics argue, are detrimental to children—they encourage poor eating habits, addictive behavior, acquisitiveness, and, ultimately, poor psychological health.

The exposure to media violence is also believed to promote aggressive behavior in young viewers. This position is forcefully advocated by the American Academy of Pediatricians (AAP) that claims that this exposure is "a significant risk to the health of children" (American Academy of Pediatricians, Joint Statement, 2000, n.p.). In its presentation to Congress, representatives from the AAP summarize their position:

> At this time, well over 1000 studies—including reports from the Surgeon General's office, the National Institute of Mental Health, and numerous studies conducted by leading figures within our medical and public health organizations … point overwhelmingly to a causal connection between media violence and aggressive behavior in some children. The conclusion of the public health community, based on over 30 years of research, is that viewing entertainment violence can lead to increases in aggressive attitudes, values and behavior, particularly in children. Its effects are measurable and long-lasting. Moreover, prolonged viewing of media violence can lead to emotional desensitization toward violence in real life. (n.p.)

Critics of the AAP position point out, however, that the increase in media violence and the emergence of home video games in the 1990s coincided with a dramatic decrease in youth crime (Juvenile Arrests for Selected Offenses, 2006), with the rate of juvenile crime at the millennium somewhat lower than it was in 1973 (Juveniles as Offenders, 1999). In other words, children today are somewhat less likely to become juvenile offenders than their grandparents were. These statistics cast some doubt on the causative weight that the APP and others assign to media culture.

One general criticism of this line of research is the depiction of children as entirely passive and malleable recipients of the messages of media culture—

and the ability of researchers to determine these effects, often without interviewing children. David Buckingham, author of *After the Death of Childhood: Growing Up in the Age of Electronic Media* (Roberts et al., 2000), summarizes this problem:

> Children, in particular, are implicitly seen to be passive and defenseless in the face of media manipulation. Audiences are not seen here as socially differentiated, or as capable of responding critically to what they watch. Television, because of its inherently "visual" nature . . . is effectively seen to bypass cognition entirely. It requires no intellectual, emotional or imaginative investment . . . no empirical evidence is offered for these assertions: they seem so self-evident, it is as though none were considered necessary. (p. 38)

One of the favored analogies of the AAP is the comparison of media violence to cigarette smoking. Smoking does not always result in lung disease because different people have different threshold or triggers for disease; in the same way media violence does not always promote actual violence because some people are more resistant to the message. The analogy, however, breaks down because lung cells cannot critically resist the effect of carcinogens, yet children are not so passive. According to researchers like Buckingham (2000) and Tobin (2000), children do make complex judgments about media, but the behaviorist "effects" paradigm of most of the media violence research fails to elicit children's judgments of the media they watch.

This anxiety about media culture and its effects on children affects profoundly the ways in which literacy instruction is approached in schools. If media culture is viewed primarily as "toxic" and exploitative—as violent, sexist, and manipulative—it logically follows that instruction will be viewed as a counterforce to the media culture, as a counterbalancing that can direct students toward a more local and neglected form of popular culture, and to high-quality print literature. Many writing workshop approaches in elementary schools actually do take this stance—prohibiting any form of violence in writing and discouraging students from "inauthentic" topics derived from the media (e.g., superhero space adventures), while promoting writing that deals with nontechnological experiences with family, friends, animals, and the natural world (e.g., Parsons, 2005). This focus, it might be argued, pushes students to define an "authentic" identity that is not preconstructed by the media. Although not didactic in the way *McGuffey* readers are, this approach to literacy instruction works to inculcate a set of values associated with serious established adult genres (e.g., memoir, nature writing, profiles)—a responsiveness to others, a sense of stewardship toward the natural world, and a particularized sense of one's own identity. Literacy and morality are intertwined: the "good reader" is not simply a skilled reader, but someone who takes on the ethical responsibility of being sensitive toward others.

EMBRACING THE MEDIA CULTURE

Over history, technological changes have profoundly affected literacy practices. These changes are often resisted by an adult generation that is comfortable and proficient in the established forms of literacy. In his dialogue, *Phaedrus*, Plato's character Socrates laments the increasing popularity of the new technology of his day—writing (Plato, 1973). He argues that writing is inferior to oral dialogue that allows for an active and continued exchange among participants (where writing says the same thing over and over again). He also claimed that because information can be stored in written form, this technology will also foster forgetfulness. Similarly, independent silent reading, made possible through the dissemination of books after the invention of the printing press, was viewed with great suspicion by religious authorities, who feared that it would lead to idiosyncratic and heretical readings of the Bible. In the first great European novel, *Don Quixote*, Cervantes plays with the common belief that excessive isolated reading of popular fiction can lead to madness.

Johnson (2005) satirizes this generational reaction by imagining the resistance to reading books if it were a literacy practice that came *after* video game playing:

> Reading books chronically underestimates the senses. Unlike the longstanding tradition of game playing—which engages the child in a vivid, three dimensional world filled with moving images and musical soundscapes, navigated and controlled with complex muscular movements—books are simply a barren string of words on a page. Only a small portion of the brain devoted to processing written language is activated during reading, while games engage the full range of sensory and motor cortices.
>
> . . . perhaps the most dangerous property of these books is the fact that they follow a fixed linear path. You can't control the narrative in any fashion—you simply sit back and have the story dictated to you. For those of us raised on interactive narratives, this property may seem astonishing. (pp. 19–20)

Johnson emphasizes that he is writing parody here—he does not endorse this condemnation of book reading. Rather, he is pointing out the ways in which adult practitioners of established literacies are insensitive to attractions of new ones and are unaware of the cognitive demands made on users.

In his book, *Everything Bad Is Good for You*, Johnson (2005) makes the contrarian argument that the media culture, and television in particular, is responsible for an *increase* in intelligence of the general population—a phenomenon he calls the "Flynn effect." James Flynn was a civil rights activist who initially set out to prove that the lower scores of African Americans were due to their environment, and not, as Arthur Jensen had argued, to genetics. In sorting through data, he discovered that the intelligence scores of African Americans had actually been steadily going up, an untold story. He also found that the scores of whites had gone up as well. In fact, the intelligence scores for the U.S. population had gone up by more than 13 points in the past 45 years, a change masked by the regular renorming of tests to keep the average at 100.

Johnson proposes three possible explanations for this increase. These include better diet, improved education, and the increasing complexity of the media environment. Neither dietary changes nor school improvement is a plausible primary explanation. The major dietary improvements ended at about the time this increase began, and there has been no major transformation in schooling to account for such a rise (as we have seen, school performance in reading has been flat). The component of the test responsible for the increase has been problem solving and the recognition of visual patterns, a form of cognition that is not likely to be affected by school learning, which tends to focus on verbal intelligence. Johnson concludes that rather than being a passive media, television is more complicated and challenging than it was in previous generations—with multiple plots, irresolution, parody, and quotation from other media (a staple of *The Simpsons*). Movies like *The Matrix* or *Harry Potter and the Goblet of Fire* would have been nearly unintelligible (not to mention terrifying) to those who crowded theaters in the 1950s to watch Fess Parker play Davy Crockett. The Pokemon card trading on school playgrounds was exponentially more complex than the trading of baseball cards decades earlier.

Video games are regularly viewed as a time-wasting pastime that detracts from academic performance, particularly among boys. Video games emerged in the early 1970s as young entrepreneurs tried to make video versions of arcade games and then later developed ways to play these games on home consoles. The first successful early game was *Pong*, which resembled ping pong, followed in 1980 by the hugely successful *Pac-Man* created by Atari, which helped bring arcade revenues to $5 billion per year (Kent, 2001). Video games became more complex with games like *Final Fantasy* and *SimCity,* and Nintendo and Sony developed affordable consoles for home video use. A literacy scholar, James Gee (2003), argues that contrary to the popular perception of this medium as mindless and instantly gratifying, video games provide stimulating learning environments. For example, video games are often calibrated for difficulty (different levels of the game) so that gamers can work on an appropriately challenging level; they provide regular feedback on performance; they require the gamer to assume a variety of identities and to imagine the game from the standpoint of these created characters. Users learn the game through playing the game, and they get meaningful and interesting practice in following the rules of the game; they tend to form collaborative communities (on-line and in person) to discuss gaming strategies. Other literacy researchers have argued that boys regularly enter a "flow state" of optimal intellectual engagement when playing video games—yet rarely feel that connection to school work (Smith and Wilhelm, 2002).

This more appreciative perspective on popular visual media suggests two problems with the orthodox approach to literacy instruction and its focus on established literary genres. First, it fails to recognize that composing in the wider culture is increasingly multimodal. The third most commonly visited Internet site is MySpace.com, which features personally designed Web sites in which contributors represent themselves through photos, links to music, friendship lists, and any other personal information they choose to provide. From a traditional standpoint, this Web site building would be seen as a distraction. Yet, scholars like Gee (2003) and other leaders of the new literacies movement, would view it as a new multimodal genre with intriguing possibilities for identity construction. With some assistance, students can also learn to create digital stories that integrate text, voice, and photographs with a musical background. Relatively simple technology allows the composer to lay down various tracks (e.g., a visual track, a sound track, a commentary track) along a timeline so they will play simultaneously. Powerpoint similarly allows for the integration of text, photographs, or any digital source that can often serve as a backdrop to an oral presentation, as Al Gore demonstrated in his presentation in *An Inconvenient Truth*. Of course, multimodality is nothing new. A traditional church service is an integration of multiple and reinforcing modes of expression—architectural, musical, literary, and visual, such as the contemplation of stories in the stained glass windows, which themselves often combine text and picture. Beginning writers typically combine drawing and writing, and they frequently accompany their composing with sound effects. This more expansive multimodal model of composing also allows students to incorporate more representational skills; for many boys, their drawing ability develops faster than their ability to write. Thus a stronger system can support a weaker or slower developing system, and the child can feel successful.

Literacy instruction that resists (or ignores) the popular culture loyalties of children may introduce a cultural and gender bias into school learning. Few educational problems are more disturbing than the gap between white and African American children, and perhaps the amount of television watching contributes to this problem, as many leaders like Bill Cosby have argued. Yet if this visual screen culture is so prominent in the family life of these children—if it constitutes the primary cultural resource that many bring to school—it would seem irresponsible to dismiss these experiences as irrelevant or detrimental to literacy learning. Television programs are, after all, usually written; they have characters, plot, dialogue, often humor, and drama. Clearly, bridges can be built from these programs to story writing in schools; often this takes no "instruction" on the part of the teacher; many students will choose this story material if they have the opportunity.

National educational assessments have also established that the literacy gap between males and females is substantial in the area of writing approaching the gap between white and African American students ("Average Writing Scores," 2002). This gap is six time larger than the advantage that boys have in mathematics, which, except at the most advanced levels, has largely disappeared. ("Trends in Average Mathematical Scale Scores by Gender," 2004).

Researchers and policy makers have offered various explanations for this gap and have even disputed the significance of it. One possible explanation centers on the tacit valuation of genre and the way that valuation coincides with certain class and gender tastes. For example, memoir and realistic fiction dealing with important social themes is often viewed as having the greatest "cultural capital"—these genre mark the student as a "serious" reader, a member of a reading elite. Not coincidentally, these genres are the staple of the reading clubs formed by professional middle and upper middle class women. Many adult men do not consider themselves "readers" at all because they are not novel readers, even though they may read regularly at work, read newspapers and magazine, and increasingly get their information from the Internet. In schools, nonfiction, which boys tend to prefer over fiction, is only recently being given prominence in literacy instruction. Genres that have been traditionally popular with males—trade magazines, comics, cartoons, satire, graphic novels, science fiction—are marginalized, if not actually proscribed. This emphasis leads boys to conclude that school reading is gendered female and does not fit the identity they are shaping for themselves, so that by the high school years, advanced placement literature classes are composed almost entirely of girls.

THE PERMEABLE CURRICULUM

The term *permeable curriculum* originated with literacy research by Dyson (1993) who uses the term to describe the complex interaction that can occur between children's "unofficial" worlds and the school curriculum, which is porous enough to allow some of the outside to come in. Dyson rejects the common deficit stereotype of urban children, which assumes that only one kind of cultural experience (e.g., being read to by parents) can lead to a good start in literacy learning. Rather, Dyson sees the urban landscape children live in as rich—with children coming in to school knowing song lyrics, plots from television and movies, jump rope rhymes, sports affiliations, and family stories. Friendship groups are maintained and defined by talk about commonly held cultural knowledge (e.g., the plot of the Disney film *The Mighty Ducks*). Unlike media critics who view children as passive victims of unhealthy cultural messages, Dyson views children as capable of appropriating and transforming these cultural resources for their own purposes. One friendship group that Dyson studied virtually adopted Coach Bombay, the hockey coach in Mighty Ducks, as a friend and topic of conversation. Group members would continually reference the movie as they worked on their writing. In other words, Dyson does not take the deterministic view of many media critics who feel confident they can predict "the effects" of media. The "effect" of a Barbie doll or a Disney movie cannot be predetermined by adult media critics. Culture circulates and is modified as it does.

The permeable curriculum allows some of these cultural affiliations into the classroom to provide a context, material, and motivation for literacy learning. Literacy instruction that is compartmentalized and separated from the unofficial worlds of children simply does not make sense, leaving the only motivation for such work to be in pleasing the teacher or "doing well." As Tolstoy once remarked, for humans only the living and complex are easy. Simplified skills tasks and worksheets are stripped of meaning-making contexts. Dyson's own painstaking analysis of texts and contexts of writing also disrupt stable conceptions of genre, as children are continually orchestrating their cultural and social resources in new ways, creating "hybrid" texts that contain traces of these multiple worlds. Each piece of student writing is, to some degree, an original modification or "remixing" of available genres.

To appreciate the conceptual power of this form of analysis, it is useful to examine actual examples of students' writing from a study that I conducted (Newkirk, 2002). The following piece was written in a 4th-grade class and was one of a series of stories written by a group of friends. In each story, the group was confronted with some danger and had to devise a plan to deal with it. The italics in the story indicate the source of the dialogue, based on an interview with the writer and the writer's teacher:

Motorcycle Mice! (the class had been reading from the Beverly Cleary Runaway Ralph series)

There once was (this opening is a literary code that places in it a fictional fairy tale space) five mice named Basil, Jimmy, Donny, Jake, and Russell (these are the actual names of his friends in the class). Basil was a crazy old mouse on a motorcycle who always took stupid risks. Basil had 1 broken leg, 1 broken arm, and 4 broken fingers! But he still rides his motorcycle. Jimmy was a mouse who always got in fights and always did stupid things. Donny is the kind of mouse that always made up these funny dances. Jake is a mouse that always takes a mouse's jacket without asking! (here the author is pointing out some of the traits of his friends in a teasing way). Russell is a mouse that always sits around and shoves cheese up his nose and then pops them out and hits us! It hurts a lot especially when it hits you on the tail or in the ear! (a touch of gross humor that singles out Russell for special attention). One day when Basil, Donny, Jake , and I (the constant reiteration of names emphasizes the friendship group)were riding our motorcycles. Basil was in front of every one of us. Basil was going so fast that his tail was wandering around so much that it got caught in the spokes of his motorcycle! So Basil's tail came right off! Now Basil looks like a hamster (the author once had a hamster as a pet). Russell was going really fast too. Too fast. He was going so fast that when he ran over Basil's tail he crashed. Bye

Bye Russell, He got ate by the cat! (again, the specialness of Russell) Everybody was so mad at that cat. They wanted to get the cat back. (A classic revenge plot.) So Jimmy, Basil, Donny, and Jake (reiteration again) made a plan to get the cat back.

So here's the plan. Jake you go get some fish from the market. Basil, Donny, and I will distract the cat while you put the fish in the cat's food bowl. Then the cat will chase us but she will stop to eat the fish. Then we can go get some mouse traps. When she is eating her fish we can sneak up behind her and snap a mouse trap on her tail. Then Donny and Basil come out on your motorcycles and run over the cat's paws. (*this kind of visual action may come from watching Tom and Jerry cartoons*). That cat will never bother us again. And she never did. But Basil Donny, Jake, and I had a funeral for Russell. We invited every mouse. And they came. And all the mice said is we will remember Russell for the rest of our lives. (*Russell is now canonized*)

This writing accomplishes a great deal of "social work"—the constant reiteration of the names of the friends, and the special place given to Russell, whose death gives him a place of honor and significance. The writing draws on literacy sources, most notably the Beverly Cleary series that the author read in class, but also in the opening that places the story in a fictional space. The visual action involving the fish and mousetrap is a staple of cartoons like the Tom and Jerry series. Those who claim that children simply *copy* media plots in their writing typically fail to recognize the orchestration and "remixing" of multiple strands of child culture. As one 1st grader, a Star Wars fan, explained, it was always more interesting when he didn't "play by the movie."

Video games can also provide young writers with a scaffold that they can use in their own story writing. For example, a common narrative of these games is to traverse a space that is filled with dangers or obstacles where the protagonist has to use skills and weapons wisely to move from setting to setting, accomplishing "tasks" along the way. This general frame allowed two boys in one 1st-grade class to invent the kinds of dangers that their characters had to face. Abe chose to have his space filled with spikes, lava pans, snakes, and his favorite danger—killer bees. Jason created "lava robots," a giant robot, and a boiling cauldron of magic potion. In their writing they described, at considerable length, the tactics the protagonist uses to navigate the dangers represented in the drawing. Although the boys mentioned two video games that helped them imagine this space (the *Frogger* series and *Dangerous Hunts II*), they were clearly inventing their own stories using elements from the games.

Examples like these show students using writing for multiple purposes: to consolidate friendship, to improvise with features of the video culture they love, and to use the scaffold and props of this video culture to accomplish the *curricular* objective of developing fluency in writing. The teacher in this particular 1st-grade class, not coincidentally, enjoyed much of the same media the children watched; she was familiar with the Star Wars series and once announced to the class that *Spongebob Squarepants* was one of her favorite shows. When I asked Abe whether he preferred writing true or made-up stories he said he "wanted it to be fake" because there was no way he could include aliens or lava robots in a true story. With these made-up adventure stories, Abe noted, "kids in the class can bring their imagination out of their bodies.

CHILDHOOD AS PROJECTION

In Richard Ford's (2006) short story, "How Was It to Be Dead?," the main character must deal with the fact that his wife's ex-husband, gone for more than 20 years and legally declared dead, had suddenly reappeared. As he copes with this difficult situation, he offers this advice:

> I should say straight out: never tell anyone that you know how he or she feels unless you happen to be, just at that second, stabbing yourself with the very same knife in the very same place in the very same heart that he or she is stabbing. Because if you're not, then you don't know how the person feels. (p. 61)

More often, the claim to understand someone else's reality is a form of projection; one group superimposes its fears, hopes, and personal histories onto another—without decentering or disengaging from one's own perspective. A young, African American male teenager with sunglasses, wearing a hooded sweatshirt and baggy pants, stands at a street corner lost in the music of his iPod. Such an image can trigger fear among whites who project their worst racial fears onto this scene and keep their distance. The music is surely violent rap about cop killers and rape; African American males in particular are seen as "dry tinder," ready to act on the slightest suggestion. Any serious analysis of popular culture requires a bracketing of these stereotypes and preconceptions if there is to be any understanding of children's attraction to it.

This caution is especially important in any examination of childhood, which itself is not a biological fact, but an adult construction. The "good reader" in the *McGuffey's* reader was not an actual child, but an expression of adult desire for children to act in a certain way. Children's books are written by adults, and the awards they receive are given by adults. The conception of children as helpless and innocent is a relatively recent cultural construction, in the same way that that in earlier eras children were thought to be innately sinful or, before the seventeenth century in Europe, thought of as young adults. James Kincaid, a scholar of childhood and critical theory, as quoted in Jenkins (1998), writes:

> The child was there waiting . . . defenseless and alluring, with no substance, no threatening history, no independent insistences. As a category created but not occupied, the child could be the repositories of cultural needs or fears not adequately disposed on elsewhere. . . . The child carries for us things we cannot carry for ourselves, sometimes anxieties we want to be divorced from and sometimes pleasures so great we could not, without the child, know how to contain them. (p. 4)

This projecting, or depositing of needs, leads to a curious form of public discourse where youth culture is viewed as discontinuous from adult culture. Child obesity is a social problem, yet children eat from the same grocery bag (or at the same fast food restaurant) as their parents. Video game playing is corrupting young males, yet the average gamer is 33 years old (*Top Ten Industry Facts*). It may be unhealthy for so many children to have televisions in their own rooms, but such an arrangement allows parents to choose their own shows without negotiation or distraction. By treating these as distinct "youth" problems, adults can "deposit" or displace anxieties about their own lifestyle onto children, and even construct a narrative of cultural decline.

Clearly, there are elements of popular culture that are harmful to some children and young adults. It is naïve to believe that eating disorders are unrelated to the relentless exposure of girls to the "ideal" of super thinness, or to ignore the role of some rap and MTV videos in glamorizing ghetto street culture for some African American males, or to deny the possibility of video games becoming addictive and isolating, or to accept the current pattern of media exposure in families as entirely healthy. It is equally unproductive, however, to ignore the appeal of this culture and the pleasure children take in participating in it—or to prejudge it as mindless without ever engaging with it. As James Gee once noted, most of the critics of the video game *Grand Theft Auto* "couldn't get the car out of the garage" (personal communication, 2004).

Several years ago, I remember watching my nephew, then in middle school, play one of the first shooter video games that came under such criticism. The "shooter" moved through a dark warehouse from room to room, with enemy shooters popping out of hiding places. My nephew would change weapons with such fluidity that it almost seemed he was playing a musical instrument. He allowed me a turn, and I helplessly fumbled with the controls, and was "dead" in short order. The appeal, it seemed to me, was not the violence, but the challenge of anticipating a situation and having the right weapon at the right time. At a stage in his life, when little else was in his control, he was master of this domain.

CONCLUSION

The central feature of contemporary American childhood is the omnipresence of media, and a key question for educators is how to deal with this "saturation." In this chapter we have explored two broadly defined responses—one that views popular culture and literacy as in opposition and the other that is more open to media affiliations and views them as resources for literacy development. In the end, both perspectives are necessary. As Postman (1987) argued in *Teaching as a Conserving Activity*, schools need to make a stand in favor of thoughtful habits of mind, of reasonableness and sensitivity (even civility) that are in opposition to the glibness and superficiality, to the easy flattery, of much that comes over the popular media. Yet a blanket dismissal of popular culture leads to a defensive, embattled kind of instruction (and parenting). The barbarians are always at the gates—or even closer than that. At the very least, educators and parents need to perform that most difficult of tasks: to attempt to understand, from the child's point of view, the attractions and pleasures of this media culture. By extension, schools should acknowledge that children can draw from the narratives of popular culture, even video games, to develop fluency and storytelling skills. From this standpoint, the hybrid texts that children create—with elements from their multiple worlds—are wonders to contemplate.

REFERENCES

American Academy of Pediatricians. (2000). *Joint statement on the impact of entertainment violence on children* Congressional Public Health Summit, July 26. http://www.aap.org/advocacy/releases/jstmtevc.htm

Average Writing Scale Scores by Gender, Grades 4, 8, 12: 1998 and 2002. National Assessment of Educational Progress. Washington: Institute of Educational Sciences. http://nces.ed.gov/nationsreportcard/writing/results2002/scalegender-all.asp

Buckingham, D. (2000). *After the death of childhood: Growing up in the age of electronic media.* Polity Press: Cambridge England.

Dyson, A. H. (1993). *The social worlds of children learning to write in an urban primary school.* New York: Teachers College Press.

Ford, R. (2006). How was it to be dead? *The New Yorker* (August 28): 58–69.

Gee, J. (2003). *What video games have to teach us about learning and literacy.* New York: Palgrave.

Jenkins, H. (Ed.). (1998). *The children's culture reader.* New York: NYU Press.

Johnson, S. (2005). *Everything bad is good for you: How today's popular culture is actually making us smarter.* New York: Riverhead Books.

Juvenile Arrests for Selected Offenses—Table 316. (2006). *The 2006 United States Statistical Abstract: The National Data Book.* Washington: United States Census Bureau.

Juveniles as Offenders. (1999). Washington: Office of Juvenile Justice and Delinquency Prevention. http://ojjdp.ncjrs.org/ojstatbb/offenders/qa03201.asp?qaDate = 19990930

Kent, S. L. (2001). *The ultimate history of video games.* New York: Three Rivers Press.

MacQuarrie, B. (2006). Park officials fear trend toward the great indoors. *The Boston Globe* (August 21): B-1.

McGuffey's Fifth Eclectic Reader, Rev. Ed. (1879). Cincinnati: Van Antwerp, Bragg, and Co.

McPherson, M., Smith-Lovin, L., & Brashears, M.(2006). Social isolation in America. *American Sociological Review, 11* (June): 354–375.

National Trends in Reading by Average Scale Scores. (2006). Washington: Institute of Educational Sciences. http://nces.ed.gov/nationsreportcard/ltt/results2004/nat-reading-scalescore.asp.

Newkirk, T. (2002). *Misreading masculinity: Boys literacy and popular culture.* Portsmouth, NH: Heinemann.

Opie, I., & Opie, P. (1969). *Children's games in street and playground.* Oxford: Clarendon Press.

Parsons, S. (2005). *First grade writers: Units of study to help children plan, organize, and structure their writing.* Portsmouth: Heinemann.

Plato. 1973. *Phaedrus and the Seventh and Eighth Letters*. Trans. Walter Hamilton. London: Penguin.

Postman, N.(1987). *Teaching as a conserving activity*. New York: Delacorte.

Putnam, R. D. (2000). *Bowling alone: The collapse and revival of American community*. New York: Simon and Schuster.

Roberts, D. F., Foehr, U. G., & Rideout, V. (2005). *Generation M: Media in the lives of 8–18 year olds*. Menlo Park, CA: Kaiser Family Foundation. http://www.kff.org/entmedia/upload/Generation-M-Media-in-the-Lives-of-8–18-Year-olds-Report.pdf

Schor, J. (2004.) *Born to buy: The commercialized child and the new consumer culture*. New York: Scribners.

Smith, M., & Wilhelm, J. (2002). *Reading don't fix no Chevys: Literacy in the lives of young men*. Portsmouth, NH: Heinemann.

Tobin, J. (2000). *"Good guys don't wear hats": Children talk about the media*. New York: Teachers College Press.

"Top Ten Industry Facts." Entertainment Software Association. http://www.theesa.com/facts/top_10_facts.php

Trends in Average Mathematical Scale Scores by Gender. National Assessment of Educational Progress. (2004). Washington: Institute of Educational Sciences. http://nces.ed.gov/nationsreportcard/ltt/results2004/sub-math-gender.asp

Chapter Twelve

RESOURCES FOR CHILDHOOD LITERACY

Denise N. Morgan and Wendy C. Kasten

The term *literacy* within education describes the teaching of reading, writing, language arts, literature, and anything else related such as spelling, grammar, or word origins. This chapter includes an overview of the kinds of literacy resources available concerning K-8 classrooms organized as guidelines and suggestions for evaluating resources, especially Internet ones; an overview of national professional organizations, which can serve as a first stop for resources; and specific topics in literacy including action research, reading and language arts, children's literature, vocabulary and word study, writing, and diversity issues. Each topic provides some "best picks" in books, online resources, periodicals, and related organizations.

SELECTING RESOURCES

Because so much information is available through resources in books, journals, or the Internet, it is difficult to determine which ones are worthy. Here are points to consider to be a critical consumer of resources and information.

Who Is the Author? What Is the Source?

When examining any source, good first questions are: Who is the author? What are the credentials of the author(s) or organization? In the case with education, is the author identified as a classroom teacher, principal, or professor? Is the organization identified as a professional society? These questions do not automatically guarantee credible information, but they are a good starting point.

Facts can be gathered to make an informed decision about the information or resource. A public library and its staff are a great resource, as are school libraries, local colleges or universities, or related nonprofit groups, such as the Parent Teachers Association or Parent Teachers Organization. An Internet search may be appropriate to find out more about a person, book, resource, or organization.

One goal in searching and querying others is to decide if a person, resource, book, or organization is a reliable, unbiased, credible source. Reliable organizations present their beliefs, sponsors, and affiliations. In journals, such information is typically presented either in the beginning or at the end.

What Is the Documentation of Sources?

One way to assess sources is to first examine their bibliography or references. *Any good resource contains references.* Although searchers aren't always familiar with the names of individual(s) or books listed, there are some definite possible problems to look for when browsing a bibliography.

First, are the entries on the bibliography quite a bit older than the resource itself? Imagine a resource purchased in 2006 in which most of the references are from the 1970s. That gap in dates should make any savvy reader beware. It's possible that much work on a topic was done in a particular time frame, but it's also likely that the authors of the resource are not consulting more current works.

Second, are the entries on the bibliography by many people, nearly all by one person, or by just a few people? Although it's possible that there are only a few experts on a niche topic, it's also likely that many have been omitted. The resource developers may have selected only experts who agree with one perspective. Too-narrow references warrant further examination.

Who Published or Sponsored the Resource?

Although there are many conscientious and responsible producers of educational resources, including commercial ones, other publishing companies may have a specific agenda. Here are some questions to consider: Does this publishing company have a reputation for publishing quality materials? What organization or individuals are involved in the company or resource?

Many good resources are published by *professional learned societies.* A professional learned society is one that consists of practicing members who pay dues, is typically nonprofit, and has as a mission to further knowledge and practice in a profession. Such organizations have structures that include elected leadership, systems of peer reviews, and periodicals and publications that inform those in the field and the public. The mission of such an organization may also be to spearhead professional development of its members and may be responsible to offer, publish, and maintain *standards* within that profession. Education has learned societies that are trustworthy resources (listed in a section that follows).

When considering organizations that are *not* learned societies, evaluation of the related resources becomes more difficult. Many organizations are altruistic, well intentioned, and produce good resources, but other organizations may have a specific nonmainstream point of view.

Knowing more about the organization and its viewpoints is an important aspect of reviewing the resources it offers. Again, public libraries and academic libraries all have reference librarians who can help locate information about publishers and organizations. For example, is a publisher a legitimate educational press with a skilled editorial staff? Or is it a "vanity press" (publishes anything for a fee), or a business owned by an individual or group? Librarians know where to locate who and what (and what money in some cases) is behind an organization.

INVESTIGATING INTERNET WEB SITES

Web sites offer their own particular challenges. Once the Internet came along, people had ready access to a wide range of resources that were previously either unavailable or secured only through a library system. Along with genuinely useful Internet resources, there are thousands of sites that are a business enterprise, or the homework of school children learning to use technology. Many libraries offer handouts for evaluating Internet Web sites. Here are some points to consider that particularly pertain to evaluating Web sites as sources for information and other resources.

Is the Resource a Sponsored Web Site?

Sponsored Web sites that have a ".org" ending are usually reliable resources. This address ending signals a nonprofit society, which rarely has anything other than good intentions. For example, www.pbs.org is a Web site with many resources published by the citizen-supported and nonprofit Public Broadcasting Network.

Similarly, another group of Web sites ends in ".gov." These sites are the domain of a federally funded agency and generally contain information of interest to the general public, as well as educators. For example, www.loc.gov is the Library of Congress Web site, with a wealth of information on U.S. history. Similarly, www.nasa.gov is a well-constructed Web site with current information about space, shuttle missions, new discoveries, and much more. Many "gov" Web sites are reliable. Consider, however, that government agencies, too, can have biases that support or criticize the current political climate.

Web sites that end in ".edu" indicate education-related sites, such as schools and universities, and can sometimes be useful sources of information. Many university sites have important accessible information for their students on their Web site that is also of interest to others. At the same time, the ".edu" ending does not ensure that the material is sound, accurate, or current. A graduate student teaching a university class could post handouts for class members that contain outdated or inaccurate material. Professors, too, make mistakes. No one knows, when simply finding materials, how the materials were intended to be used. Caution should be used when consulting ".edu" Web sites.

Web addresses ending in ".com" are commercial. Some commercial sites may still be helpful and useful, but the consumer needs to proceed with caution, keeping in mind that the function of the Web site is to make money. For example, many books and DVDs are sold through www.amazon.com. Amazon does not choose only products that someone agrees are of high quality or conform to certain standards. They sell a vast array of materials. What they do offer are "customer reviews," which are not regulated in any way but can still offer consumers varied perspectives on a book, film, or product under consideration. Consequently, a Web site like Amazon can be a viable resource when the consumer is conscientious about reviewing possible products of interest.

Is the Information Current?

Not all Web sites are well maintained. A Web site that was posted 10 years ago might still be available and functioning, but it may have had no updating. Material on a Web site needs to be current in terms of up-to-date facts, as well as having updated editions of books, links that actually work, and more.

PROFESSIONAL ORGANIZATIONS

Teaching is a profession guided and governed by learned societies. Professional scholarly organizations play important roles in the advancement and dissemination of knowledge. Professional organizations are probably one of the best and easiest places to begin a search on a particular literacy related topic, with a variety of teacher resources including journals, books, and various online and Web-based materials.

Many organizations offer at least one research-based scholarly journal, often denoted by the word *research* in the title, and perhaps one aimed at the practical application of ideas. These journals are peer reviewed, meaning that all articles published are "blind reviewed" by fellow educators (names and affiliations are removed when being considered) to help ensure quality. Many organizations offer online access to journals for subscribers. Most organizations offer position statements, which offer the organization's stand on educational-related issues, including controversial ones. These organizations also publish many resources including books, pamphlets, video/DVDs, and more.

Professional organizations hold annual conferences where attendees can learn from fellow educators about current ideas and practices in the field. Most national organizations also have state affiliates, so interested individuals can attend more local conferences. Learned societies serve as a means of professional development and growth for their members. The professional organizations with a specific focus on literacy are listed first followed by organizations that deal with a wider range of literacy-related topics.

International Reading Association (www.reading.org)

For more than 50 years, the International Reading Association (IRA) has served as a membership organization for literacy professionals. Worldwide literacy issues are among the mission of IRA. IRA holds an annual conference in late April/early May and a worldwide conference in a country outside the United States every other year. IRA publishes four journals. Of particular interest for information on students in grades kindergarten to 8th grade are the following publications:

> *The Reading Teacher:* This journal focuses on literacy with children up to age 12. This journal offers monthly articles about literacy teaching.
> *Journal of Adolescent and Adult Literacy:* This journal focuses on teaching *middle grade* students (generally ages 8–14), *adolescents* (generally ages 14–18), and *adults.*
> *Reading Research Quarterly:* This is a research journal reporting on current scholarship about literacy teaching.
> *Lectura y Vida:* IRA also offers a quarterly journal that is written in Spanish.

IRA also offers Web resources providing visitors with information related to issues in literacy and teaching tools to use in classroom practice. In addition, IRA publishes *Reading Today,* a bimonthly newspaper, addressing current issues in education around the country. IRA offers an electronic journal, *Reading Online,* addressing issues of literacy for students ages 5 to 18. Also available are books, videos, and other materials for purchase. The IRA Web site has much to offer to inform the public and policy makers concerned with literacy.

National Council of Teachers of English (www.ncte.org)

Since 1911, the National Council of Teachers of English (NCTE), a learned society of educators, has worked toward advancing English language arts education and is open to anyone interested in that mission, which includes all matters related to reading, writing, language learning, English language teaching, and public policy. NCTE holds an annual conference in November and publishes 12 journals. Of particular interest to those involved in literacy issues for children in grades kindergarten through 8th grade are the following publications:

> *Language Arts*: This journal offers peer-reviewed articles targeting English language arts-related topics spanning from elementary to middle school.
>
> *Voices from the Middle*: This quarterly journal is devoted to issues related to the teaching of English-language arts in middle school.
>
> *Research in the Teaching of English*: This journal is also published four times a year. It accepts original research about English-language arts and focuses on a preschool–adult audience.

NCTE also publishes *School Talk,* a quarterly newsletter focusing on a particular topic, and the quarterly *Classroom Notes Plus* written by teachers for teachers, aimed at teachers of middle, junior, and senior high school students. *Talking Points* is a subsection's online journal for members particularly interested in holistic instruction. Members can receive an e-newsletter, *NCTE Inbox,* providing links to important articles. Updates about the organization are available from *The Council Chronicle monthly newspaper.* NCTE also publishes professional books and teacher resource materials.

National Writing Project (www.writingproject.org)

The National Writing Project (NWP) founded in 1974, is a professional organization devoted to improving writing instruction at all levels of schooling and offers summer institutes for teachers of students in grades kindergarten through grade 12. *The Quarterly,* once a print publication of NWP, is now offered as an online journal. This journal addresses exemplary teaching practices and cutting-edge issues in the teaching of writing. NWP also offers *The Voice,* the project's newsletter, and *E-Voice,* an e-mail newsletter. NWP offers many books and additional publications on its Web site.

College Reading Association (www.collegereadingassociation.org)

Founded in 1958, the College Reading Association (CRA) is another scholarly organization, primarily of reading researchers and professors. CRA publishes a bimonthly research journal, *Reading Research and Instruction,* and also publishes the *College Reading Association Yearbook,* a book of conference proceedings, along with a newsletter twice a year.

National Reading Conference (www.nrconline.org)

Primarily made up of literacy professors and researchers, members of the National Reading Conference (NRC) have a primary interest in literacy research. NRC sponsors an annual conference in December and publishes the quarterly *Journal of Literacy Research,* dedicated to sharing original research and scholarly papers. NRC also publishes the *Yearbook of the National Reading*

Conference. Its Web site has information available to teachers and other interested individuals.

American Library Association (www.ala.org)

The American Library Association (ALA) was founded in 1876 with a goal of promoting library quality and public access to information. Its membership is open to persons and organizations interested in library service. ALA offers an annual conference in the summer. Its Web site offers books, posters, bookmarks, and pamphlets. Visitors can access professional papers on a variety of topics and can engage in online discussions. ALA offers several journals. Of particular interest is *Booklinks: Connecting Books, Libraries, and Classrooms.* This publication helps inform teachers, parents, and other individuals about high-quality books for children and provides interviews with authors and illustrators and annotated booklists on a wide variety of topics.

Association for Childhood Education International (www.acei.org)

Since 1892, this veteran organization and learned society of the Association for Childhood Education International (ACEI) has been devoted to issues related to the improvement of instruction for teachers and others who provide educational services for young children through adolescence. ACEI publishes two journals.

> *Childhood Education:* This journal focuses on school and home-related issues.
> *Journal of Research in Childhood Education:* This journal offers an exchange of research ideas.

In addition, ACEI offers an international conference and several quarterly publications that focus on specific age ranges. ACEI also offers books and various resources for parents and teachers on its Web site.

National Association for the Education of Young Children (www.naeyc.org)

Since 1926, the National Association for the Education of Young Children (NAEYC) has been concerned with the education and care of younger learners. NAEYC offers an annual conference in November and has state affiliate organizations. Of particular interest are the following publications:

> *Young Children:* This journal highlights topics of importance in the field of early childhood education.
> *Early Childhood Research Quarterly:* This is a journal devoted to the dissemination of scholarly work in the field of early childhood development.

NAEYC publishes *Beyond the Journal,* an online journal that features materials not included in the print issues of *Young Children.* It sponsors publications and training materials and offers books, brochures, DVDs, and CDs.

Association for Supervision and Curriculum Development (www.ascd.org)

Founded in 1943, the Association for Supervision and Curriculum Development (ASCD) has been a community of educators with interest in all areas of the curriculum. ASCD offers an annual conference, various events, on-site training, online resources, and various products, including films and DVDs related to professional development in a wide variety of specialties. ASCD includes state affiliate organizations. ASCD publishes *Educational Leadership*, a journal focusing on teaching and learning from prekindergarten through higher education.

SELECT LITERACY TOPICS

Childhood literacy is a vast field with many specialties within it. What follows here are selected topics under the umbrella of literacy. Included are action research, reading and language arts, children's literature, vocabulary and word study, writing, and diversity issues.

RESOURCES FOR ACTION RESEARCH

Professional development is the term for lifelong learning in a profession. All those that enter teaching are expected, by virtue of their professional affiliation, to continue to learn and grow throughout their career. The resources that follow assist teachers of literacy in doing this in general as opposed to one specific area of literacy by supporting and enabling teachers to form and inquire into their own questions unique to their setting or practice. Listed here are some useful resources for those interested in action research:

Best Picks in Books

Holly, M. L., Arhar, J. A., & Kasten, W. C. (2005). *Action research for teachers: Traveling the Yellow Brick Road.* Columbus, OH: Pearson Education.
   With a basis of literacy examples, this text takes the reader through some history of research, and then acts as a practical guide through the action research process by enabling teachers to design simple studies in their classrooms to solve or illuminate unique problems. Five different cases are developed through the book, addressing a variety of age ranges and issues.
Mills, G. (2007). *Action research: A guide for the teacher-researcher* (3rd ed.). Columbus, OH: Pearson Education.
   This is another concise guide that takes readers through steps in the process to complete the action research experience.
Moore, R. A. (2004). *Classroom research for teachers: A practical guide.* Norwood, MA: Christopher-Gordon Publishers.
   This is a slim volume of essentials that takes the reader through the major steps and trials of an action research study.

Patterson, L., Santa, C. M., Short, K. G., & Smith, K. (Eds.). (1993). *Teachers are researchers: Reflection and action.* Newark, DE: International Reading Association.
This book frames teaching as opportunities for inquiry and tells the stories of successful and often inspiring studies conducted by teachers in their own classroom settings. Teachers of all age groups are included.

Online Resources

http://literacy.kent.edu/—This State of Ohio funded site features articles for families and teachers, pathways toward getting a GED, various programs available, and much more (note: Most states have their own literacy resource Web site).
http://www.nelrc.org/—Similar to the Ohio Literacy Resource Center, this site is a collaborative of all New England states, offering classroom ideas, articles, the ability to find expertise in a niche area, and announcements of regional literacy events.

Periodicals

Action Research—This is a refereed journal published in the United Kingdom that showcases action research, and is sponsored by Sage publications. It is available at: http://arj.sagepub.com
Action Research International Journal—This is an online refereed journal of action research with Australian sponsorship. It is available at: http://www.scu.edu.au/schools/gcm/ar/ari/arihome.html
Action Research Journal—This is another refereed journal devoted to action research sponsored by Montana State University. It is available at: http://www.montana.edu/arexpeditions/index.php
Educational Action Research—This journal was introduced in 2006, and is published by Taylor & Francis, and supported by C.A.R.N. (Collaborative Action Research Network) an organization in the United Kingdom and is available at: http://www.tandf.co.uk/journals/titles/09650792.asp

RESOURCES FOR READING AND LANGUAGE ARTS

There are numerous books on various aspects of literacy instruction. These resources help to provide an understanding of both theory and practice.

Best Picks in Books

Braunger, J., & Lewis, J. (2006). *Building a knowledge base in reading* (2nd ed.). Portland, OR: Northwest Regional Education Laboratory's Curriculum and Instruction Services *and* International Reading Association *and* National Council of Teachers of English.
Every discipline needs to compile and acknowledge its own body of science that informs further work, research, policy, & practice. This concise volume does just that.

Codell, E. R. (2003). *How to get your child to love reading.* New York: Algonquin Books of Chapel Hill.

In this 474-page book, Codell provides books grouped by different categories of possible interest, ranging from books that have a baking theme, books that deal with sleep, to more traditional grouping of books that are about the Civil War.

Fountas, I. C., & Pinnell, G. S. (1996). *Guided reading: Good first teaching for all children.* Portsmouth, NH: Heinemann.

Fountas and Pinnell focus on guided reading and aspects related to instruction, such as grouping for instruction, selecting, and introducing books.

Fox, M. (2001). *Reading magic: Why reading aloud to our children will change their lives forever.* San Diego, CA: Harcourt.

In this quick, easy-to-read book, Fox speaks to the power of reading aloud to children frequently and with passion. She details what children learn from a simple read-aloud encounter.

Harvey, S., & Goudvis, A. (2000). *Strategies that work: Teaching comprehension to enhance understanding.* York, ME: Stenhouse.

Well described in the title, this book explicates successful strategies that are consistent with theory and research in a teacher-friendly format.

Keene, E. O., & Zimmermann, S. (1997). *Mosaic of thought: Teaching comprehension in a reader's workshop.* Portsmouth, NH: Heinemann.

This favorite book of teachers handles comprehension in ways that develop depth with readers and addresses critical thinking about texts.

New Zealand Ministry of Education. (1991). *Reading in junior classes* Wellington, NZ. (distributed by Richard C. Owen, Katonah, NY).

This is a concise, reader-friendly guide to implementing major reading strategies. It appeals even to the most novice teacher. Graphics contribute to the appeal.

Routman, R. (2003). *Reading essentials: The specifics you need to teach reading well.* Portsmouth, NH: Heinemann.

Routman has written many books; this most recent one details the different kinds of instructional experiences students need to progress to as readers.

Taberski, S. (2000). *On solid ground: Strategies for teaching reading K-3.* Portsmouth, NH: Heinemann.

Taberski discusses in detail her daily instruction in reading. She paints a clear picture of what she does, providing her rationale and research to support her decisions.

Weaver, C. (2002). *Reading process and practice: From socio-psycholinguistics to whole language* (3rd ed.). Portsmouth, NH: Heinemann.

This is a most comprehensive and readable text to help teachers and others understand the process of reading and the practice that applies that understanding.

Online Resources

www.readwritethink.org—This joint venture between the IRA and NCTE provides instructional practices and resources for teachers.

Periodicals

Reading and Writing Quarterly: Overcoming Learning Difficulties. This quarterly specializes in issues and topics related to struggling readers or those who need more help than is typical. It is available at: (http://www.tandf.co.uk/journals/authors/urwlauth.asp).

RESOURCES FOR CHILDREN'S LITERATURE

The backbone of an effective learning environment is high-quality books of all kinds that support curriculum in every way. Resources for Children's Literature are resources to locate and use high-quality books in fiction, poetry, nonfiction, traditional literature, reference, etc.

Best Picks in Books

Gambrell, L. B., & Almasi, J. F. (Eds.). (1996). *Lively discussions! Fostering engaged reading.* Newark, DE: IRA Publications.
   This is one of several excellent and popular books on teaching literature with age-appropriate novels. This book has chapters written by various people, including classroom teachers who share successful practices.

Harris, V. J. (Ed.). (1993). *Teaching multicultural literature in grades K-8.* Norwood, MA: Christopher-Gordon Publishers.
   One of the leading experts on this topic, Harris offers chapters by most of the well-known professionals in multicultural literature and promotes teaching toward a wealth of understanding and appreciation of multicultural issues.

Hill, B. C., Johnson, N. J., & Schlick-Noe, K. L. (1995). *Literature circles and response.* Norwood, MA: Christopher-Gordon Publishers.
   This is a well-organized book for teachers to implement literature circles, a popular strategy in literature teaching using heterogeneous student-led groups reading age-appropriate novels. This book includes strategies for use with students in responding to literature.

Huck, C. S., Hepler, S., Hickman, J., & Kiefer, B. Z. (2006). *Children's literature in the elementary school* (9th ed.). Boston, MA: McGraw-Hill.
   This tome has been the mainstay of texts for courses in many children's literature courses, as Charlotte Huck pioneered and advocated knowledge and attention to children's literature in the United States. The book is a comprehensive look at literature for children by genre.

Kasten, W. C., Kristo, J. V., & McClure, A. A. (2005). *Living literature: Using children's literature to support reading and language arts.* Columbus, OH: Pearson Education.
   Unlike most other literature resources, this book focuses on teaching literature. Genre information is included, but concise. A database of 13,000 titles is included, as well as other resources on the accompanying CD and a companion Web site.

Kristo, J. V., & Bamford, R. A. (2004). Nonfiction in focus: A comprehensive framework for helping students become independent readers and writers of nonfiction, K-6. New York: Scholastic.
   In this book, Kristo and Bamford provide an in-depth analysis of nonfiction literature and how this genre can be used throughout the instructional day.

Laminack, L. L., & Wadsworth, R. M. (2006). *Learning under the influence of language and literacy: Making the most of read-alouds across the day.* Portsmouth, NH: Heinemann.

This book is filled with read aloud suggestions and provides a vast collection of book titles with annotations, pointing out subtle nuances in art or language that a teacher or parent might want to share with students.

McClure, A. A., & Kristo, J. V. (Eds). (2002). *Adventuring with books: A booklist for pre-K-grade 6* (13th ed.). Urbana, IL: National Council of Teachers of English.

An NCTE initiative conducted every two years, this book is a compilation of newer titles; annotations are included by categories as a resource for teachers.

Wilhelm, J. D. (1997). *"You gotta BE the book:" Teaching engaged and reflective reading with adolescents*. New York, NY: Teachers College Press/NCTE.

Wilhelm's contributions are substantial to the teaching of children's literature by motivating students to become highly involved with drama and other sorts of deep engagement with texts.

Online Resources

www.childslit.com—This commercial Web site includes book reviews, interviews with authors, links to authors' Web sites, and bestsellers.

www.ucalgary.ca/~dkbrown—This Web site has been around a while. It is well maintained by a Canadian university with an extensive database.

www.carolhurst.com—This is an example of a known literature expert sponsoring a Web site that offers lesson plans, book reviews, activity ideas, a free newsletter, and more.

www.bookhive.org—This library-sponsored Web site offers read alouds of stories and book reviews, recommendations, and more.

www.falcon.jmu.edu—This university-sponsored Web site isn't fancy, but it has lots of information packed into it, including extensive booklists, organized by content topics, and a database.

Periodicals

Dragon Lode—This quarterly scholarly journal is sponsored by the Children's Literature Special Interest Group of the International Reading Association and is available at: www.reading.ccsu.edu/TheDragonLode/default.html

Horn Book—This journal offers articles, editorials, and reviews of children's and young adult's literature and is available at: www.hbook.com

Journal of Children's Literature—This scholarly journal is offered by the Children's Literature Assembly of the National Council of Teachers of English and is available at: www.childrensliteratureassembly.org

Organizations

There are several professional organizations devoted to children's literature and instruction in literacy.

Children's Literature Assembly (CLA)—This is a special-interest group within the NCTE devoted to literature in K-8 classrooms.

Society for Children's Book Writers and Illustrators (SCBWI)—This is a society of writers and illustrators for children's literature and those interested in writing, illustrating, and publishing. National and local conferences and issues about writing and publishing are addressed. It is available at: www.scbwi.org

RESOURCES FOR VOCABULARY AND WORD STUDY

A popular and important area of literacy is the world of words. Learning about words, decoding them, finding about their origins, learning their meanings—all of these contribute to word study. Here is a list of books devoted to vocabulary.

Best Picks in Books

Bear, D. R., Invernizzi, M., Templeton, S., & Johnston, F. (2003). *Words their way: Word study for phonics, vocabulary, and spelling instruction* (3rd ed.). Columbus, OH: Pearson Education.
   This attractive book is popular with teachers, guides orthographic assessment, and identifying patterns in learners. The various chapters recommend word learning strategies for learners in different categories according to these assessments.
Blachowicz, C., & Fisher, P. (2006). *Teaching vocabulary in all classrooms* (3rd ed.). Upper Saddle River, NJ: Merrill/Prentice Hall.
   This research-based book includes strategies, ideas, and Web sites for developing vocabulary in all content areas. Many of the techniques explored in this book have the broader goal of enhancing the acquisition of content knowledge within vocabulary instruction.
Nagy, W. E. (1988). *Teaching vocabulary to improve reading instruction.* Urbana, IL: Eric Clearinghouse on Reading and Communication Skills, and National Council of Teachers of English, and International Reading Association.
   In this slim book, Nagy discusses vocabulary's link to reading comprehension and then presents effective and efficient methods of vocabulary instruction.
Rasinski, T., & Padak, N. (2001). *From phonics to fluency: Effective teaching of decoding and reading fluency in the elementary school.* New York: Longman.
   These former editors of *The Reading Teacher* include issues such as fluency and using authentic texts, as well as practical strategies like word sorts, language experience, spelling, and teaching advanced word patterns.
Tompkins, G., & Blachfield, C. L. (2004). *Teaching vocabulary: 50 creative strategies, grades k-12.* Upper Saddle River, NJ: Pearson/Merrill Prentice Hall.
   This book addresses specific learning needs. The strategies included are time-tested and classroom proven, according to the authors, and include students K-12, and ESL suggestions as well.
Wilde, S. (1997). *What's a schwa sound, anyway?: A holistic guide to phonetics, phonics, and spelling.* Portsmouth, NH: Heinemann.
   This is a book about phonics that situates phonics within the linguistic framework including language history and origin. With delightful examples and a bit of humor, this book is popular with teachers and teacher education students, as it has a great deal of substance and is presented attractively.

Online Resources

http://www.vocabulary.com/VUcrosswordS139L1.html—Although a commercial Web site, a fair amount of workbook-type activities are offered for free and can be printed, such as fill-in-the blank and matching activities. This resource is suitable for students in intermediate and higher grades.

http://wordsurfing.co.uk—This is an impressive Web site suitable for English language learners or other language learning. Among other features, an audio pictionary lists many categories of words and each is pronounced when the mouse is placed on the picture. This feature is offered in 11 different languages.

http://wordorigins.org—This site is used like a dictionary, alphabetically tabbed on the side, so that users can select a word of their interest and find facts about its origin, including the family of languages from which it evolved.

Organizations

One major resource is the International Reading Association Special Interest Group (SIG) on Phonics. See www.reading.org for links.

RESOURCES FOR WRITING

The teaching of writing has changed since the 1980s with what is termed a more "process approach." Teachers today want students to write with confidence and develop a way to study well-known authors to better develop their own writing. The following resources approach the teaching of writing as described here.

Best Picks in Books

Atwell, N. (1998). *In the middle: New understandings about writing, reading, and learning.* (2nd ed.). Portsmouth, NH: Heinemann.
   In this classic book, Atwell takes readers into her classroom as she uses a workshop approach to teaching writing (and reading).
Fletcher, R., & Portalupi, J. (2001). *Writing workshop: The essential guide.* Portsmouth, NH: Heinemann.
   This book provides an overview of writing workshop and how to get it started in the classroom in an easy, no-fuss manner.
Graves, D. H. (1994). *A fresh look at writing.* Portsmouth, NH: Heinemann.
   Graves, considered one of the pioneers in implementing writing workshops in elementary classrooms, offers a collection of actions for teachers to take to support their teaching of writing.
Noden, H. (1999). *Image grammar: Using grammatical structures to teach writing.* Portsmouth, NH: Heinemann.
   This is a book about writing that looks at grammar as a tool for the artistic expression of language. Noden includes lessons that he used in his own classroom.
Ray, K. W. (2006). *Study driven: A framework for planning units of study in the writing workshop.* Portsmouth, NH: Heinemann.
   In this book, Ray describes a predictable approach or structure for studying any genre to support students in learning from authors who write those genres well.
Short, K. G., Harste, J. C., & Burke, C. (1996). *Creating classrooms for authors and inquirers.* Portsmouth, NH: Heinemann.
   In this lengthy book, the process of writing is integrated with other areas of learning and presents writing as a cycle as it relates to inquiry and the learning community.

Turbill, J. (Ed). (1982). *No better way to teach writing.* Rozelle, Australia.: Primary English Teaching Association.
>A logical description of writing in a teacher-friendly format. This book has been a favorite of teachers because it is theoretically sound and practical.

RESOURCES FOR DIVERSITY EDUCATIONAL ISSUES

Educators recognize that today's students vary greatly in their backgrounds, ethnicity, heritage, culture, and learning abilities. The job of educators is to do what's best to meet the needs of all learners. Meeting all learners' needs is dynamically challenging and works only with knowledge about the myriad issues involved. Below are some resources that can help.

Best Picks in Books

Au, K. (2006). *Multicultural issues and literacy achievement.* Mahwah, NJ: Erlbaum.
>Au is a leader in multicultural literacy, and this book synthesizes the author's knowledge about diverse cultures in a way that other educators can benefit.

Brown, D. (2002). *Becoming a successful urban teacher.* Portsmouth, NH: Heinemann.
>Urban schools in the United States typically have students with diverse backgrounds. African American teachers who have used this book have stated that all urban teachers and their administers should read this book because Brown does a remarkable and honest treatment of urban issues.

Delpit, L. (1995). *Other peoples' children: Cultural conflict in the classroom.* New York: The New Press.
>This book deals with the frequent mismatch between students of African American, Hispanic, Asian American, and Native American cultures and their experiences in schools. Delpit argues that culture matters in school, because schooling practices often collide with students' values and beliefs.

Freeman, D. E., & Freeman, Y. (2001). *Between worlds: Access to second language acquisition.* (2nd ed.). Portsmouth, NH: Heinemann.
>Probably the gurus of bilingual education issues, the Freemans offer this and other books of theirs that explain, lead, and evaluate programs and issues related to bilingual or dual language education.

Gilliland, H. (1988). *Teaching the Native American.* New York: Kendall/Hunt.
>Of all minority cultures in the United States, Native American children are the ones who are least likely to succeed in schools. Although this is an older book, it's still the best single source of understanding for some very complex cultural issues that impact students' learning.

Minami, M., & Kennedy, B. (Eds.). (1991). *Language issues in literacy and bilingual/multicultural education.* Cambridge, MA: Harvard Educational Review.
>This book contains 18 chapters by leading authors in diversity topics. These chapters all previously appeared as papers in the prestigious *Harvard Educational Review* journal and address a wide range of critical topics.

Nieto, S. (2002). *Language, culture, and teaching: Critical perspectives for a new century.* Mahwah, NJ: Erlbaum.
>This book by a leader in diversity issues does exactly what it says—it educates the reader about issues of language and culture and why these issues cannot be ignored in schools.

Shor, I. (Ed.). (1987). *Freire for the classroom: A sourcebook for liberatory teaching.* Portsmouth, NH: Heinemann.

> Based on the ideals of the late Paolo Freire, a South American educator and thinker, the chapters within address some stunning ideas that raise questions about the status quo in many schools and the issues that are rarely addressed or questioned, especially where minority voices are concerned.

Periodicals

Bilingual Research Journal—This is a quarterly scholarly journal of the National Association of Bilingual Educators and is available at: http://www.nabe.org

Rethinking Schools—This is a monthly journal for teachers, which dares to be different and bold with teaching ideas, raising important critical issues and providing material for thinking about topics and teaching differently. It is available at: www.rethinkingschools.org

Teaching Tolerance—This is a magazine that is free to teachers and is published by the Southern Poverty Law Center. It includes books, articles, and ideas to assist teachers who include issues of tolerance and diversity in their teaching. It is available at: www.teachingtolerance.org

Online Resources

Edchange—This is a nonprofit and online source for book titles, and teaching resources promoting multicultural understanding. It is available at: http://www.edchange.org/multicultural.

Oyate.org—This Web site is managed by Native American women who review children's literature with American Indian/ Native American topics or images and provide their candid opinions of those books. This site is also a clearinghouse for purchasing books on Native American issues and topics. It is available at: www.oyate.org.

North Central regional educational library—This is a nonprofit resource of papers and resources related to multicultural awareness and practices. It is available at: http://www.ncrel.org/sdrs/areas/issues/educatrs/presrvce/pe3lk1.htm

Organizations

The National Association of Bilingual Educators—This professional organization is a learned society dedicated to bilingual education. It is available at: http://www.nabe.org

National Association of Multicultural Education—This is an organization that coordinates issues, resources, hot topics, articles, and conferences around multicultural issues anywhere on the globe. It is available at: http://www.nameorg.org

International Reading Association Special Interest Group (SIG) on *Concerned Educators of Black Students.* It is available at: www.reading.org/association/about/sigs_concerned_educators.html

There are a vast number of resources that are related to literacy. The resources listed in this chapter should serve as a quick overview of some of the materials available.

INDEX

ABOUT THE CONTRIBUTORS

BARBARA J. GUZZETTI is a professor of language and literacy at Arizona State University in the Mary Lou Fulton College of Education. She is also an affiliated faculty member in the College of Liberal Arts and Sciences in women's and gender studies. Her research interests include gender and literacy, science education and literacy, adolescent literacy, popular culture, and the new literacies, including digital literacies.

JOBETH ALLEN conducts collaborative action research with teachers who are exploring issues of educational equity and social justice in relation to literacy teaching and learning. A professor at the University of Georgia in language and literacy education, she is the codirector of the Red Clay Writing Project where she is involved in an inquiry on literacy and social class. Her most recent book is *Creating Welcoming Schools: A Practical Guide to Home-School Partnerships with Diverse Families*. She has also published *Class Action: Teaching for Social Justice in Elementary and Middle School*.

EMMA BAILEY is a graduate of the University of Georgia where she completed her master's degree in children's literature and language arts. A former 2nd- and 4th-grade teacher in a small southeastern college town, Bailey currently participates in the Red Clay Writing Project where her involvement has led to opportunities to facilitate professional development for county teachers. Bailey also works collaboratively with teachers to improve instruction in writing workshops and other language arts areas.

JAMES F. BAUMANN is a professor in the Department of Elementary and Early Childhood Education at the University of Wyoming. He formerly was an elementary classroom teacher in grades 2–4. His research interests include elementary reading instruction trends and techniques for teaching students to expand their reading vocabularies and to comprehend text.

JOHN BISHOP is currently working on his doctorate degree at the University of Georgia in language and literacy education. He has taught elementary and middle school, and continues to work with both practicing and preservice elementary teachers in the areas of writing instruction and children's literature. His research focuses on multimodal forms of literacy instruction, and he presently works as the technology liaison for the Red Clay Writing Project, a local chapter of the National Writing Project.

RANDY BOMER is associate professor in the language and literacy studies program at the University of Texas at Austin. He conducts research in literacy classrooms and about the politics of literacy, and he is the author of *Time for Meaning* and *For a Better World*. In 2005, he was president of the National Council of Teachers of English.

ROBERT C. CALFEE, Distinguished Professor Emeritus at University of California, Riverside's Graduate School of Education, is a cognitive psychologist with interests in the effect of schooling on the intellectual potential of individuals and groups. He has studied literacy assessment, effective instructional practices for helping all students become competent readers and writers, and methods for assisting schools to become learning communities. He has authored more than 200 published research articles and numerous books in the fields of education and psychology.

AMY CARTER is a doctoral student in curriculum and instruction at Clemson University. Her current research interests are focused on literacy, technology, and diverse populations. She is a research assistant on a project entitled Teaching Internet Comprehension to Adolescents (TICA), funded by the Institute of Education Sciences, U.S. Department of Education.

JAMES V. HOFFMAN is a professor of language and literacy studies at The University of Texas at Austin where he directs the undergraduate reading specialization program in elementary teacher education and where his research interests focus on beginning reading and teacher education. He has served as president of the National Reading Conference and as a member of the board of directors of the International Reading Association. He has also served as editor of the *Yearbook of the National Reading Conference* and *The Reading Research Quarterly.*

BOB IVES is an assistant professor in special education at the University of Nevada, Reno. He teaches undergraduate and graduate courses in instructional methods for students with mild/moderate disabilities, assessment, and educational research methods, and also conducts research in these same areas. Bob is cofounder and codirector of the Educational Research in Romania program.

JERRY L. JOHNS, Distinguished Teaching Professor Emeritus at Northern Illinois University, is a past president of the International Reading Association. He has published nearly 300 articles and research studies, as well as more than 20 books, including his most recent *Fluency: Strategies & Assessments* (3rd edition) and *Basic Reading Inventory* (9th edition). He currently consults with schools in the United States and serves as a speaker for professional organizations and Reading First conferences.

BARBARA KAPINUS, PhD, is a senior policy analyst at the National Education Association. She has taught reading courses at the University of Maryland, The Johns Hopkins University, Western Maryland College, Trinity College, and the Catholic University and has served as the director of the Curriculum and Instructional Improvement Program at the Council of Chief State School Officers where she worked on projects related to standards implementation, assessment, reading, workplace readiness, early learning, and Title I. Kapinus's experience also includes 8 years as the specialist for reading and communication skills at the Maryland State Department of Education and 16 years in Prince George's county public schools in several roles including classroom teacher, reading specialist, and curriculum specialist.

WENDY C. KASTEN is a professor of curriculum and instruction in literacy at Kent State University. She is the coauthor of *Living Literature: Using Children's Literature to Support Reading and Language Arts* and *Action Research for Teachers: Traveling the Yellow Brick Road.* Kasten teaches courses at Kent State University and does extensive international work on literacy projects as well.

DENISE N. MORGAN is an assistant professor in the Department of Teaching, Leadership, and Curriculum Studies at Kent State University. She teaches literacy courses in both undergraduate and graduate programs. Her research interests include teacher education, understanding children's development as readers and writers, and long-term professional development.

THOMAS NEWKIRK is a professor of English at the University of New Hampshire where he directs the New Hampshire Literacy Institutes. He is the author of *The Performance of Self in Student Writing*, which won the David Russell Award from the National Council of Teachers of English. His most recent book is *Misreading Masculinity: Boys, Literacy, and Popular Culture*.

KIMBERLY A. NORMAN is associate professor in the College of Education at the University of California, Fullerton. Her research interests include literacy development, the content and pedagogy of teacher education, and the role of classroom discourse in promoting reflection and conceptual understanding. Her articles have appeared in *Teachers College Record* and *Teacher Education Quarterly*, among other publications.

JANET L. PARIZA, assistant professor at Northeastern Illinois University, teaches courses in diagnosis and remediation of reading problems. She has published articles on vocabulary development and was a 2002 College Reading Association distinguished finalist for dissertation of the year.

DAVID REINKING is the Eugene T. Moore Professor of Teacher Education at Clemson University. He has been the coeditor of *Reading Research Quarterly*, one of the most highly regarded research journals in the field of education. He has published widely on the topic of digital literacies, and he is currently a coprincipal investigator on a project entitled Teaching Internet Comprehension to Adolescents (TICA), funded by the Institute of Education Sciences, U.S. Department of Education.

MISTY SAILORS is an assistant professor of literacy education in the Department of Interdisciplinary Learning and Teaching in the College of Education and Human Development at the University of Texas at San Antonio. A former elementary teacher and author of several book chapters and numerous peer-reviewed articles, Sailors is active in national and international literacy organizations and currently teaches undergraduate and graduate literacy education courses with a focus on comprehension instruction and the interdisciplinary inclusion of technology into teaching and learning. She has worked in South Africa for several years, conducting research on high-performing schools in rural areas and is currently overseeing the development of supplementary learning materials for elementary learners in conjunction with the Republic of South Africa Department of Education and several South African nongovernmental organizations.

TERRY SALINGER is a managing director and chief scientist for reading research at the American Institutes for Research. Currently the project direc-